CW00362020

How to Pass
Practical Computing

FIRST, SECOND AND THIRD LEVELS

How to Pass
Practical
Computing

LCCI
EXAMINATIONS
BOARD

FIRST, SECOND AND THIRD LEVELS

Pam Smith

BA Hons PGCE

T Jacqueline Appleton

BA (Admin)

London Chamber of Commerce and Industry Examinations Board
Athena House
112 Station Road
Sidcup
Kent DA15 7BJ
United Kingdom

First published 1999
Reprinted with corrections 2001

British Library Cataloguing-in-Publication Data
Smith, Pam
   How to pass practical computing : first, second and third levels
   1.Computer science – Examinations – Study guides
   I.Title II.Appleton, T Jacqueline
   004

ISBN 1 86247 031 6

**This is the only book endorsed by LCCIEB for use by students
of this LCCIEB examination subject at these levels. No other book
is endorsed by LCCIEB for this subject at these levels.**

10   9   8   7   6   5   4   3   2

Typeset by the London Chamber of Commerce
and Industry Examinations Board
Printed in Hong Kong
Reprinted in The United Kingdom by Astron Limited, Huntingdon, Cambridgeshire

Contents

Contents

About the authors

Pam Smith is currently a Lecturer in the School of Information Processing at North West Kent College in Dartford. She has also taught in colleges in Bournemouth, Bristol and Hertfordshire. A linguist by training, she has over 20 years' experience of teaching in England and Spain. She now teaches secretarial skills, information technology and languages to students of all ages.

Pam is Chief Examiner in Practical Word Processing for the LCCIEB and has been closely involved in the development of the practical assessment schemes. She is also a Chief Examiner for two other examinations boards.

Jacqueline Appleton has had considerable experience in teaching information technology to classes of college students of different age groups and to individuals.

She is currently Chief Examiner in Practical Computing for the LCCIEB and has helped to develop the higher levels of database, spreadsheet and presentation graphics assessments. In addition she sets and marks examination papers for other examining boards.

Note on product names

This book includes some names that are or are claimed to be owned by certain commercial organisations. For legal purposes, the inclusion of these words does not suggest that they are no longer owned by a specific company or that they have passed into general use, nor is any other understanding implied regarding their legal status. Every effort has been made by the Publisher to seek the permission of the owners to include their product names in this book. The Publisher will rectify any credit omissions or errors in a subsequent edition of this book, should notification of any such error be made at any time.

Introduction

In today's electronic workplace, many skills are demanded of the computer user. Word processing, or the manipulation of text, is no longer the only type of work undertaken. Additional skills are required which demonstrate the employee's competence in other software packages such as spreadsheet, database and presentation graphics. In many offices, expertise in such areas is rapidly becoming an essential skill.

A highly regarded qualification in a range of software applications is proof of such skill, and the LCCI Examinations Board offers Practical Computing assignments at three levels to enable candidates to gain a formal qualification.

Objective

This book is designed to help candidates in their preparation for the LCCI Examinations Board assignments in Spreadsheet, Database, Word Processing and Presentation Graphics at **First, Second** and **Third Levels**.

After working through the sets of assignments contained in this book, candidates should be able to approach their course assessments with confidence.

The Practical Computing scheme

The aim of this assessment scheme is to test the candidate's practical ability across the key areas of:

- spreadsheet
- database
- word processing
- presentation graphics.

The target audience for the scheme includes those who are:

- wishing to acquire the fundamental practical IT skills for modern business
- starting a career in industry and need the IT skills to support that career
- returning to work or business and need to update their IT skill base
- requiring an expanded skill set for job enhancement or promotion.

Format of assignments

At **First Level**, each set of assignments comprises six tasks which may, or may not, be directly related to each other. They will, however, all address the same theme and the candidate will be given background information which details the organisation for whom the work is intended. The total time allowance for each set of assignments at **First Level** is 1 hour and 30 minutes, after which time the work produced by the candidate must be handed in to the tutor for marking.

Second Level assignment sets comprise 4 tasks which must be completed within 2 hours. These are more complex and require additional skills. All work must be handed in to the tutor for marking.

The **Third Level** assignment sets also comprise 4 tasks. The time allowance for **Third Level** assignments is 2 hours and 30 minutes. These assignments not only test the candidate on a full range of software functions, but also demand a high level of speed and accuracy.

The sets of assignments are designed to be taken when the candidate and the tutor agree that the candidate possesses the necessary skill to complete the tasks to a satisfactory standard within the time allowance. In this way, the candidate can progress at his or her own pace, irrespective of the rest of the group.

All work is marked and graded by the tutor and sent for moderation to the LCCI Examinations Board.

The scheme is available on demand, which means it is perfect for courses of study which do not necessarily fall within the standard academic year for testing.

Syllabus functions

Within the section of this book which is devoted to a specific software application, you will be given a full list of the syllabus functions required at each level. It is important that candidates demonstrate skill in the listed functions before attempting a set of assignments.

There is a steady progression between levels: **First Level** assignments test the basic functions of the software whilst **Third Level** assignments cover advanced features. At **Second** and **Third Level** it is assumed that the candidate can confidently undertake all the functions required at the lower level. Such functions will automatically be tested within the sets of assignments.

The assignments cannot, of course, test *every* function listed. However, candidates should expect that *any* function could appear in *any* set of assignments at the appropriate level.

The assignments used in this book cover a broad range of the listed functions. They are presented in the same way as 'live' assignments which will be provided by the LCCI Examinations Board for assessment purposes.

However, it would not be wise to concentrate *only* on the functions tested here. You should be prepared to perform any of the functions listed at each level.

How to use this workbook

Before using this book, candidates should already have a basic keyboarding ability and be able to perform basic functions within the software packages they intend to be assessed in. They should also have developed good proofreading and error-correction skills.

This book will enable candidates for each of the three levels of Spreadsheet, Database, Word Processing and Presentation Graphics assignments to check on what is required for each level and practise the functions that will later be tested under examination conditions.

Correct versions of all assignments are given at the end of each section so that candidates can check on progress made.

1

General guidelines

By the end of this section you will be able to:

1 *recognise the need for the sensible use of your time;*

2 *recognise the need for the inclusion of your name on each print-out;*

3 *recognise the need to save your work regularly;*

4 *recognise the need for instructions to be followed carefully;*

5 *identify the abbreviations that may be used;*

6 *identify the correction signs used when working from manuscript;*

7 *identify the need for careful proofreading of your work;*

8 *recognise the need for an accurate printout to be produced for marking.*

Using your time sensibly

When you are ready for assessment, your tutor will present you with a set of assignments in your subject area. You will be given a time allowance in which to complete the tasks and be told when to begin. It is important that you keep within the time allowance. You must hand in all your work when your tutor tells you that the time allowance has ended.

Each set of assignments at each level has a time allowance which relates directly to how much work is involved. **First Level** assignments must be completed within 1 hour and 30 minutes. **Second Level** assignments are given a 2-hour allowance whilst **Third Level** assignments, which can be quite complex, must be completed within 2 hours and 30 minutes. The time allowance for each set of assignments is stated clearly on the front page.

Within the time allocated to you, it is sensible to spend some time reading through the tasks carefully before you begin. Fifteen minutes spent planning your work at the beginning should ensure that you progress through the tasks without difficulty.

It is also important to spend time checking your work before you hand it to your tutor for marking. Once your work has been handed in, it cannot be amended in any way. Many candidates fail because they hand in work which has been hastily completed at the last minute.

Naming your work

It is very important that your work is identifiable when it leaves the printer, so you are asked to print your name on each document. Many candidates include this information in the header or footer area of the document produced. At **First Level**, no specific instructions will be given relating to where your name should appear. In assignments at **Second** and **Third Level**, you are told exactly where your name must appear. Make sure that your full name appears on each document handed in for marking.

Saving your work

It is most important that you save your work to disk under the filename that will be given to you. Sometimes you will be asked to retrieve a document that you produced earlier and it is vital that you can find the document quickly and easily. It is sensible to save your work regularly so that no work is lost. When working on Database assignments, you may also choose to make a copy of your original database just in case you make a mistake. In all cases, your work must be saved so that you can produce a final copy of your assignment for marking.

Following instructions

It is very important that you follow all the instructions given within each set of assignments. It is sensible to read through the tasks and underline or highlight what you must do. Tick off each instruction when it has been done.

Instructions will always appear in clear and simple English. Sometimes they are given as numbered points, but they may appear in continuous text. They will not be ambiguous and they should not confuse. They are designed to check that you are competent in the functions printed in the syllabus. They will not test any functions which are not included in the syllabus.

Here is an example of a set of instructions from a **Second Level** Word Processing assignment:

> 1 Key in the text below and edit as shown.
>
> 2 Insert today's date.
>
> 3 Expand abbreviations.
>
> 4 Insert a hard page break at the appropriate point in the text.
>
> 5 Key in your name at the bottom of the document.
>
> 6 Save the document as [WP2ASS1] and print out a copy of your work.

The following instructions appear in a **Second Level** Presentation Graphics assignment:

> Find pictures of a computer and a globe of the world and combine them to show the computer on top of the world. Then insert the new image into the following piece of text which should be typed with margins of 50 cm (2 inches) on each side and be fully justified.

Although the above instructions appear in continuous text it is, nevertheless, very clear what the candidate has to do.

Second and **Third Level** Word Processing assignments may also include handwritten and marginal instructions which appear next to the text to be amended. Such instructions will always be written clearly and an arrow or a bracket will indicate which text must be changed.

Figure 1.1 shows an example of a handwritten marginal instruction in a **Second Level** Word Processing assignment:

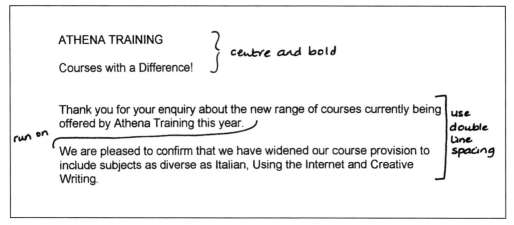

Figure 1.1   Example of a handwritten marginal instruction

In this case the headings must be centred and emboldened and the first paragraph changed from single to double line spacing. Handwritten instructions will appear *only* in Word Processing assignments.

Working from manuscript

Word Processing assignments at all levels will include text which is handwritten. The handwriting will always be clear and easy to read. At **First Level**, the words used will be simple and any additions and amendments will be accompanied by the appropriate correction sign. The correction sign will appear in the left or right margin. At **Second** and **Third Levels**, much of the text will be handwritten and correction signs will be used to indicate how the text should be changed.

Figure 1.2 is a list of correction signs that will be used throughout Word Processing assignments at all levels:

Sign in Margin	Meaning	Instruction	Example
Lc	lower case	change capital letter(s) into small letter(s)	The cat Sat on the mat
uc or caps	upper case	change small letter(s) into capital letter(s)	United states of America
NP	new paragraph	divide continuous text at point indicated by / or [	... end of the working day. [It was apparent that ...
run on	run on	join the two paragraphs together as shown	... working during college hours. Staff will be offered ...
trs	transpose	change the order of two items, vertically or horizontally	pepper and salt Britain Brazil
delete	delete	leave out the word(s) crossed through	many people were very worried about ...
insert	insert	include the word(s) indicated	absolutely I was delighted to ....
Close up	close up	reduce the amount of space between words	... the message took a long time ...
stet	stet (let it stand)	leave in place the word(s) originally crossed through	anxious He was very worried

Figure 1.2   Correction signs

Where correction signs are used, there will be a mark in the text and an instruction in the margin on the same line.

Handwritten text and correction signs are *not* used in Spreadsheet, Database or Presentation Graphics assignments.

Using abbreviations

With the exception of assignments in Word Processing at **Second** and **Third Levels**, abbreviations should not be expanded. If a Database assignment has *No* and *Street* as one of its field titles, you do not need to expand *No* to *Number*. Leave the word in its shortened form. You will not be penalised for copying from the assignment.

However, if you work on **Second** and **Third Level** Word Processing assignments, abbreviations must be expanded because the correct expansion of certain abbreviations is one of the functions tested.

Here is a full list of abbreviations which must be expanded within Word Processing assignments at **Second** and **Third Level**:

Abbreviations used at First Level

Abbreviation	Word in full	Abbreviation	Word in full
Common words			
approx	approximately	org	organisation
asap	as soon as possible	poss	possible
cat	catalogue	ref	reference
co(s)	company/ies	shd	should
dept	department	temp	temporary
dr	dear	th	that
immed	immediately	tho'	though
info	information	wd	would
no	number	yr	year/your
Dates			
Mon	Monday	Jan	January
Tue	Tuesday	Feb	February
Wed	Wednesday	Mar	March
Thur	Thursday	Apr	April
Fri	Friday	May	May
Sat	Saturday	Jun	June
Sun	Sunday	Jul	July
		Aug	August
		Sept	September
		Oct	October
		Nov	November
		Dec	December

Abbreviation	Word in full	Abbreviation	Word in full
Addresses			
Ave	Avenue	Pl	Place
Cres	Crescent	Rd	Road
Dr	Drive	Sq	Square
Pk	Park	St	Street
Complimentary closes			
Yrs ffly	Yours faithfully	Yrs sncly	Yours sincerely

You are not required to expand words which do not appear in the above list.

Proofreading

It is essential that you proofread your work carefully and amend any errors before handing your work in for marking as each error found will incur a penalty. Most candidates who fail have been careless when checking their work.

Take care when you key in your text. It does not matter whether you are working on a Word Processing, Spreadsheet, Database or Presentation Graphics assignment. Every word you key in must be accurate.

Check your work carefully against the assignment instruction sheet. Use an on-line spellcheck if you wish, but do not rely on the spellcheck facilities as the only method of proofreading. Candidates frequently miss out words or include extra words in their assignments. Each omitted or extra word is an error.

If you find an error, you must correct it and print out your document again. There is no restriction on how many copies of a document you can print, but it is sensible to check your work carefully on screen before sending the document to the printer. Use a document holder so that your assignment instruction sheet is level with your screen. Check your work word by word.

Printing

Some assignments will require several printouts as evidence that you have been able to satisfactorily achieve all the functions being tested, but most assignments will require only one copy of each printout. In Spreadsheet assignments, however, you may have to print out one copy of the spreadsheet showing the figures and another showing the formulae you have used. Do not forget to print out the formulae as that is the only way your tutor will know that the correct formulae have been used. Make sure that all the formulae, including the final brackets, can be seen clearly.

Many assignments will fit easily on to one sheet of A4 paper. At **First Level**, all assignments should fit on to one sheet, although you may choose to print out in landscape format (wide edge at the top), particularly when producing spreadsheet printouts. It is acceptable to reduce the font size so that the spreadsheet fits on to one page, but remember that the text must be legible. If the font size is so small that it is difficult to read, print the work on two pages.

Second Level and **Third Level** Word Processing assignments may ask for two or three-page documents. You should not try to fit these on to one page. Use a standard font size and print out a multi-page document as instructed. Most other assignments at **Second** and **Third Level** (Spreadsheet, Presentation Graphics and Database) can be reduced to fit on to one page.

As stated earlier, your name must appear on each printout.

HELPFUL HINTS

- **Read through each assignment carefully before starting work.**

- **Follow each instruction carefully.**

- **Save your work regularly under the appropriate filename.**

- **Learn to recognise manuscript correction signs for Word Processing assignments.**

- **Learn the list of abbreviations for Second and Third Level Word Processing assignments.**

- **Proofread your work for errors – each error will be penalised.**

- **Check that you have included your name on each document.**

- **Print out a final copy of the assignment for marking.**

2

Spreadsheets

Introduction

Spreadsheet software allows the user to enter text and numbers into a grid of cells, add formulae to make calculations and save and print out a copy of the results. Each cell is identified by a unique cell reference which relates to its location on the grid. Rows and columns are marked numerically and alphabetically and the cell reference reflects this (ie A4, G35). Data contained within cells can be amended, and changes to numbers and formulae are automatically recalculated for the user.

This makes a spreadsheet an ideal tool for statistical forecasting and budgeting, and spreadsheet software is widely used in business. The data produced on the spreadsheet can also be translated into graphs or charts for ease of interpretation.

Spreadsheets which have been stored to disk can be recalled to screen, amended and printed out when needed.

This section of the workbook will guide you through the LCCIEB's three levels of Spreadsheet assignments. On the following pages you will find typical **First, Second** and **Third Level** Spreadsheet assignments. Each assignment is broken down into its composite parts and guidance is given as to how to approach the tasks.

This is what you should do:

1 First of all, check that you can perform all the functions that are listed for each level.
2 Read the accompanying text and follow the instructions carefully.
3 Work through each assignment at your own speed.
4 When you have completed the assignment, check your work with the specimen answer which appears at the end of this section.
5 When you feel confident that you can competently perform all the functions for the next level, continue through the workbook.

A full version of each assignment appears in Chapter 7.

First Level

For success in a First Level Spreadsheet assignment, you must be able to:

1 *Create and save a spreadsheet;*

2 *Retrieve and open a spreadsheet;*

3 *Enter text and data;*

4 *Edit data – delete and replace text and figures;*

5 *Edit the spreadsheet – insert and delete rows and columns;*

6 *Enter formulae and calculate data;*

7 *Recognise and perform corrections;*

8 *Print the spreadsheet;*

9 *Sort data into categories or alphabetical/numerical order;*

10 *Change the column width.*

Check that you can perform all these basic functions before you continue.

The **First Level** assignment set comprises six assignments which you must complete within 1 hour and 30 minutes. You are required to print out six versions of your spreadsheet, each printout being proof that you have accurately completed the tasks demanded of you. Always check to make sure that you have six printouts for marking.

Background

Before you begin work on your spreadsheet, there is an introductory section which gives you background information about the work you are about to undertake. You will be told the name of the company you are working for and the reason you are required to produce the work.

Figure 2.1 gives the background information for this set of assignments.

BACKGROUND

You work for Athena Electrical PLC, a retail company selling electrical goods to the general public. You have been assigned to the Market Research Department to help with the preparation of reports and statistics. Today you have been asked to use your spreadsheet package to present information relating to sales of certain electrical items. Please carry out the following instructions:

Figure 2.1   Background information for First Level spreadsheet assignments

ASSIGNMENT 1

Assignment 1 involves the simple keying in of a spreadsheet. It will contain text and figures and there will be no more than 20 rows and 12 columns. The original spreadsheet will be in typescript and you must follow the copy exactly. It is a good idea to position the words and numbers exactly as the original copy shows you. However, you will not be penalised at **First Level** if you choose not to embolden the text or align the headings.

Do not forget to:

- use each column – do not leave empty columns between data
- widen your column(s) if the words or figures will not fit in (this is often shown as a row of ####### within a cell – it simply means that your column is not wide enough to contain all the figures)
- check your work very carefully as you enter the data and again when you have completed the task
- save your work under the filename which is given on the instruction sheet
- make sure that your name appears on the spreadsheet (at the top or the bottom).

Figure 2.2 shows your first assignment.

ASSIGNMENT 1

Create a spreadsheet using the following layout (please format Item Cost figures to 2 decimal places):

ATHENA ELECTRICAL PLC

SALES FOR JANUARY – MARCH [YEAR]

Item Code	Item Description	Item Cost £	January	February	March
WM652	Washing Machine	349.99	219	230	264
WD438	Washer Dryer	620.20	124	100	145
DW871	Dishwasher	359.00	78	102	95
FR308	Larder Fridge	319.50	245	201	220
VC276	Upright Cleaner	69.50	145	202	164
MW283	Microwave Oven	249.99	213	302	265
VR994	Video Recorder	229.50	234	267	280
CC639	Camcorder	449.99	221	245	324
PR200	Deskjet Printer	145.00	456	403	387
TV880	Portable Television	199.50	521	530	568

Save this sheet as SS1 and print a copy entitled ASSIGNMENT 1.

Figure 2.2   First Level spreadsheet assignment 1

Did you remember to:

- insert this year's date in the sub-heading?
- follow capitalisation for headings and text entries?
- widen Column B so that all the words can be seen clearly?
- make sure that Column C shows figures to 2 decimal places?
- right align the headings over the figures in Columns C, D, E and F?
- embolden headings and column headings as copy?
- save your work to disk and print out a copy?

Check your work against the worked version which appears as Figure 2.18 on page 36.

ASSIGNMENT 2

Assignment 2 asks you to make changes to the original spreadsheet that you have saved and printed. You will be asked to amend words and figures within the rows and columns you have already entered. You may also be required to delete rows and add additional rows to the spreadsheet.

Do not forget to:

- be consistent with the positioning of words and figures when adding new data to your spreadsheet
- be consistent with the number of decimal places when displaying the new data
- delete the entire row as instructed so that no sign remains on the screen
- make all the changes listed.

Figure 2.3 gives your next set of instructions.

ASSIGNMENT 2

Unfortunately some of the information was not correct. Please make the following changes:

1 The Washing Machine now sells at £359.99.
2 The January sales of Microwave Ovens was 241.
3 The Upright Cleaner should not appear on this list. Delete the record.
4 The Deskjet Printer should be called the Deskjet Colour Printer.
5 Five new records need to be added to the table, as follows:

Item Code	Item Description	Item Cost £	January	February	March
TD456	Tumble Dryer	189.50	300	286	265
CF294	Chest Freezer	110.00	402	459	521
CM113	Coffee Maker	54.50	78	61	89
UF667	Upright Freezer	149.50	145	120	210
HC312	Home Cinema	859.00	86	65	78

Save this sheet as SS2 and print a copy entitled ASSIGNMENT 2.

Figure 2.3   First Level spreadsheet assignment 2

Did you remember to:

- delete the entire row containing details of the Upright Cleaner?
- extend the width of Column B to accommodate the insertion of the word Colour in Deskjet Colour Printer?
- make all the necessary changes?
- add the final five rows ensuring consistency of capitalisation and figures?

Check your printout against the worked version which appears as Figure 2.19 on page 36.

ASSIGNMENT 3

Assignment 3 asks for an additional column to be added to the spreadsheet. The position of the column may be within the spreadsheet or it may be added to the edge of the spreadsheet. You will also be asked to create formulae which will calculate the sum of certain cells. You will only be required to use the following formulae:

addition	=(cell reference)+(cell reference)	eg	=C6+F6
	=sum(range)	eg	=sum(C6:F6)
multiplication	=(cell reference)*(cell reference)	eg	=C6*F6
subtraction	=(cell reference)-(cell reference)	eg	=C6-F6
division	=(cell reference)/(cell reference)	eg	=C6/F6

No other formulae need be used. Always check that the formula used is correct before copying it to other cells.

Do not forget to:

- insert the extra column in the correct location on the spreadsheet
- make sure that the heading for the new column is displayed consistently with the existing headings
- test your formula on one row before repeating it on the remainder of the spreadsheet.

Figure 2.4 gives your next assignment:

ASSIGNMENT 3

In the cell to the right of the March column, type **Total Sales**. In that column, create a suitable formula to show the value of sales for each product.

Save this sheet as SS3 and print a copy entitled ASSIGNMENT 3.

Figure 2.4   First Level spreadsheet assignment 3

Did you remember to:

- position the new column at the far left hand side of the spreadsheet?
- format the heading so that it matches the other headings?
- use the correct formula – which will be something like =sum(D8:F8)*C8.

Check your printout with Figure 2.20 on page 37.

ASSIGNMENT 4

In Assignment 4 you will be asked to insert further columns in the spreadsheet. One of the columns will contain figures which will affect the totals you have already calculated, so you must be prepared to change the formula to incorporate the changes you have made. You may enter the new data manually or by copying from existing rows and columns. Use whichever method you are happiest with. Always check that the cells contain the correct words and figures.

Do not forget to:

- insert the new columns in the correct position and check the formatting
- ensure consistency with the display and capitalisation of the column headings
- check that the formulae used include all cells within the range
- check that the spreadsheet will still fit neatly on to one page.

Figure 2.5 gives your instructions for Assignment 4.

ASSIGNMENT 4

Sales for April are thought to be the same as those for March. Insert a new column between March and Total Sales, label it **April (Projected)** and enter the figures for each product. Ensure that the Total Sales column now shows the figures for the first four months of the year.

Insert a column between Item Code and Item Description and label it **Item Category**. Insert the word **Entertainment** alongside Video Recorder, Camcorder, Deskjet Colour Printer, Portable Television and Home Cinema. Insert the word **Domestic** alongside the other records.

Save this sheet as SS4 and print a copy entitled ASSIGNMENT 4.

Figure 2.5   First Level spreadsheet assignment 4

Did you remember to:

- enter the columns in the correct positions?
- right align the heading in the April (Projected) column and extend the column width?

- change the formulae in the Total Sales column to include the additional column?
- insert the words Entertainment and Domestic (correctly spelled) in the correct rows?
- change the paper orientation to landscape?

Good, now check your printout with the worked version which appears as Figure 2.21 on page 38.

ASSIGNMENT 5

Assignment 5 involves the sorting of data into alphabetical or numerical order. Two sorts will normally be required; the first to sort the data into groups, and the second to rearrange the data within the groups into the correct order. Always make sure that you sort all columns at the same time. It is sensible to make sure that your work has been carefully saved to disk before attempting the sort function.

You will also be asked to insert additional rows within the spreadsheet so that sub-totals can be included. You will be given clear instructions as to where these extra rows should be positioned and where the row heading should appear.

Once again, formulae will be required. You may choose to produce these figures by manually keying in the formulae or, if your spreadsheet software allows, you may choose to use the autosum function (which appears on your toolbar as Σ). Whichever method you choose, you should check that you have added together the correct range of cells.

Do not forget to:

- select the rows that you wish to sort – do not include empty rows or headings within your selection
- sort on the correct column (in this case, the Item Category column)
- insert and label the additional rows in the appropriate position
- check that your formulae produce the required sub-totals and grand totals
- format the totals rows to 2 decimal places.

Your instructions for Assignment 5 are shown in Figure 2.6.

ASSIGNMENT 5

Sort the table so that all the Domestic items are together and all the Entertainment items are under them. Within each grouping, the items should be arranged alphabetically.

Below each group insert a row showing the word **Sub-Total** in the first column. Use formulae to produce the sub-totals for both groups in all columns except Item Cost.

At the bottom of the spreadsheet type **Grand Total** in the first column. Use formulae to produce the grand total for all columns except Item Cost.

Save the completed spreadsheet as SS5 and print a copy entitled ASSIGNMENT 5.

Figure 2.6   First Level spreadsheet assignment 5

Did you remember to:

- sort the spreadsheet twice?
- produce sub-totals for all the numerical columns except **Item Cost**?
- produce a grand total for all numerical columns except **Item Cost**?

If so, check your work carefully against the worked version given in Figure 2.22 on page 39.

ASSIGNMENT 6

Assignment 6 is always the shortest assignment in the set. All that is required is a second printout of your final spreadsheet, showing the formulae instead of the figures. Check that you can do this procedure quickly and easily on your spreadsheet software.

It is a good idea to print out the column and row headings on this particular spreadsheet, so that your tutor can more easily check that your formulae are correct.

If your printer will allow, try to fit this particular spreadsheet on to one page only. You may be able to do this by automatically reducing the font size or you may have to perform the task manually. Do not worry if some of the words on the spreadsheet seem to disappear – this is not an error and you will not be penalised. However, you must check that all the formulae (including the final brackets) can be seen.

Do not forget to:

- print out the column and row headings
- reduce the font size so that the whole spreadsheet fits on to one page
- change the heading at the top of the assignment to Assignment 6.

Assignment 6 is given in Figure 2.7.

ASSIGNMENT 6

Print a copy of the completed spreadsheet, showing the formulae you have used in your calculations. This printout should be entitled ASSIGNMENT 6.

Figure 2.7   First Level spreadsheet assignment 6

Did you remember to:

- check that there was room in the columns for all the formulae to be seen?

Now check your formulae with those on the final printout shown in Figure 2.23 on page 40.

HELPFUL HINTS

- Use each column of the spreadsheet – do not leave empty columns.

- Ensure that all your text is visible by widening columns as required.

- Be consistent with the positioning of text and figures.

- Show figures to the required number of decimal places.

- Save each version of your spreadsheet under a separate filename.

- Make sure that your name appears on each printout.

- Check that you have included a printout showing the formulae used.

Second Level

For success in a Second Level Spreadsheet assignment, you must be able to perform all the functions tested at First Level:

1 *Create and save a spreadsheet;*

2 *Retrieve and open a spreadsheet;*

3 *Enter text and data;*

4 *Edit data – delete and replace text and figures;*

5 *Edit the spreadsheet – insert and delete rows and columns;*

6 *Enter formulae and calculate data;*

(continued)

---

7 *Recognise and perform corrections;*

8 *Print the spreadsheet;*

9 *Sort data into categories or alphabetical/numerical order;*

10 *Change the column width.*

You must also be able to:

1 *Use complex formulae to calculate data;*

2 *Define absolute and relative cells;*

3 *Format data;*

4 *Use simple spreadsheet formulae functions;*

5 *Print the spreadsheet or a defined section.*

Check that you can perform all these functions before you continue.

The **Second Level** assignment set comprises four assignments which must be completed within a 2-hour period. This more advanced spreadsheet will contain more complex data which will require careful checking prior to printing out. Specific formatting instructions will be given with regard to the inclusion of headers and footers, the alignment of headings and the use of multi-line headings. You should follow all instructions very carefully.

Background

As with the **First Level** Spreadsheet assignments, there is an introductory section which gives you information about the work you are about to undertake. This is to familiarise you with the organisation for whom you work and tells you why the spreadsheet is needed.

Figure 2.8 gives the background information for this **Second Level** set of assignments.

BACKGROUND

You work for Athena College which offers a range of courses to students of all ages. The Principal has asked you to prepare a set of figures showing the current course provision. Please follow the instructions below and prepare the necessary spreadsheets.

Figure 2.8   Background information for Second Level spreadsheet assignments

ASSIGNMENT I

Assignment 1 gives instructions relating to the creation of the original spreadsheet. You will be told which headings to use and instructions will be given regarding the formatting of text and numbers. You will also be asked to insert a cell with an absolute cell reference which will be used later for calculations. You may position this cell wherever you wish. Specific instructions relating to the completion of a header and a footer will also be given.

Do not forget to:

- use each column – do not leave empty columns between data
- follow instructions relating to the use of headings and the alignment of text
- follow copy regarding capitalisation (unless alternative instructions are given)
- check your work very carefully before saving to disk and printing out a copy for marking.

Figure 2.9 shows Assignment 1.

ASSIGNMENT 1

1 Prepare a spreadsheet with the main heading **ATHENA COLLEGE**. Include a sub-heading – **COURSE PROVISION**.
2 On the next row enter a cell to show a Lecturer Charge (per hour) of £25.
3 Enter the data given below on this page and embolden the two main headings.
4 Embolden the column headings and right justify those containing figures. Fees and charges should be shown as currency. Wrap the text so that longer headings appear on two lines (as below).
5 Insert a header to show your name and a footer with today's date.
6 Save a copy of the spreadsheet as AC1.
7 Print a copy of the spreadsheet on A4 landscape.

Course Title	Course Reference	Length (hours)	No in Group	Room Fee	Catering Charge
Time Management	BU4357	8	12	100	120
Assertiveness Training	BU3876	6	12	100	120
Health and Safety	BU8721	12	15	200	180
Communication Skills	BU9876	12	15	200	180
Internet Skills	TE3298	15	18	150	50
Presentation Skills	TE4597	12	20	200	50
Practical Computing	TE3390	20	18	180	50
Desktop Publishing	TE2190	25	18	250	50
Creative Writing	LE5572	30	20	150	0
Spanish for Beginners	LE9703	48	20	200	0
Holiday Italian	LE4497	48	20	200	0
Basic Japanese	LE2265	48	20	200	0
Practical Bookkeeping	VO2408	45	15	150	0
Business Administration	VO9765	45	15	150	0
Accounting	VO1437	45	15	150	0

Figure 2.9   Second Level spreadsheet assignment 1

Did you remember to:

- embolden the headings as instructed?
- include the information relating to the lecturer charge?
- wrap the text within Columns B–F to produce multi-line headings?
- extend the width of Column A to accommodate the longer course titles?
- follow copy regarding the capitalisation of the course titles?
- format Columns E and F for currency (with or without 2 decimal places)
- include a header and footer as requested?

Check your printout against the worked version shown in Figure 2.24 on page 41.

ASSIGNMENT 2

Assignment 2 involves further additions to the spreadsheet produced in Assignment 1, including the insertion of additional columns and the use of formulae to calculate totals and percentages. You may be asked to use any of the following formulae:

addition	=(cell reference)+(cell reference)	eg	=C6+F6
	=sum(range)	eg	=sum(C6:F6)
multiplication	=(cell reference)*(cell reference)	eg	=C6*F6
subtraction	=(cell reference)-(cell reference)	eg	=C6-F6
division	=(cell reference)/(cell reference)	eg	=C6/F6
average	=average(range)	eg	=average(C6:F6)
percentage	=(cell reference)/100*percentage	eg	=C6/100*10

However, you must relate at least one of the formulae to the cell with the absolute cell reference. Absolute cell references usually include the $ sign as an indicator. Thus an absolute reference would be $C$4.

Clear instructions will be given as to how to format the figures which result from the formulae you have used. You may be asked to show all figures to 2 decimal places. Alternatively you may be required to show all figures as integers (whole numbers). Be sure to follow the instructions carefully.

Do not forget to:

- check that the formulae you use produce the correct answers
- show all figures according to instructions
- be consistent in the display of text and figures when inserting new columns
- check that all text and figures can be easily read; extend column widths if necessary.

Figure 2.10 shows Assignment 2.

ASSIGNMENT 2

1   Insert a column after the **No in Group** column and give it the heading **Lecturer Costs**.

2   Enter a formula to calculate the lecturer costs on each course by multiplying the length in hours by the lecturer charge per hour. Show these figures as currency.

3   Add a column to the right of the **Catering Charge** column and give it the heading **Total Overheads**.

4   Enter a formula to calculate the total overheads for each course. Show these figures as whole numbers.

5   The College fees are calculated on a 50% markup on the total overhead figures. Add a further column and give it the heading **Total Charge**. Calculate the figures for each course and show the figures as whole numbers.

6   Insert a column after the **Course Reference** column and give it the heading **Course Fee**.

7   For each course calculate the course fee by dividing the total charge by the number in the group. Show each course fee as currency but without decimal places.

8   Ensure all column widths are adjusted to fit headings.

9   Adjust the spreadsheet to fit on one sheet of A4 landscape.

10   Save the spreadsheet as AC2.

11   Print a copy of the calculated spreadsheet on A4 landscape. Include the header and footer as in Assignment 1, point 5.

Figure 2.10 Second Level spreadsheet assignment 2

Did you remember to:

- ensure that the new column headings are displayed on two lines like the original headings?
- enter the correct formula to calculate the lecturer costs by using an absolute cell reference?
- enter the correct formula to calculate the 50% markup charge for the college fees?
- display all figures in the required format?
- check that your extended spreadsheet fits on to one sheet of A4 landscape?

Check your printout against the worked version as shown in Figure 2.25 which appears on page 42.

ASSIGNMENT 3

This assignment asks you to sort the spreadsheet into categories and then once again into a strict order (numerical or alphabetical). You are also asked to insert additional rows so that sub-totals can be calculated. You will also be asked to use a formula to work out the average number of a range of items. You will be given clear instructions and you should follow them carefully.

Do not forget to:

- sort the spreadsheet on the correct column
- insert additional rows in the correct locations
- use the correct formulae to calculate the necessary totals
- check that the spreadsheet will still fit on to one sheet of A4 landscape.

Figure 2.11 shows Assignment 3.

ASSIGNMENT 3

1   Sort the spreadsheet into alphabetical order of course reference.

2   Create four sections by inserting a row under each of the following courses:

Communication Skills
Spanish for Beginners
Presentation Skills

3   Sort each section into alphabetical order of course title.

4   Entitle each of the new rows **Total** and add a final row entitled **Total**. Embolden these titles.

5   Calculate the totals for lecturer costs and total overheads only. Embolden these two sets of figures.

6   Insert a further row underneath the four **Total** rows and entitle each of these rows **Average Course Fee**.

7   Use the Average function to calculate the average course fee.

8   Display the average figures in bold.

9   Save the spreadsheet as AC3.

10   Print a copy of the calculated spreadsheet on A4 landscape. Include the header and footer as in Assignment 1, point 5.

Figure 2.11   Second Level spreadsheet assignment 3

Did you remember to:

- sort the spreadsheet twice (on different columns)?
- insert the new rows in the correct locations?
- make all the necessary calculations?
- correctly use the average formula to calculate the average course fee?

Check your printout against the worked version shown in Figure 2.26 on page 43.

ASSIGNMENT 4

The final part of the assignment asks for some additional calculations to complete the spreadsheet. It also asks you to print out two copies of the spreadsheet, one showing the final figures and the second showing the formulae you have used. This is so that your tutor can check that your formulae are correct. It is a good idea to print out the column and row headings so that your tutor can check your work more easily. Do not forget to print out the additional copy; you will be penalised if you do not produce a total of five printouts for this set of assignments.

Do not forget to:

- display the figures in the format requested
- use the appropriate formulae to arrive at the correct totals
- print out two copies of your spreadsheet: one showing figures, one showing formulae.

Figure 2.12 shows Assignment 4.

ASSIGNMENT 4

1 The Principal wants to know how many students would be needed to cover the total overheads. Add a further column and give it the title **Break-Even Student No**.

2 Calculate the number of students needed to cover costs by dividing the total overheads by the course fee. Display the figures as whole numbers.

3 Leave a clear row at the bottom of the spreadsheet and then add the heading **TOTALS** in the first column. Embolden and italicise this heading.

4 Calculate totals for the columns headed **No in Group, Lecturer Costs, Room Fee, Catering Charge, Total Overheads** and **Total Charge**.

5 Display these figures in bold and italic.

6 Adjust the spreadsheet to fit on one sheet of A4 landscape.

7 Save the spreadsheet as AC4.

8 Print a copy of the calculated spreadsheet on A4 landscape. Include the header and footer as in Assignment 1, point 5.

9 Print a copy of the spreadsheet showing the formulae you have used. Display the column and row headings. Include the header and footer as in Assignment 1, point 5.

Figure 2.12 Second Level spreadsheet assignment 4

Did you remember to:

- widen column widths as required to display all figures clearly?
- ensure that the second printout shows all your formulae clearly and legibly?
- check that each spreadsheet fits on to one sheet of A4 landscape?

Now check your printouts with the worked versions as shown in Figures 2.27 and 2.28 on pages 44 and 45.

HELPFUL HINTS

- Use each column of the spreadsheet – do not leave empty columns.

- Ensure that all your text is visible by widening columns as required.

- Follow instructions relating to the use of headings.

- Be consistent with the positioning of text and figures.

- Include the appropriate header and footer on each printout.

- Check that you are familiar with the formulae being tested.

- Make sure that your printouts fit on to one sheet of A4 landscape.

Third Level

For success in a Third Level Spreadsheet assignment, you must be able to perform the functions tested at First Level:

1 *Create and save a spreadsheet;*

2 *Retrieve and open a spreadsheet;*

3 *Enter text and data;*

4 *Edit data – delete and replace text and figures;*

5 *Edit the spreadsheet – insert and delete rows and columns;*

6 *Enter formulae and calculate data;*

7 *Recognise and perform corrections;*

8 *Print the spreadsheet;*

9 *Sort data into categories or alphabetical/numerical order;*

10 *Change the column width.*

You must also be able to carry out the functions tested at Second Level:

1 *Use complex formulae to calculate data;*

2 *Define absolute and relative cells;*

3 *Format data;*

4 *Use simple spreadsheet formulae functions;*

5 *Print the spreadsheet or a defined section.*

You must also be able to:

1 *Create and use a spreadsheet template;*

2 *Create graphical representations of spreadsheet data;*

3 *Enter formulae using date functions;*

4 *Combine and link spreadsheets;*

5 *Enter conditional statements;*

6 *Use standard statistical spreadsheet functions;*

7 *Print graphs.*

Check that you can perform all these functions before you continue.

The **Third Level** assignment set comprises four assignments which must be completed within a time allowance of 2 hours and 30 minutes. The basis of the assignments is the production of a spreadsheet template containing formulae which, once saved, will be customised for three different clients. Extreme care should be taken to follow all instructions. You will be given more choice in the way you display the data within the spreadsheets, but the data must be formatted consistently. Information will be supplied which should be used throughout the assignment.

Background

As with assignments at **First** and **Second Level**, there is an introductory section which gives you information about the work you are to undertake. The information given at **Third Level** is more complicated than at previous levels and it is vital that you read it through carefully before designing your spreadsheet.

Figure 2.13 gives the background information for this **Third Level** Spreadsheet assignment.

BACKGROUND

You work for Athenaware Computer Supplies who provide computer equipment and accessories to educational establishments. You have been asked to prepare the August sales figures and analyse the sales of printers using the following two data tables:

SALES TO CUSTOMERS IN AUGUST

Date	Customer	Quantity	Item
6 August	Regency College	3	inkjet printers
6 August	Regency College	4	laserjet printers
6 August	Regency College	100	box 3.5" diskettes
9 August	Excelsior College	15	box 3.5" diskettes
9 August	Excelsior College	20	CD recordable disks
9 August	Excelsior College	10	box zip disks
10 August	Regency College	20	box zip disks
10 August	Regency College	6	box laser labels
10 August	Regency College	5	box inkjet labels
10 August	Central College	50	box 3.5" diskettes
10 August	Central College	10	box zip disks
12 August	Regency College	6	inkjet colour printers
12 August	Regency College	2	colour flatbed scanners
13 August	Central College	12	box laser labels
13 August	Central College	15	box inkjet labels
13 August	Central College	5	inkjet printers
15 August	Excelsior College	4	laserjet printers
15 August	Excelsior College	5	inkjet colour printers
15 August	Excelsior College	6	inkjet printers
21 August	Central College	8	laserjet printers
21 August	Central College	8	inkjet colour printers
21 August	Central College	2	flatbed scanners
23 August	Excelsior College	2	flatbed scanners
23 August	Excelsior College	10	box laser labels

ATHENAWARE COMPUTER SUPPLIES – PRICE LIST (EXCLUSIVE OF VAT)

Item	Unit of Supply	Price (£)
3.5" diskettes	box	11.45
CD-recordable disks	box	15.70
zip disks	box	81.25
inkjet labels	box	16.45
laser labels	box	18.25
flatbed scanner	each	85.50
colour flatbed scanner	each	159.00
inkjet printer	each	139.00
inkjet colour printer	each	209.50
laserjet printer	each	232.50

Figure 2.13 Background information for Third Level spreadsheet assignment

Follow the instructions given and create the spreadsheets.

Each spreadsheet must be in A4 landscape orientation adjusted to fit on one sheet. Insert a header showing the assignment number at the left of the page and your name at the right. Insert today's date at the bottom of the page in the centre. Headings and columns must be formatted and aligned consistently. Currency columns should be formatted to 2 decimal places. Headings and data may be in capitals or initial capitals and lower case.

1   Colleges are eligible for a 5% discount on each item if the total price for the item exceeds £150.

2   VAT (Value Added Tax) of 17.5% is not included in the price per item.

3   Orders equal to or in excess of a grand total of £5000 will not be liable to pay a delivery charge. Orders under £5000 will be charged a flat rate of £50. This is added to the final **Net Total + VAT** to make the **Grand Total**.

Figure 2.13 (continued)

Read the above information very carefully, particularly that which relates to the layout and formatting of the spreadsheet and the use of headers and footers.

Note also that points 1–3 in Figure 2.13 will be needed as you begin to insert formulae into the spreadsheet.

ASSIGNMENT I

Assignment 1 gives instructions relating to the creation of a spreadsheet template needed for the production of three customised spreadsheets. There will be no data included in this template but it must be saved under the filename given. The template will include the basic structure of the spreadsheet and the formulae which will be used to calculate the totals on the three customised spreadsheets. You will not be required to print out a copy of the template for marking, but you may find a printout helpful for your own use.

For this assignment you will need to refer once again to the Background Information which gives information relating to the calculation of VAT, the addition of the delivery charge and the deduction of the 5% discount.

The formulae used within the template could include any of the following:

addition	=(cell reference)+(cell reference)	eg	=C6+F6
	=sum(range)	eg	=sum(C6:F6)
multiplication	=(cell reference)*(cell reference)	eg	=C6*F6
subtraction	=(cell reference)-(cell reference)	eg	=C6-F6
division	=(cell reference)/(cell reference)	eg	=C6/F6
average	=average(range)	eg	=average(C6:F6)
percentage	=(cell reference)/100*percentage	eg	=C6/100*10

You will also be required to use 'IF' statements to create logical expressions and perform one of two operations depending on a condition. For example, a typical IF statement could be:

=IF(A6=>100,(A6+D6),0)

which would mean: if the value of cell A6 is equal to or greater than 100, add to its value the value of cell D6 and enter the sum into the active cell. If the value of cell A6 is less than 100, enter a value of 0 into the active cell.

You should not attempt this assignment if you are unsure about how to incorporate IF statements into a spreadsheet. If you *are* unsure, ask your tutor for assistance.

Do not forget to:

- insert the header and footer and change the page orientation to landscape
- use each column – do not leave empty columns between data
- leave sufficient space within columns for the longest item to fit comfortably
- choose whether to use capitals or lower case and initial capitals for your headings – and format them consistently
- insert the appropriate formulae in the columns which will need to be calculated for each client (columns headed Total Price, –5% Discount, VAT, Net Total + VAT, Delivery and Grand Total)
- include an apostrophe (') before the text if you have difficulty entering the column heading '–5% Discount'
- test the formulae used by inserting one line of data from the tables provided
- proofread the spreadsheet very carefully before saving it to disk.

Figure 2.14 gives Assignment 1.

ASSIGNMENT 1

Refer to the data in the two tables given above.

1   Set up the August spreadsheet template to be used to show Athenaware Computer Supplies' sales to each of the three named colleges.

2   Insert a suitable heading and include a space for the name of the college.

3   Use the following column headings suitably formatted: **Date, Quantity, Item Description, Price Each, Total Price, -5% Discount, VAT, Net Total + VAT, Delivery** and **Grand Total**. The figures for **Delivery** and **Grand Total** should be shown only at the base of the last two columns (on the **Totals** row referred to in Point 4 below).

4   In Assignment 2 there will be 8 rows of data to input. After these 8 rows, in the **Date** column, add a heading **Totals**. Sum the totals for all columns except **Date, Quantity, Item Description** and **Price Each**. On this row insert the figures for **Delivery** and **Grand Total**.

5   Save this template as SALES1. No printout is required.

Figure 2.14 Third Level spreadsheet assignment 1

Did you remember to:

- use a suitable heading, perhaps 'ATHENAWARE COMPUTER SUPPLIES – AUGUST SALES'?
- widen columns to accommodate the column headings and/or the data which will later be entered?
- format headings consistently? You will see that the headings of the columns containing figures have been right aligned.
- format currency columns to 2 decimal places (with or without the £ sign)?
- display the spreadsheet as instructed, leaving 8 rows between the column headings and the row containing totals?
- insert the header and footer as requested?
- check that the template fits on to one sheet of A4 landscape?

Check your template against the printouts which appear in Figures 2.29 and 2.30 on pages 46 and 47. Note that the first printout shows the layout of the template whilst the second printout shows the formulae and IF statements that have been used. You are *not* required to print out your template in the real assessment.

ASSIGNMENT 2

Assignment 2 relates to the input of data to the spreadsheet template; thus creating three personalised spreadsheets, one for each of the three colleges. You will need to refer to the Background Information for a list of the items to include in each spreadsheet. You must ensure that you save each spreadsheet separately, as they will be needed later for the purpose of linking.

Do not forget to:

- complete the top line of the first order to make sure that the formulae work
- include eight items for each college in date order
- check your work very carefully as you input the data – do not make any errors
- change the header so that the assignment number is now 2
- save each spreadsheet as instructed
- print out a copy, making sure that each one fits on to one sheet of A4 landscape.

The instructions for Assignment 2 are shown in Figure 2.15.

ASSIGNMENT 2

1   Use the template created in Assignment 1 to enter the relevant data from the tables above in order to compile 3 individual college order sheets for Regency College, Excelsior College and Central College.

2   Save your work as SALES2 (1), SALES2 (2) and SALES2 (3).

3   Print out the 3 individual order sheets.

4   Print a further copy of SALES2 (1) showing the formulae used.

Figure 2.15 Third Level spreadsheet assignment 2

Did you remember to:

- include the name of the college on each spreadsheet?
- tick off each item on the Sales sheet as you entered it?
- enter the data in strict date order?
- widen the columns as appropriate so that all words and numbers can be seen?
- print out a copy of each of the three spreadsheets, plus a further copy to show the formulae used?

Now check your three spreadsheets with those which appear in Figures 2.31, 2.32, 2.33 and 2.34 on pages 48–51.

ASSIGNMENT 3

Assignment 3 asks you to devise another spreadsheet (also in landscape format) which includes figures which have already been calculated on the previous spreadsheets. Therefore, you must link the new spreadsheet with cells in each of the spreadsheets relating to the three colleges.

Check that you are confident that you can successfully link spreadsheets before you continue. Once again, ask your tutor for assistance if you cannot successfully import data from one spreadsheet into another.

Do not forget to:

- include a suitable heading
- format the column headings and row titles consistently
- check that the links formed represent the correct information
- print out two copies, one showing the figures and one showing the formulae and links used.

Figure 2.16 gives the instructions for Assignment 3.

ASSIGNMENT 3

You are asked to analyse the sales of inkjet, inkjet colour and laserjet printers to the 3 colleges in August.

1	Create a spreadsheet to show the sub-totals for these 3 items for each customer. This spreadsheet will be linked to the 3 previous individual order spreadsheets.
2	Set up the spreadsheet using the headings **Item Description, Net Total + VAT – Regency, Net Total + VAT – Excelsior** and **Net Total + VAT – Central**. Add a column for the **Final Total**.
3	After the last entry in the **Item Description** column, add a label **Total Spent on Printers**.
4	Leave a blank row and then label the next row **Grand Total for Each College**.
5	Create links between the individual order spreadsheets so that the **Grand Total** on each college's August order sheet is automatically inserted into the relevant cells on this new spreadsheet. Calculate all totals.
6	Once the totals have been inserted leave a blank row and then label the next row **Percentage Spent on Printers**. Calculate to the nearest whole number what percentage of each college's entire order was spent on the purchase of printers.
7	Leave a row and then label the next row **Average Spent on Printers**. Calculate this and insert the answer under the **Final Total** column.
8	Save your work as SALES3.
9	Print a copy of this spreadsheet.
10	Print a copy of this spreadsheet showing the links and formulae you have used.

Figure 2.16 Third Level spreadsheet assignment 3

Did you remember to:

- allow sufficient space within each column to show all text and figures clearly?
- format some cells to 2 decimal places (those showing currency values) and others to integers (those showing percentages)?
- position the average figure in the correct cell location?

Check your printouts with those in Figures 2.35 and 2.36 on pages 52 and 53.

ASSIGNMENT 4

The final assignment at **Third Level** gives you the opportunity to produce graphs which represent some of the figures already calculated. The choice of graph or chart is left to you, but once again, you should ensure that you are consistent in your approach to formatting and that you include all the information required. You may produce a new spreadsheet on which to base your charts if you wish. Alternatively you may wish to select the relevant cells of an existing spreadsheet. The choice is yours. Choose whichever method guarantees the correct results.

Do not forget to:

- check that the figures on which your charts are based are accurate, particularly if you choose to enter them again on a new spreadsheet (you may wish to cut and paste this information into a new spreadsheet)
- use integers instead of 2 decimal places
- include a heading and labels for your charts
- ensure that your name and other details appear in the headers and footers as instructed
- print a copy of the two charts – you do not need to include the spreadsheet in your printout.

Figure 2.17 gives the instructions for Assignment 4.

ASSIGNMENT 4

1   Prepare 2 graphs (or charts) as follows:

    a   a graph or chart to show only the total figure from Assignment 3 spent on printers by each college (use whole numbers)

    b   a graph or chart to show a comparison of the Net Total + VAT for each type of printer in Assignment 3 bought by each of the colleges in August. Once again, use whole numbers.

    The graphs/charts can be in any format – pie chart, bar chart etc. Give each graph a suitable heading and label the data with the figures. Label both axes. Adjust and format where necessary.

2   Print one copy of each of these 2 graphs/charts.

Figure 2.17 Third Level spreadsheet assignment 4

Did you remember to:

- choose a graph which clearly shows the figures you wish to demonstrate? In the worked assignments you will see a pie chart and a bar graph.
- use sensible chart headings?
- ensure that the figures used were expressed as integers?
- use a legend for each graph to identify more clearly the data displayed?
- include your details within the header and footer zone?

Now look at the graphs shown in Figures 2.37 and 2.38 on pages 54 and 55. There is also a printout of the table used to formulate these charts for you to check your figures, shown in Figure 2.39 on page 56.

HELPFUL HINTS

- **Read all the background information carefully before starting work on your template spreadsheet – it contains valuable advice relating to the formulae you will be using.**

- **Use appropriate headings for your spreadsheets (use your common sense).**

- **Lay out the template ensuring consistency of capitalisation and formatting.**

- **Ensure that the longest item in each column can be accommodated by the column width.**

- **Key in all the formulae and test that they work correctly (you may wish to use a calculator to check that your final figures are accurate).**

- **Include the header and footer details as instructed and check the spreadsheet orientation (landscape).**

- **Check that each spreadsheet fits neatly on to one sheet of A4 landscape.**

- **Produce printouts of the formulae you have used.**

- **Save each spreadsheet under the filename given.**

- **Ensure that the graphs have unambiguous headings and are clearly labelled.**

Worked assignments

On the following pages, you will find the answers to the Spreadsheet assignments at **First, Second** and **Third Level**.

Check your work carefully against these correct versions.

ASSIGNMENT 1

	A	B	C	D	E	F
1	ATHENA ELECTRICAL PLC					
2						
3	SALES FOR JANUARY - MARCH [YEAR]					
4						
5	Item Code	Item Description	Item Cost	January	February	March
6			£			
7						
8	WM652	Washing Machine	349.99	219	230	264
9	WD438	Washer Dryer	620.20	124	100	145
10	DW871	Dishwasher	359.00	78	102	95
11	FR308	Larder Fridge	319.50	245	201	220
12	VC276	Upright Cleaner	69.50	145	202	164
13	MW283	Microwave Oven	249.99	213	302	265
14	VR994	Video Recorder	229.50	234	267	280
15	CC639	Camcorder	449.99	221	245	324
16	PR200	Deskjet Printer	145.00	456	403	387
17	TV880	Portable Television	199.50	521	530	568

Figure 2.18 Worked assignment 1 – First Level spreadsheet

ASSIGNMENT 2

	A	B	C	D	E	F
1	ATHENA ELECTRICAL PLC					
2						
3	SALES FOR JANUARY - MARCH [YEAR]					
4						
5	Item Code	Item Description	Item Cost	January	February	March
6			£			
7						
8	WM652	Washing Machine	359.99	219	230	264
9	WD438	Washer Dryer	620.20	124	100	145
10	DW871	Dishwasher	359.00	78	102	95
11	FR308	Larder Fridge	319.50	245	201	220
12	MW283	Microwave Oven	249.99	241	302	265
13	VR994	Video Recorder	229.50	234	267	280
14	CC639	Camcorder	449.99	221	245	324
15	PR200	Deskjet Colour Printer	145.00	456	403	387
16	TV880	Portable Television	199.50	521	530	568
17	TD456	Tumble Dryer	189.50	300	286	265
18	CF294	Chest Freezer	110.00	402	459	521
19	CM113	Coffee Maker	54.50	78	61	89
20	UF667	Upright Freezer	149.50	145	120	210
21	HC312	Home Cinema	859.00	86	65	78

Figure 2.19 Worked assignment 2 – First Level spreadsheet

ASSIGNMENT 3

	A	B	C	D	E	F	G
1	ATHENA ELECTRICAL PLC						
2							
3	SALES FOR JANUARY - MARCH [YEAR]						
4							
5	Item Code	Item Description	Item Cost	January	February	March	Total Sales
6			£				
7							
8	WM652	Washing Machine	359.99	219	230	264	256672.87
9	WD438	Washer Dryer	620.20	124	100	145	228853.80
10	DW871	Dishwasher	359.00	78	102	95	98725.00
11	FR308	Larder Fridge	319.50	245	201	220	212787.00
12	MW283	Microwave Oven	249.99	241	302	265	201991.92
13	VR994	Video Recorder	229.50	234	267	280	179239.50
14	CC639	Camcorder	449.99	221	245	324	355492.10
15	PR200	Deskjet Colour Printer	145.00	456	403	387	180670.00
16	TV880	Portable Television	199.50	521	530	568	322990.50
17	TD456	Tumble Dryer	189.50	300	286	265	161264.50
18	CF294	Chest Freezer	110.00	402	459	521	152020.00
19	CM113	Coffee Maker	54.50	78	61	89	12426.00
20	UF667	Upright Freezer	149.50	145	120	210	71012.50
21	HC312	Home Cinema	859.00	86	65	78	196711.00

Figure 2.20 Worked assignment 3 – First Level spreadsheet

ASSIGNMENT 4

	A	B	C	D	E	F	G	H	I
1	ATHENA ELECTRICAL PLC								
2									
3	SALES FOR JANUARY - MARCH [YEAR]								
4									
5	Item Code	Item Category	Item Description	Item Cost	January	February	March	April	Total Sales
6				£				(Projected)	
7									
8	WM652	Domestic	Washing Machine	359.99	219	230	264	264	351710.23
9	WD438	Domestic	Washer Dryer	620.20	124	100	145	145	318782.80
10	DW871	Domestic	Dishwasher	359.00	78	102	95	95	132830.00
11	FR308	Domestic	Larder Fridge	319.50	245	201	220	220	283077.00
12	MW283	Domestic	Microwave Oven	249.99	241	302	265	265	268239.27
13	VR994	Entertainment	Video Recorder	229.50	234	267	280	280	243499.50
14	CC639	Entertainment	Camcorder	449.99	221	245	324	324	501288.86
15	PR200	Entertainment	Deskjet Colour Printer	145.00	456	403	387	387	236785.00
16	TV880	Entertainment	Portable Television	199.50	521	530	568	568	436306.50
17	TD456	Domestic	Tumble Dryer	189.50	300	286	265	265	211482.00
18	CF294	Domestic	Chest Freezer	110.00	402	459	521	521	209330.00
19	CM113	Domestic	Coffee Maker	54.50	78	61	89	89	17276.50
20	UF667	Domestic	Upright Freezer	149.50	145	120	210	210	102407.50
21	HC312	Entertainment	Home Cinema	859.00	86	65	78	78	263713.00

Figure 2.21 Worked assignment 4 – First Level spreadsheet

ASSIGNMENT 5

	A	B	C	D	E	F	G	H	I
1	ATHENA ELECTRICAL PLC								
2									
3	SALES FOR JANUARY - MARCH [YEAR]								
4									
5	Item Code	Item Category	Item Description	Item Cost	January	February	March	April	Total Sales
6				£				(Projected)	
7									
8	CF294	Domestic	Chest Freezer	110.00	402	459	521	521	209330.00
9	CM113	Domestic	Coffee Maker	54.50	78	61	89	89	17276.50
10	DW871	Domestic	Dishwasher	359.00	78	102	95	95	132830.00
11	FR308	Domestic	Larder Fridge	319.50	245	201	220	220	283077.00
12	MW283	Domestic	Microwave Oven	249.99	241	302	265	265	268239.27
13	TD456	Domestic	Tumble Dryer	189.50	300	286	265	265	211482.00
14	UF667	Domestic	Upright Freezer	149.50	145	120	210	210	102407.50
15	WD438	Domestic	Washer Dryer	620.20	124	100	145	145	318782.80
16	WM652	Domestic	Washing Machine	359.99	219	230	264	264	351710.23
17	Sub-Total				1832	1861	2074	2074	1895135.30
18	CC639	Entertainment	Camcorder	449.99	221	245	324	324	501288.86
19	PR200	Entertainment	Deskjet Colour Printer	145.00	456	403	387	387	236785.00
20	HC312	Entertainment	Home Cinema	859.00	86	65	78	78	263713.00
21	TV880	Entertainment	Portable Television	199.50	521	530	568	568	436306.50
22	VR994	Entertainment	Video Recorder	229.50	234	267	280	280	243499.50
23	Sub-Total				1518	1510	1637	1637	1681592.86
24	Grand Total				3350	3371	3711	3711	3576728.16

Figure 2.22 Worked assignment 5 – First Level spreadsheet

39

	A	B	C	D	E	F	G	H	I
1	ATHENA ELECTRICAL PLC								
2									
3	SALES FOR JANUARY - MA								
4									
5	Item Code	Item Category	Item Description	Item Cost	January	February	March	April	Total Sales
6				£				(Projected)	
7									
8	CF294	Domestic	Chest Freezer	110	402	459	521	521	=SUM(E8:H8)*D8
9	CM113	Domestic	Coffee Maker	54.5	78	61	89	89	=SUM(E9:H9)*D9
10	DW871	Domestic	Dishwasher	369	78	102	95	95	=SUM(E10:H10)*D10
11	FR308	Domestic	Larder Fridge	319.5	245	201	220	220	=SUM(E11:H11)*D11
12	MW283	Domestic	Microwave Oven	249.99	241	302	265	265	=SUM(E12:H12)*D12
13	TD456	Domestic	Tumble Dryer	189.5	300	286	265	265	=SUM(E13:H13)*D13
14	UF667	Domestic	Upright Freezer	149.5	145	120	210	210	=SUM(E14:H14)*D14
15	WD438	Domestic	Washer Dryer	620.2	124	100	145	145	=SUM(E15:H15)*D15
16	WM652	Domestic	Washing Machine	359.99	219	230	264	264	=SUM(E16:H16)*D16
17	Sub-Total				=SUM(E8:E16)	=SUM(F8:F16)	=SUM(G8:G16)	=SUM(H8:H16)	=SUM(I8:I16)
18	CC639	Entertainment	Camcorder	449.99	221	245	324	324	=SUM(E18:H18)*D18
19	PR200	Entertainment	DeskJet Colour Printer	145	456	403	387	387	=SUM(E19:H19)*D19
20	HC312	Entertainment	Home Cinema	859	86	65	78	78	=SUM(E20:H20)*D20
21	TV880	Entertainment	Portable Television	199.5	521	530	568	568	=SUM(E21:H21)*D21
22	VR994	Entertainment	Video Recorder	229.5	234	267	280	280	=SUM(E22:H22)*D22
23	Sub-Total				=SUM(E18:E22)	=SUM(F18:F22)	=SUM(G18:G22)	=SUM(H18:H22)	=SUM(I18:I22)
24	Grand Total				=E17+E23	=F17+F23	=G17+G23	=H17+H23	=I17+I23

Figure 2.23 Worked assignment 6 – First Level spreadsheet

Candidate's Name

	A	B	C	D	E	F
1	ATHENA COLLEGE					
2						
3	COURSE PROVISION					
4	Lecturer Charge (per hour)	£25.00				
5						
6	Course Title	Course Reference	Length (hours)	No in Group	Room Fee	Catering Charge
7						
8	Time Management	BU4357	8	12	£100	£120
9	Assertiveness Training	BU3876	6	12	£100	£120
10	Health and Safety	BU8721	12	15	£200	£180
11	Communication Skills	BU9876	12	15	£200	£180
12	Internet Skills	TE3298	15	18	£150	£50
13	Presentation Skills	TE4597	12	20	£200	£50
14	Practical Computing	TE3390	20	18	£180	£50
15	Desktop Publishing	TE2190	25	18	£250	£50
16	Creative Writing	LE5572	30	20	£150	£0
17	Spanish for Beginners	LE9703	48	20	£200	£0
18	Holiday Italian	LE4497	48	20	£200	£0
19	Basic Japanese	LE2265	48	20	£200	£0
20	Practical Bookkeeping	VO2408	45	15	£150	£0
21	Business Administration	VO9765	45	15	£150	£0
22	Accounting	VO1437	45	15	£150	£0

Today's Date

Figure 2.24 Worked assignment 1 – Second Level spreadsheet

	A	B	C	D	E	F	G	H	I	J
1	ATHENA COLLEGE									
2										
3	COURSE PROVISION									
4	Lecturer Charge (per hour)	£25.00								
5										
6	Course Title	Course Reference	Course Fee	Length (hours)	No in Group	Lecturer Costs	Room Fee	Catering Charge	Total Overheads	Total Charge
7										
8	Time Management	BU4357	£53	8	12	£200	£100	£120	£420	£630
9	Assertiveness Training	BU3876	£46	6	12	£150	£100	£120	£370	£555
10	Health and Safety	BU8721	£68	12	15	£300	£200	£180	£680	£1,020
11	Communication Skills	BU9876	£68	12	15	£300	£200	£180	£680	£1,020
12	Internet Skills	TE3298	£48	15	18	£375	£150	£50	£575	£863
13	Presentation Skills	TE4597	£41	12	20	£300	£200	£50	£550	£825
14	Practical Computing	TE3390	£61	20	18	£500	£180	£50	£730	£1,095
15	Desktop Publishing	TE2190	£77	25	18	£625	£250	£50	£925	£1,388
16	Creative Writing	LE5572	£68	30	20	£750	£150	£0	£900	£1,350
17	Spanish for Beginners	LE9703	£105	48	20	£1,200	£200	£0	£1,400	£2,100
18	Holiday Italian	LE4497	£105	48	20	£1,200	£200	£0	£1,400	£2,100
19	Basic Japanese	LE2265	£105	48	20	£1,200	£200	£0	£1,400	£2,100
20	Practical Bookkeeping	VO2408	£128	45	15	£1,125	£150	£0	£1,275	£1,913
21	Business Administration	VO9765	£128	45	15	£1,125	£150	£0	£1,275	£1,913
22	Accounting	VO1437	£128	45	15	£1,125	£150	£0	£1,275	£1,913

Today's Date

Figure 2.25 Worked assignment 2 – Second Level spreadsheet

	A	B	C	D	E	F	G	H	I	J
1	ATHENA COLLEGE									
2										
3	COURSE PROVISION									
4	Lecturer Charge (per hour)	£25.00								
5										
6	Course Title	Course Reference	Course Fee	Length (hours)	No in Group	Lecturer Costs	Room Fee	Catering Charge	Total Overheads	Total Charge
7										
8	Assertiveness Training	BU3876	£46	6	12	£150	£100	£120	£370	£555
9	Communication Skills	BU9876	£68	12	15	£300	£200	£180	£680	£1,020
10	Health and Safety	BU8721	£68	12	15	£300	£200	£180	£680	£1,020
11	Time Management	BU4357	£53	8	12	£200	£100	£120	£420	£630
12	Total					£950			£2,150	
13	Average Course Fee		£59							
14	Basic Japanese	LE2265	£105	48	20	£1,200	£200	£0	£1,400	£2,100
15	Creative Writing	LE5572	£68	30	20	£750	£150	£0	£900	£1,350
16	Holiday Italian	LE4497	£105	48	20	£1,200	£200	£0	£1,400	£2,100
17	Spanish for Beginners	LE9703	£105	48	20	£1,200	£200	£0	£1,400	£2,100
18	Total					£4,350			£5,100	
19	Average Course Fee		£96							
20	Desktop Publishing	TE2190	£77	25	18	£625	£250	£50	£925	£1,388
21	Internet Skills	TE3298	£48	15	18	£375	£150	£50	£575	£863
22	Practical Computing	TE3390	£61	20	18	£500	£180	£50	£730	£1,095
23	Presentation Skills	TE4597	£41	12	20	£300	£200	£50	£550	£825
24	Total					£1,800			£2,780	
25	Average Course Fee		£57							
26	Accounting	VO1437	£128	45	15	£1,125	£150	£0	£1,275	£1,913
27	Business Administration	VO9765	£128	45	15	£1,125	£150	£0	£1,275	£1,913
28	Practical Bookkeeping	VO2408	£128	45	15	£1,125	£150	£0	£1,275	£1,913
29	Total					£3,375			£3,825	
30	Average Course Fee		£128							

Today's Date

Figure 2.26 Worked assignment 3 – Second Level spreadsheet

	A	B	C	D	E	F	G	H	I	J	K
			Course Fee	Length (hours)	No in Group	Lecturer Costs	Room Fee	Catering Charge	Total Overheads	Total Charge	Break-Even Student No
1	ATHENA COLLEGE										
2											
3	COURSE PROVISION										
4	Lecturer Charge (per hour)	£25.00									
5											
6	Course Title	Course Reference	Course Fee	Length (hours)	No in Group	Lecturer Costs	Room Fee	Catering Charge	Total Overheads	Total Charge	Break-Even Student No
7											
8	Assertiveness Training	BU3876	£46	6	12	£150	£100	£120	£370	£555	8
9	Communication Skills	BU9876	£68	12	15	£300	£200	£180	£680	£1,020	10
10	Health and Safety	BU8721	£68	12	15	£300	£200	£180	£680	£1,020	10
11	Time Management	BU4357	£53	8	12	£200	£100	£120	£420	£630	8
12	Total					£950			£2,150		
13	Average Course Fee		£59								
14	Basic Japanese	LE2265	£105	48	20	£1,200	£200	£0	£1,400	£2,100	13
15	Creative Writing	LE5572	£68	30	20	£750	£150	£0	£900	£1,350	13
16	Holiday Italian	LE4497	£105	48	20	£1,200	£200	£0	£1,400	£2,100	13
17	Spanish for Beginners	LE9703	£105	48	20	£1,200	£200	£0	£1,400	£2,100	13
18	Total					£4,350			£5,100		
19	Average Course Fee		£96								
20	Desktop Publishing	TE2190	£77	25	18	£625	£250	£50	£925	£1,388	12
21	Internet Skills	TE3298	£48	15	18	£375	£150	£50	£575	£863	12
22	Practical Computing	TE3390	£61	20	18	£500	£180	£50	£730	£1,095	12
23	Presentation Skills	TE4597	£41	12	20	£300	£200	£50	£550	£825	
24	Total					£1,800			£2,780		
25	Average Course Fee		£57								
26	Accounting	VO1437	£128	45	15	£1,125	£150	£0	£1,275	£1,913	10
27	Business Administration	VO9765	£128	45	15	£1,125	£150	£0	£1,275	£1,913	10
28	Practical Bookkeeping	VO2408	£128	45	15	£1,125	£150	£0	£1,275	£1,913	10
29	Total					£3,375			£3,825		
30	Average Course Fee		£128								
31											
32	TOTALS				253	£10,475	£2,580	£800	£13,855	£20,783	

Today's Date

Figure 2.27 Worked assignment 4 – Second Level spreadsheet

	A	B	C	D	E	F	G	H	I	J	K
1	ATHENA COLLEGE										
2											
3	COURSE PROVISION										
4	Lecturer Charge (per hour)	25									
5											
6	Course Title	Course Reference	Course Fee	Length (hours)	No in Group	Lecturer Costs	Room Fee	Catering Charge	Total Overheads	Total Charge	Break-Even Student No
7											
8	Assertiveness Training	BU3876	=J8/E8	6	12	=D8*$B$4	100	120	=SUM(F8:H8)	=I8/100*150	=I8/C8
9	Communication Skills	BU9876	=J9/E9	12	15	=D9*$B$4	200	180	=SUM(F9:H9)	=I9/100*150	=I9/C9
10	Health and Safety	BU8721	=J10/E10	12	15	=D10*$B$4	200	180	=SUM(F10:H10)	=I10/100*150	=I10/C10
11	Time Management	BU4357	=J11/E11	8	12	=D11*$B$4	100	120	=SUM(F11:H11)	=I11/100*150	=I11/C11
12	Total					=SUM(F8:F11)			=SUM(I8:I11)		
13	Average Course Fee		=AVERAGE(C8:C11)								
14	Basic Japanese	LE2265	=J14/E14	48	20	=D14*$B$4	200	0	=SUM(F14:H14)	=I14/100*150	=I14/C14
15	Creative Writing	LE5572	=J15/E15	30	20	=D15*$B$4	150	0	=SUM(F15:H15)	=I15/100*150	=I15/C15
16	Holiday Italian	LE4497	=J16/E16	48	20	=D16*$B$4	200	0	=SUM(F16:H16)	=I16/100*150	=I16/C16
17	Spanish for Beginners	LE9703	=J17/E17	48	20	=D17*$B$4	200	0	=SUM(F17:H17)	=I17/100*150	=I17/C17
18	Total					=SUM(F14:F17)			=SUM(I14:I17)		
19	Average Course Fee		=AVERAGE(C14:C17)								
20	Desktop Publishing	TE2190	=J20/E20	25	18	=D20*$B$4	250	50	=SUM(F20:H20)	=I20/100*150	=I20/C20
21	Internet Skills	TE3298	=J21/E21	15	18	=D21*$B$4	150	50	=SUM(F21:H21)	=I21/100*150	=I21/C21
22	Practical Computing	TE3390	=J22/E22	20	18	=D22*$B$4	180	50	=SUM(F22:H22)	=I22/100*150	=I22/C22
23	Presentation Skills	TE4597	=J23/E23	12	20	=D23*$B$4	200	50	=SUM(F23:H23)	=I23/100*150	=I23/C23
24	Total					=SUM(F20:F23)			=SUM(I20:I23)		
25	Average Course Fee		=AVERAGE(C20:C23)								
26	Accounting	VO1437	=J26/E26	45	15	=D26*$B$4	150	0	=SUM(F26:H26)	=I26/100*150	=I26/C26
27	Business Administration	VO9765	=J27/E27	45	15	=D27*$B$4	150	0	=SUM(F27:H27)	=I27/100*150	=I27/C27
28	Practical Bookkeeping	VO2408	=J28/E28	45	15	=D28*$B$4	150	0	=SUM(F28:H28)	=I28/100*150	=I28/C28
29	Total					=SUM(F26:F28)			=SUM(I26:I28)		
30	Average Course Fee		=AVERAGE(C26:C28)								
31											
32	TOTALS				=SUM(E8:E28)	=F12+F18+F24+F29	=SUM(G8:G28)	=SUM(H8:H28)	=I12+I18+I24+I29	=SUM(J8:J28)	

Today's Date

Figure 2.28 Formulae for worked assignment 4 – Second Level spreadsheet

Assignment 1

SALES 1

	A	B	C	D	E	F				
1	ATHENAWARE COMPUTER SUPPLIES									
2										
3	AUGUST SALES									
4										
5	College									
6										
7	Date	Quantity	Item Description	Price Each	Total Price	-5% Discount	VAT	Net Total + VAT	Delivery	Grand Total
8					£0.00	£0.00	£0.00	£0.00		
9										
10										
11										
12										
13										
14										
15										
16	Totals				£0.00	£0.00	£0.00	£0.00	£50.00	£50.00

Today's Date

Figure 2.29 Template for assignment 1 – Third Level spreadsheet

	A	B	C	D	E	F	G	H	I	J
1	ATHENAWARE COM									
2										
3	AUGUST SALES									
4										
5	College									
6										
7	Date	Quantity	Item Description	Price Each	Total Price	-5% Discount	VAT	Net Total + VAT	Delivery	Grand Total
8					=D8*B8	=IF(E8>=150,(E8*95%),E8)	=F8*17.5%	=F8+G8		
9										
10										
11										
12										
13										
14										
15										
16	Totals				=SUM(E8:E15)	=SUM(F8:F15)	=SUM(G8:G15)	=SUM(H8:H15)	=IF(H16<=5000,(50),0)	=H16+I16

Today's Date

Figure 2.30 Formulae template for assignment 1 – Third Level spreadsheet

	A	B	C	D	E	F	G	H	I	J
1	ATHENAWARE COMPUTER SUPPLIES									
2										
3	AUGUST SALES									
4										
5	College	REGENCY								
6										
7	Date	Quantity	Item Description	Price Each	Total Price	-5% Discount	VAT	Net Total + VAT	Delivery	Grand Total
8	06/08/--	3	Inkjet printers	£139.00	£417.00	£396.15	£69.33	£465.48		
9	06/08/--	4	Laserjet printers	£232.50	£930.00	£883.50	£154.61	£1,038.11		
10	06/08/--	100	Box 3.5" diskettes	£11.45	£1,145.00	£1,087.75	£190.36	£1,278.11		
11	10/08/--	20	Box zip disks	£81.25	£1,625.00	£1,543.75	£270.16	£1,813.91		
12	10/08/--	6	Box laser labels	£18.25	£109.50	£109.50	£19.16	£128.66		
13	10/08/--	5	Box inkjet labels	£16.45	£82.25	£82.25	£14.39	£96.64		
14	12/08/--	6	Inkjet colour printers	£209.50	£1,257.00	£1,194.15	£208.98	£1,403.13		
15	12/08/--	2	Colour flatbed scanners	£159.00	£318.00	£302.10	£52.87	£354.97		
16	Totals				£5,883.75	£5,599.15	£979.85	£6,579.00	£0.00	£6,579.00

Today's Date

Figure 2.31 Worked assignment 2 (Regency) – Third Level spreadsheet

	A	B	C	D	E	F	G	H	I	J
								Net Total +		Grand
				Price						
	Date	Quantity	Item Description	Each	Total Price	-5% Discount	VAT	VAT	Delivery	Total
1	ATHENAWARE COMPUTER SUPPLIES									
2										
3	AUGUST SALES									
4										
5	College	EXCELSIOR								
6										
7	Date	Quantity	Item Description	Price Each	Total Price	-5% Discount	VAT	Net Total + VAT	Delivery	Grand Total
8	09/08/--	15	Box 3.5" diskettes	£11.45	£171.75	£163.16	£28.55	£191.72		
9	09/08/--	20	CD recordable disks	£15.70	£314.00	£298.30	£52.20	£350.50		
10	09/08/--	10	Box zip disks	£81.25	£812.50	£771.88	£135.08	£906.95		
11	15/08/--	4	Laserjet printers	£232.50	£930.00	£883.50	£154.61	£1,038.11		
12	15/08/--	5	Inkjet colour printers	£209.50	£1,047.50	£995.13	£174.15	£1,169.27		
13	15/08/--	6	Inkjet printers	£139.00	£834.00	£792.30	£138.65	£930.95		
14	23/08/--	2	Flatbed scanners	£85.50	£171.00	£162.45	£28.43	£190.88		
15	23/08/--	10	Box laser labels	£18.25	£182.50	£173.38	£30.34	£203.72		
16	Totals				£4,463.25	£4,240.09	£742.02	£4,982.10	£50.00	£5,032.10

Today's Date

Figure 2.32 Worked assignment 2 (Excelsior) – Third Level spreadsheet

49

	A	B	C	D	E	F	G	H	I	J
1	ATHENAWARE COMPUTER SUPPLIES									
2										
3	AUGUST SALES									
4										
5	College	CENTRAL								
6										
7	Date	Quantity	Item Description	Price Each	Total Price	-5% Discount	VAT	Net Total + VAT	Delivery	Grand Total
8	10/08/--	50	Box 3.5" diskettes	£11.45	£572.50	£543.88	£95.18	£639.05		
9	10/08/--	10	Box zip disks	£81.25	£812.50	£771.88	£135.08	£906.95		
10	13/08/--	12	Box laser labels	£18.25	£219.00	£208.05	£36.41	£244.46		
11	13/08/--	15	Box inkjet labels	£16.45	£246.75	£234.41	£41.02	£275.43		
12	13/08/--	5	Inkjet printers	£139.00	£695.00	£660.25	£115.54	£775.79		
13	21/08/--	8	Laserjet printers	£232.50	£1,860.00	£1,767.00	£309.23	£2,076.23		
14	21/08/--	8	Inkjet colour printers	£209.50	£1,676.00	£1,592.20	£278.64	£1,870.84		
15	21/08/--	2	Flatbed scanners	£85.50	£171.00	£162.45	£28.43	£190.88		
16	Totals				£6,252.75	£5,940.11	£1,039.52	£6,979.63	£0.00	£6,979.63

Today's Date

Figure 2.33 Worked assignment 2 (Central) – Third Level spreadsheet

	A	B	C	D	E	F	G	H	I	J
1	ATHENAWARE C(									
2										
3	AUGUST SALES									
4										
5	College	REGENCY								
6										
7	Date	Quantity	Item Description	Price Each	Total Price	-5% Discount	VAT	Net Total + VAT	Delivery	Grand Total
8	06/08/--	3	Inkjet printers	139	=D8*B8	=IF(E8>=150,(E8*95%),E8)	=F8*17.5%	=F8+G8		
9	06/08/--	4	Laserjet printers	232.5	=D9*B9	=IF(E9>=150,(E9*95%),E9)	=F9*17.5%	=F9+G9		
10	06/08/--	100	Box 3.5" diskettes	11.45	=D10*B10	=IF(E10>=150,(E10*95%),E10)	=F10*17.5%	=F10+G10		
11	10/08/--	20	Box zip disks	81.25	=D11*B11	=IF(E11>=150,(E11*95%),E11)	=F11*17.5%	=F11+G11		
12	10/08/--	6	Box laser labels	18.25	=D12*B12	=IF(E12>=150,(E12*95%),E12)	=F12*17.5%	=F12+G12		
13	10/08/--	5	Box inkjet labels	16.45	=D13*B13	=IF(E13>=150,(E13*95%),E13)	=F13*17.5%	=F13+G13		
14	12/08/--	6	Inkjet colour printers	209.5	=D14*B14	=IF(E14>=150,(E14*95%),E14)	=F14*17.5%	=F14+G14		
15	12/08/--	2	Colour flatbed scanners	159	=D15*B15	=IF(E15>=150,(E15*95%),E15)	=F15*17.5%	=F15+G15		
16	Totals				=SUM(E8:E15)	=SUM(F8:F15)	=SUM(G8:G15)	=SUM(H8:H15)	=IF(H16<=5000,(H6+50),0)	=H16+I16

Today's Date

Figure 2.34 Formulae for assignment 2 – Third Level spreadsheet

51

SALES3

	A	B	C	D	E
1	ATHENAWARE COMPUTER SUPPLIES				
2					
3	SALES OF PRINTERS IN AUGUST				
4					
5	Item Description	Net Total + VAT - Regency	Net Total + VAT - Excelsior	Net Total + VAT - Central	Final Total
6	Inkjet Printers	£465.48	£930.95	£775.79	£2,172.22
7	Inkjet Colour Printers	£1,403.13	£1,169.27	£1,870.84	£4,443.23
8	Laserjet Printers	£1,038.11	£1,038.11	£2,076.23	£4,152.45
9	Total Spent on Printers	£2,906.72	£3,138.34	£4,722.85	£10,767.91
10					
11	Grand Total for Each College	£6,579.00	£5,032.10	£6,979.63	
12					
13	Percentage Spent on Printers	44	62	68	
14					
15	Average Spent on Printers				£3,589.30

Today's Date

Figure 2.35 Worked assignment 3 – Third Level spreadsheet

	A	B	C	D	E
1	ATHENAWARE COMPUTER SUPPLIES				
2					
3	SALES OF PRINTERS IN AUGUST				
4					
5	Item Description	Net Total + VAT - Regency	Net Total + VAT - Excelsior	Net Total + VAT - Central	Final Total
6	Inkjet Printers	='C:\[SALES2(1).xls]Sheet1'!$H$8	='C:\[SALES2(2).xls]Sheet1'!$H$13	='C:\[SALES2(3).xls]Sheet1'!$H$12	=SUM(B6:D6)
7	Inkjet Colour Printers	='C:\[SALES2(1).xls]Sheet1'!$H$14	='C:\[SALES2(2).xls]Sheet1'!$H$12	='C:\[SALES2(3).xls]Sheet1'!$H$14	=SUM(B7:D7)
8	Laserjet Printers	='C:\[SALES2(1).xls]Sheet1'!$H$9	='C:\[SALES2(2).xls]Sheet1'!$H$11	='C:\[SALES2(3).xls]Sheet1'!$H$13	=SUM(B8:D8)
9	Total Spent on Printers	=SUM(B6:B8)	=SUM(C6:C8)	=SUM(D6:D8)	=SUM(B9:D9)
10					
11	Grand Total for Each College	='C:\[SALES2(1).xls]Sheet1'!$J$16	='C:\[SALES2(2).xls]Sheet1'!$J$16	='C:\[SALES2(3).xls]Sheet1'!$J$16	
12					
13	Percentage Spent on Printers	=B9/B11*100	=C9/C11*100	=D9/D11*100	
14					
15	Average Spent on Printers				=AVERAGE(B9:D9)

Today's Date

Figure 2.36 Formulae for assignment 3 – Third Level spreadsheet

53

GRAPH A

SALES OF PRINTERS TO COLLEGES IN AUGUST

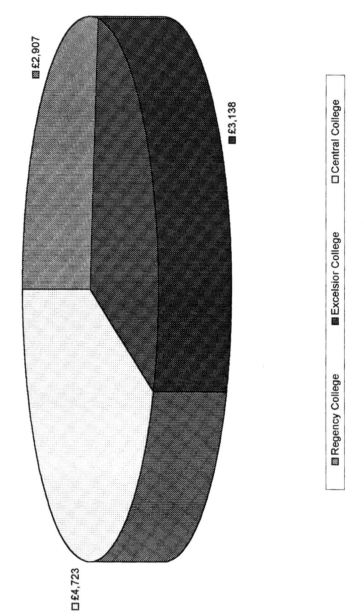

Regency College   Excelsior College   Central College

Today's Date

Figure 2.37 Pie chart for assignment 4 – Third Level spreadsheet

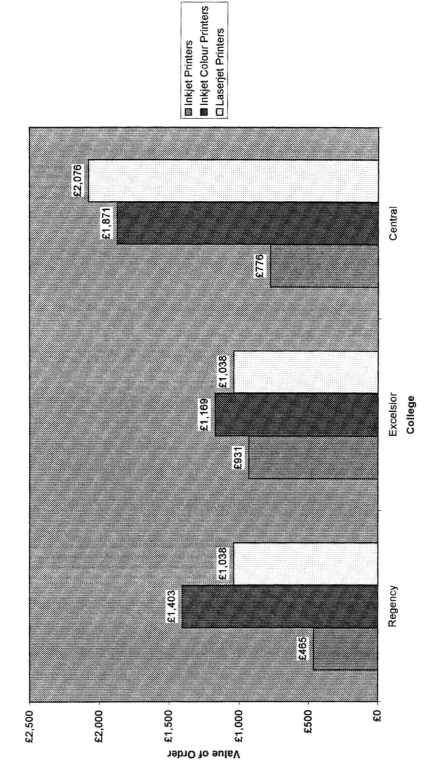

COMPARISON OF PRINTER TYPES BOUGHT BY COLLEGES IN AUGUST

Today's Date

Figure 2.38   Bar chart for assignment 4 – Third Level spreadsheet

GRAPHS

	A	B	C	D	E	F	G
1	CHART A			CHART B			
2					Regency	Excelsior	Central
3	Regency College	£2,907		Inkjet Printers	£465	£931	£776
4	Excelsior College	£3,138		Inkjet Colour Printers	£1,403	£1,169	£1,871
5	Central College	£4,723		Laserjet Printers	£1,038	£1,038	£2,076

Today's Date

Figure 2.39 Table for assignment 4 – Third Level spreadsheet

3

Databases

Introduction

We all use databases. The telephone directory is a database, catalogues are databases, inventories are databases and so are other structured lists. There are very many business uses for databases so it is advisable to know something about them, how to set them up and how to extract information from them. As well as business uses, there are leisure and home uses for databases. Databases can be set up to keep records of many personal hobbies and activities such as collecting CDs, videos, stamps or books and to monitor activities such as personal fitness or gardening.

A database package enables the user to enter text, numbers and other data to form records which make up a file in the database. This data can be saved to disk and printed out as hard copy on paper. The database file can be amended, edited, added to, queried, sorted and specific records selected. The data can be printed out in different formats such as tables, forms and reports.

Any database package can be used, for example Microsoft Access, Lotus Approach or Corel Paradox.

This section of the workbook will guide you through the LCCIEB's three levels of Database assignments. On the following pages you will find typical **First, Second** and **Third Level** sets of Database assignments. Each assignment is broken down into its composite parts and guidance is given as to how to approach the tasks.

This is what you should do:

1 First of all, check that you can perform all the functions that are listed for each level.
2 Read the accompanying text and follow the instructions carefully.
3 Work through each assignment at your own speed.
4 When you have completed the assignment, check your work with the specimen answer which appears at the end of this section.
5 When you feel confident that you can competently perform all the functions for the next level, continue through the section.

A full version of each set of assignments at all three levels appears in Chapter 7.

First Level

> **For success in a First Level Database assignment you should be able to:**
>
> 1 *Manage files by creating, storing and retrieving data;*
>
> 2 *Set up a simple database table;*
>
> 3 *Add data to a table;*
>
> 4 *Edit data in a table;*
>
> 5 *Delete data from a table;*
>
> 6 *Re-order or sort the data in a table;*
>
> 7 *Search a table and retrieve information;*
>
> 8 *Print lists;*
>
> 9 *Format and print reports.*

Check that you can perform all these basic functions before you continue.

On the following pages is a **First Level** Database paper consisting of six assignments to be completed within 1 hour 30 minutes. You will need to produce six printouts, each one being proof that you have accurately completed all tasks. Always check that you have printed out these six tasks.

To get the best from this paper, work through the assignments one at a time. Read the "Do not forget to" tips for each assignment. Do the assignment and re-read your work, then look at the "Did you remember to" checklist. When you have checked that your answer conforms as far as possible to the checklist, look up the worked assignment which appears at the end of this section and compare it with your version.

ASSIGNMENT 1

This involves the keying in of 12 records under 5 field headings. All the text and figures are given in the table. However, you must first set up the database fields before you can enter this data. Give the fields the names given in the table and set them up as text, numbers, currency or date as appropriate. Some database applications do not allow you to include more than 8 characters in the field headings. You will not be penalised if you have to abbreviate the headings in this case. However, if you misspell the abbreviated heading, this would be penalised.

Do not forget to:

- enter the fields in the order given
- for each field specify the correct property, eg text, date, numeric or memo
- enter data in full; data must not be abbreviated although field headings may have to be in a shortened form
- make sure that the columns are wide enough to show all data.

Figure 3.1 shows your first assignment.

ASSIGNMENT 1

It is sale time again and Athena House Handicrafts has asked you to set up a database in order to prepare the Sale Price list to be sent to customers.

1 Create the database using the specified field headings and enter the records which are given below.

Kit Ref	Item	Manufacturer	Usual Price	Sale Price
BA2	African Bead Kit	Ringold Bead Co plc	£26.99	£19.99
BN1	Naranja Indian Bead Kit	Ringold Bead Co plc	£28.99	£22.99
BS3	Sioux Indian Bead Kit	Ringold Bead Co plc	£27.99	£21.99
DB1	Sailor Teddy Bear Kit	Diana's Miniature Bears	£24.50	£19.50
DB2	Cricketer Teddy Bear Kit	Diana's Miniature Bears	£19.50	£24.50
MB1	Model Boat Kit	Mariposa Model Co	£35.00	£30.50
MH2	Model House Kit	Mariposa Model Co	£37.50	£32.50
PC1	Alice Porcelain Doll Kit	Annette's Unique Dolls	£50.00	£40.00
PC2	Emma Porcelain Doll Kit	Annette's Unique Dolls	£55.00	£47.99
TA3	Apron Cross Stitch Kit	Cassandra Crafts	£23.50	£19.00
TC1	Cushion Tapestry Kit	Cassandra Crafts	£37.25	£27.00
TS2	Stool Tapestry Kit	Cassandra Crafts	£29.99	£21.00

2 Prices should be formatted for currency and 2 decimal places.

3 Some database applications automatically sort the records after entry. Check this and sort your records in ascending order on **Kit Ref** if your data entry has not been automatically sorted for you.

4 Save your work using the filename **Hand1**.

5 Print this table.

Figure 3.1   First Level database assignment 1

How did you get on? Before you look at the correct version, take time to go through the work you have just done and check the following points.

Did you remember to:

- set up the correct number of fields, ie five?
- classify the **Kit Ref, Item** and **Manufacturer** fields as text?

- classify the **Usual Price** and the **Sale Price** fields as number fields formatted for currency or as currency fields with 2 decimal places?
- enter all the data with no abbreviations?
- widen the column(s) where necessary so that all the data appears in full?
- format the columns (text aligned on the left; currency with 2 decimal places and numbers with commas for thousands, both aligned on the right)?
- preview your work to see what it would be like prior to printing? If so, you may have found that you needed to set the page orientation to landscape.
- save your work with the correct reference **Hand1**?
- print your work in table format?

Now check your work against the worked assignment which appears in Figure 3.17 on page 94.

USEFUL TIP

Make a copy of this first file **Hand1**. Should anything go wrong you can return to this first copy which has already been set up with field headings and actual records and so save yourself valuable time by not having to re-enter data.

ASSIGNMENT 2

Assignment 2 asks you to make changes to the original database which you have saved and printed. You will be asked to amend data, add records and delete a record.

Do not forget to:

- carry out the instructions in the order given
- choose the correct records to amend
- carry out all the amendments
- delete the correct record
- enter all five of the new records.

Your next assignment is given in Figure 3.2.

PRACTICAL COMPUTING – DATABASE
FIRST LEVEL
CANDIDATE'S COPY

ASSIGNMENT 2

There are some errors in the database and these need to be amended. There are also additional records to be added.

1   In record BN1 the name "Naranja" is wrong and should be amended to Navajo.

2   In record DB2 the **Usual Price** and the **Sale Price** have been reversed. Amend these 2 prices.

3   The Alice Porcelain Doll Kit (PC1) proved so popular that all the stock has now been sold. Delete this record.

4   Add the following 5 new records to the list as the items have been reduced in price:

Kit Ref	Item	Manufacturer	Usual Price	Sale Price
XDB3	Footballer Teddy Bear Kit	Diana's Miniature Bears	£28.00	£23.00
XDB4	Lawyer Teddy Bear Kit	Diana's Miniature Bears	£29.50	£25.00
XMC3	Model Car Kit	Mariposa Model Co	£33.50	£28.50
XPC3	Carmen Porcelain Doll Kit	Annette's Unique Dolls	£60.00	£52.00
XPC4	Tosca Porcelain Doll Kit	Annette's Unique Dolls	£60.00	£50.00

5   Sort the table on the **Manufacturer** field in ascending order.

6   Save your work using the filename **Hand2.**

7   Print this table.

Figure 3.2   First Level database assignment 2

Did you remember to:

- follow instructions in the order they are given?

- amend "Naranja" to Navajo?

- choose the correct record (DB2) to transpose **Usual Price** and **Sale Price**?

- delete the correct doll record (PC1) for the item out of stock?

- really delete the record? Just blanking out data in each field is not the correct method of deleting a record and can cause problems later.

- add details of the 5 new records?

- sort the table on the correct field, **Manufacturer**?

- save your work?

- print your work in table format, showing all fields and their associated data?

Now check the printout with the worked assignment in Figure 3.18 on page 94.

ASSIGNMENT 3

This assignment asks you to sort the data.

Do not forget to:

- recall a copy of the file **Hand2**
- sort the correct field
- carry out a descending sort
- make sure the data in the columns match their records
- save your work
- print your work in table format, showing all the fields and their associated data.

USEFUL TIP

Again, make a copy of the amended file from Assignment 2 because if anything goes wrong, you can call up this amended **Hand2** and carry on from there. **Hand1** should not be used from now on as it does not contain the latest amendments.

The instructions for Assignment 3 are given in Figure 3.3.

ASSIGNMENT 3

Recall the table saved as **Hand2** (or a copy) to the screen.

1 Sort the **Usual Price** field so that the highest price is at the top and the lowest at the bottom of the list (descending sort). Make sure all the data is sorted.

2 Save your work under the filename **Hand3.**

3 Print this table.

Figure 3.3   First Level database assignment 3

Did you remember to:

- sort on the correct field, namely **Usual Price?**
- sort in the correct order, ie a descending sort with the highest price at the top and ending with the lowest?
- make sure all the data was sorted with the sort field, so that the data in every field still matches the sorted column?
- print all the fields?

Now check your printout with the worked assignment in Figure 3.19 on page 95.

ASSIGNMENT 4

In this assignment you are asked to select records and to sort on one field. You will have to set up a query table to enable the correct records to be selected. At the same time, you can also set the field to be sorted.

Do not forget to:

- first set up the query table in order to search the database file
- sort on the correct field
- check that all the data is sorted
- print all the field headings and associated data
- save your work.

The next assignment is shown in Figure 3.4.

ASSIGNMENT 4

The manager wishes to know how many kits manufactured by Diana's Miniature Bears are in the sale.

1 Select these records.

2 Sort them in descending order on the **Item** field.

3 Save your work using the filename **Hand4.**

4 Print these selected records.

Figure 3.4   First Level database assignment 4

Did you remember to:

- first set up a query table?
- choose the correct field, ie **Manufacturer**, to select the records?
- set the sort on the **Item** field in a descending sort, ie from Z to A?
- save your work?
- print your work?

Now check your work with the worked assignment in Figure 3.20 on page 95.

ASSIGNMENT 5

In this assignment you are asked to add a new field and enter dates in this field, taken from the data given in the table.

Do not forget to:

- add a field and set it up as a date field
- set up the format you wish to use to enter the date in this field
- sort the dates in ascending order in this new field.

Figure 3.5 gives Assignment 5.

ASSIGNMENT 5

The manager needs a record of the dates the usual prices were reduced for each item and added to the sale list. Using the file **Hand3** (or a copy).

1   To the right of the **Sale Price** field add a new field called **Date** and enter the dates from the table below.

Kit Ref	Item	Usual Price	Sale Price	Date
BA2	African Bead Kit	£26.99	£19.99	12/6/98
BN1	Navajo Indian Bead Kit	£28.99	£22.99	12/6/98
BS3	Sioux Indian Bead Kit	£27.99	£21.99	12/6/98
DB1	Sailor Teddy Bear Kit	£24.50	£19.50	19/4/98
DB2	Cricketer Teddy Bear Kit	£24.50	£19.50	19/4/98
MB1	Model Boat Kit	£35.00	£30.50	3/4/98
MH2	Model House Kit	£37.50	£32.50	15/9/98
PC2	Emma Porcelain Doll Kit	£55.00	£47.99	4/7/98
TA3	Apron Cross Stitch Kit	£23.50	£19.00	19/4/98
TC1	Cushion Tapestry Kit	£37.25	£27.00	19/4/98
TS2	Stool Tapestry Kit	£29.99	£21.00	27/4/98
XDB3	Footballer Teddy Bear Kit	£28.00	£23.00	31/8/98
XDB4	Lawyer Teddy Bear Kit	£29.50	£25.00	31/8/98
XMC3	Model Car Kit	£33.50	£28.50	15/9/98
XPC3	Carmen Porcelain Doll Kit	£60.00	£52.00	15/9/98
XPC4	Tosca Porcelain Doll Kit	£60.00	£50.00	15/9/98

2   Sort the **Date** field in ascending order.

3   Save your work as **Hand5**.

4   Print your work showing only the **Item, Manufacturer** and **Date** fields.

Figure 3.5   First Level database assignment 5

Did you remember to:

- add a new field in the correct place?
- set the property of this field to a date field?
- enter the dates against the correct records?
- sort the dates in ascending order, ie from the oldest to the newest?
- check that the sorted data matches the data in the other fields?
- only use the **Item, Manufacturer** and **Date** fields in your work?
- save your work?
- print your work showing only the requisite 3 fields with relevant data?

Now check your work with the worked assignment in Figure 3.21 on page 95.

ASSIGNMENT 6

This assignment asks you to set out your work in an entirely different format. It asks for the report format, not a table format. You must be able to present your database file in report format. In addition, you may be asked to use data based on the amended table in Assignment 2, or you may be asked to use data from a query table.

The table used for this report is not Table 2 (or **Hand2**). This report is based on the query which you prepared in Assignment 4. Though this query was originally based on the amended Table 2, it is on this query (saved as **Hand4**) that you must base your report when you comply with Assignment 6. If you had abbreviated your field headings before, you must now enter them in full and you may be asked to rename the headings.

Do not forget to:

- read the assignment closely as you are asked to do many tasks
- only show 3 fields in your report
- alter the headings and enter them with the correct wording and in upper case (capital letters)
- insert a heading
- insert a date
- show selected records only
- carry out an ascending sort.

Assignment 6, the final assignment at **First Level**, is given in Figure 3.6.

ASSIGNMENT 6

A customer has asked for a list of Teddy Bear kits in the sale. Using the information saved under filename **Hand4,** prepare this list in report format:

1 Head the report **ATHENA HOUSE TEDDY BEAR KITS**.

2 Insert today's date on the report.

3 There should be 3 fields only, **Kit Ref, Item** and **Sale Price.** Rename these fields as **Reference, Name of Item** and **Discount Sale Price.** These field headings should be in block capitals.

4 Sort the **Name of Item** field in ascending order (A – Z).

5 Add the words **GRAND TOTAL** at the base of the columns and insert the total for the **Discount Sale Price** under that column.

6 Print this report.

Figure 3.6   First Level database assignment 6

Did you remember to:

- select the report format, not a table format, based on **Hand4**?
- insert the heading?
- have a large enough heading, but not so big that it does not fit on the page?
- make sure that the columns are wide enough to take all the data?
- insert the correct field headings using their new names? As these are not exactly the same field headings as when you first set up the database, they must be altered in accordance with instructions.
- check that these headings are in the appropriate format, in this case block capitals?
- check that there is a date inserted in the report?
- check that you have sorted on the correct field (**Name of Item**) and from A–Z?
- save your work as **Hand6**?
- print the report using only the three fields specified?

Now check your work with the worked assignment in Figure 3.22 on page 96.

HELPFUL HINTS

- If possible, use a modern database package; they have many features which make database design and data entry much easier to use than the older packages. This book is not linked to any specific database application package so most modern database packages can be used.

- Know your package and practise using it.

- Use any software features and aids in your application package. If you use Wizards in class, use them for this paper.

- Familiarise yourself with the Help menus so that you can quickly go to the section you need for assistance.

- Read through the paper carefully before you tackle the assignments.

- Mentally allocate the time you are going to spend on each assignment. If you spend too much time on one task you may find yourself unable to finish the paper.

- In each assignment, highlight instructions and phrases you consider important so that you remember to cover them in your work.

- Highlight any instruction to print, so that you have a quick method of checking the number of printouts needed.

Second Level

> **For success in a Second Level Database assignment, you should be able to perform the functions tested at First Level, namely:**
>
> 1 *Manage files by creating, sorting and retrieving data;*
>
> 2 *Set up a simple database table;*
>
> 3 *Add data to a table;*
>
> 4 *Edit data in a table;*
>
> 5 *Delete data from a table;*
>
> 6 *Re-order or sort the data in a table;*
>
> 7 *Search a table and retrieve information;*
>
> 8 *Print lists;*
>
> 9 *Format and print reports.*
>
> **In addition you should be able to carry out the functions tested at Second Level, namely:**
>
> 1 *Set up a more complex database with fields and records;*
>
> 2 *Change the structure of the table;*
>
> 3 *Create a data entry screen;*
>
> 4 *Retrieve complex information;*
>
> 5 *Use multiple fields;*
>
> 6 *Prepare a report on grouped data.*

Before attempting this paper consider the following points:

- You may have to alter the design or structure of a table. For instance, where a field is set up to take numbers only you may be asked to change that field to take text only. You may have to change a number field to a currency field.

- A different format is required for some data. A data entry screen must be created to make data entry easier for the operator.

- You must know how to create a lookup table for one field when setting up the structure of the database file.

Check that you can perform all these basic functions before you continue.

The **Second Level** paper comprises four assignments (or tasks) which you must complete within 2 hours. You will need to print six printouts for this paper, each printout being proof that you have accurately completed the tasks. Always check to make sure that you have the correct number of printouts for marking.

The background information for this set of assignments is shown in Figure 3.7.

BACKGROUND

You work for Comlon's Cattery. Today you have been asked to set up a database to record information about the cats which are listed on Comlon's register. Please carry out the following instructions.

Figure 3.7   Background information for Second Level database assignments

---

USEFUL TIP

If asked to insert a Yes/No field, check whether later on you will have to set up a query based on this field. If so, choose a Yes/No text field rather than a check box field as the ticked check box may be difficult to reproduce in a query.

ASSIGNMENT 1

Assignment 1 involves setting up a database structure using text, numeric and currency properties. You will also be required to create a new format, the Form view or Data Entry screen format. In addition, you will need to set up a lookup table on one of the fields of the table.

Do not forget to:

- read the instructions carefully and refer to them constantly when setting up data screens and lookup tables
- create the lookup column as set out in the assignment
- set up the **Cat Ref** field with the correct property.

Your first assignment is shown in Figure 3.8.

ASSIGNMENT 1

Turn to the next page where you will find a table giving details of seventeen records to be entered in this new Feline Register table.

1   Create a database table to include the following 10 fields: a numeric **Cat Ref, Cat Type, Cat Name, Birth Date, Breed, Colour Details, Gender, Breeder, Address** and **Price**. The **Price** field should be formatted for currency but with no decimal places.

2   Set up a lookup table linked to the Address field. You will need to create a 2 columns x 5 rows lookup table. You should enter the following information in this table: town and county, followed by the breeder's name.

> Stockport, Cheshire; Cuddly Cats plc
> Framley, Barset; Barset Cat Breeders
> Ashton, Somerset; Jaswinder's Topcats
> Brixton, London; Tamara's Exotic Felines
> Leeds, Yorkshire; Pat Cloggs Moggies

By accessing the lookup table on the Address field you can automatically enter the correct address for the breeder.

3   Create an entry screen based on the table you have designed, to enable you to enter data into the table. Give the screen a title COMLON'S CATTERY DATA ENTRY SCREEN. In the **Gender** field specify that only Male or Female should be entered. Enlarge and embolden the text, to make it clearer.

4   Enter the first record. Save your work as **Cat1Scrn**.

5   Print a copy of the entry screen to show this first record.

6   Now enter the remaining 16 records.

7   Save your work as **Cat1Tab**.

8   Print a copy of this complete database table in landscape orientation.

Figure 3.8   Second Level database assignment 1

Cat Ref	Cat Type	Cat Name	Birth Date	Breed	Colour Details	Gender	Breeder	Address	Price
601	Tortoiseshell	Felicity	15/10/98	Tortoiseshell	Red/Black	Female	Tamara's Exotic Felines	Brixton, London	£255
602	Siamese	Beauty	16/2/99	Siamese	Seal Point	Female	Jaswinder's Topcats	Ashton, Somerset	£350
603	Angora	Zara	22/1/99	Angora	Lilac/White	Female	Barset Cat Breeders	Framley, Barset	£395
604	Ocicat	Nanamay	14/4/99	Ocicat	White	Female	Barset Cat Breeders	Framley, Barset	£340
605	Tortie Tabby	Dumpling	17/3/99	Tortie Tabby	Blue/Silver	Female	Cuddly Cats plc	Stockport, Cheshire	£345
608	Manx	Pushkin	31/3/99	Manx	White	Male	Jaswinder's Topcats	Ashton, Somerset	£320
612	Tabby	Shamus	6/2/99	Tabby	Red	Male	Barset Cat Breeders	Framley, Barset	£345
614	Burmese	King John	14/2/99	Burmese	Brown	Male	Tamara's Exotic Felines	Brixton, London	£385
615	Tortoiseshell	Gingerbread	3/2/99	Tortoiseshell	Red/Black/White	Female	Tamara's Exotic Felines	Brixton, London	£295
616	Persian	Vanilla	27/1/99	Persian	White	Female	Pat Cloggs Moggies	Leeds, Yorkshire	£315
617	Persian	Bella	21/2/99	Persian	Black Smoke	Female	Cuddly Cats plc	Stockport, Cheshire	£325
618	Siamese	Milor	23/2/99	Siamese	Cream Point	Female	Jaswinder's Topcats	Ashton, Somerset	£298
619	Maine Coon	Whiskey	17/1/99	Maine Coon	Brown/White	Male	Pat Cloggs Moggies	Leeds, Yorkshire	£220
625	Tortie Tabby	Candyrue	1/3/99	Tortie Tabby	Blue/Silver	Female	Cuddly Cats plc	Stockport, Cheshire	£355
627	Siamese	Torquil	16/4/99	Siamese	Cream Point	Male	Jaswinder's Topcats	Ashton, Somerset	£325
644	Persian	Xanadu	13/4/99	Persian	Black	Male	Pat Cloggs Moggies	Leeds, Yorkshire	£350
666	Somali	Little Caesar	19/3/99	Somali	Lilac	Male	Cuddly Cats plc	Stockport, Cheshire	£305

Figure 3.8 (continued)

70

Did you remember to:

- specify the correct column in the lookup table so that that the breeder's address was entered in the **Address** column and not the breeder's name?
- check that the **Cat Ref** field is a numeric field (it should align to the right)?
- set up a Data Entry Screen with the correct main heading?
- alter fonts, point sizes and adjust label widths so that all the information appears on the screen and is readable?
- print just one record first of all so as to check for ease of entry?
- count the records, when you have entered all of them, to see that you really have entered 17 records?
- widen the columns in the table so that all the records are completely visible in every field?

Check your work against the worked assignments which appear in Figures 3.23 and 3.24 on pages 96 and 97.

ASSIGNMENT 2

Because Assignment 2 asks you to make so many changes to the original database which you have saved and printed, it is advisable, as at the **First Level**, to make a copy of the original table saved as **Cat1Tab** and use the copy for Assignment 2. The changes will include altering a field's structure, deleting a field, inserting a field, deleting a record and amending words and figures within the records. You will be required to add additional records to the database file and then sort them in date order.

Do not forget to:

- carry out the instructions in the order given
- delete the correct field
- add a field in the correct place
- choose the correct records to amend
- delete the correct record
- carry out all the amendments
- enter all eight of the new records
- sort the records on the date field.

Your next set of instructions is given in Figure 3.9.

ASSIGNMENT 2

On inspecting the database, certain amendments are required. Carry out the following:

1 A new system of coding is coming into operation so change the **Cat Ref** to an alphanumeric field instead of a numeric one to cope with future references.

2 As the data entered into the **Cat Type** column is identical to the **Breed** data, delete the **Cat Type** field from the database.

3 A new field called **Long Hair?** should be inserted between the **Colour Details** and the **Gender** columns. This indicates if the cat is a long-haired cat or a short-haired one. Make this a Yes/No field (not a check box field). All the cats bred by Cuddly Cats plc and by Pat Cloggs Moggies are long-haired cats. The other three breeders only supply short-haired cats.

4 As Shamus the tabby (Cat Ref 612) has now been sold, delete the record from the database.

5 Milor, the cream point Siamese (Cat Ref 618), is a male cat so amend this record.

6 Amend the colour details for the Ocicat, Cat Ref 604. This cat is chocolate coloured and not white.

7 In the past few months, 8 new kittens have been acquired by Comlon Cattery. Details are given in the table on the next page. Add these records to the database.

8 The database should be in **Birth Date** order so once all 24 records are entered, sort the records starting with the oldest date first.

9 Save your work as **Cat2Tab**.

10 Print the amended table.

Figure 3.9   Second Level database assignment 2

Cat Ref	Cat Name	Birth Date	Breed	Colour Details	Gender	Breeder	Address	Price
671	Sultana	5/3/99	Turkish Van	Auburn	Female	Tamara's Exotic Felines	Brixton, London	£340
672	Cookienet	3/4/99	Angora	Chocolate	Female	Barset Cat Breeders	Framley, Barset	£325
673	Rolypoly	31/3/99	Persian	Cream/White	Male	Pat Cloggs Moggies	Leeds, Yorkshire	£300
676	Sterlingworth	3/4/99	Tabby	Silver	Male	Cuddly Cats plc	Stockport, Cheshire	£350
677	Caramba	24/3/99	Tortoiseshell	Red/Black	Female	Jaswinder's Topcats	Ashton, Somerset	£310
678	Saroola	4/4/99	Singapura	Sable Brown	Male	Barset Cat Breeders	Framley, Barset	£325
679	Frisky	13/4/99	Siamese	Red Point	Male	Jaswinder's Topcats	Ashton, Somerset	£330
680	Martina Babbage	14/4/99	Persian	Blue	Female	Tamara's Exotic Felines	Brixton, London	£340

Figure 3.9 (continued) New records for Assignment 2

Did you remember to:

- amend the structure of the **Cat Ref** field? It should now be a text field to accept letters as well as numbers, and the data should be left aligned.
- delete the **Cat Type** column and all its data?
- insert the new column between the **Colour Details** and **Gender** columns? This is a different type of property from the usual text or numeric columns and you should have followed the instructions to make this a Yes/No type field and not a check box field. You will see why when you start to plan your work on Assignment 3.
- delete the **Cat Ref 612** record?
- alter **Cat Ref 618** and **Cat Ref 604**?
- count the records to see that there are 24 records including the new kittens?
- remember to sort on the **Birth Date**?
- check that all the fields are still wide enough to show all the data including the new records and amendments?

Check your printout against the worked assignment which appears in Figure 3.25 on page 98.

ASSIGNMENT 3

Assignment 3 is in two parts, both of which involve querying the database file.

Part 1 involves a multiple criteria selection, together with the requirement to print only 4 of the fields with the associated data.

Part 2 is a query based on two criteria together with the requirement to print limited fields. One criterion is based on a Yes/No field, and it is easier to set up this field for selection with a Yes/No format, rather than choosing a check box format. This is why you were advised in the notes to Assignment 2 to set up that field's property in the Yes/No format. In this query, you are asked to sort the data.

Do not forget to:

- set up query forms based on the correct table for both queries
- only print certain fields with their associated data
- sort the query in Part 2 before printing.

Your next assignment is given in Figure 3.10.

ASSIGNMENT 3

1) A customer is interested in purchasing a blue and silver Tortie Tabby cat born after 10 March 1999. Search the database and when you have made your selection:

        (i) save your work as **Cat3Q1**

        (ii) print your work in table format showing only the **Cat Ref, Cat Name, Birth Date** and **Gender** fields.

2) The manager would like a list of all long-haired cats on the Register who were born before 1 April 1999. Search the database and when you have made your selection:

        (i) sort your records in ascending price order

        (ii) save your work as **Cat3Q2**

        (iii) print a list in table format showing only the **Cat Ref, Cat Name, Birth Date, Gender, Breeder** and **Price** fields

---

Figure 3.10 Second Level database assignment 3

Did you remember to:

- set up a query form for each query?
- base each of these queries on the amended table which you produced at the end of Assignment 2?
- sort on the price in Query 2 with the lowest price at the beginning?
- restrict the fields for each printout?

Good. Now check your printout with the worked assignments which appear in Figures 3.26 and 3.27 on page 99.

ASSIGNMENT 4

In Assignment 4 instead of displaying data in the table format you have been using until now, a new format has to be set up to display the data. This is a report format. A heading is specified for the report and instructions are given as to how the data should be grouped in the report. A simple format is as acceptable as a more complicated one. You will be asked to do a primary sort and a secondary sort. This time, you will have to calculate data on a specified field and insert sub-totals for each group and a final grand total covering all the groups. You must set up a footer to show the current date, and also a label for you to add your name.

Do not forget to:

- base the report on the table which you amended in Assignment 2
- select the fields which you want in the report
- set up each group under the breeder's name and address

- sort the breeders in alphabetical order
- sort the cats grouped under each breeder in date order
- set up for each group a sub-total calculated on the **Price** field
- set up the grand total for each group
- add a footer and your name.

Your instructions for Assignment 4 are given in Figure 3.11.

ASSIGNMENT 4

1 Create a report showing all the cats on the Feline Register. Head this report COMLON CATTERY – BREEDERS.

2 Group the cats by Breeder. Use the full name and address of the breeder for each group heading.

3 Sort the groups alphabetically from A – Z and under each group sort the cats in **Birth Date** order.

4 Restrict the fields to **Cat Ref, Birth Date, Cat Name, Breed, Gender** and **Price**.

5 Give sub-totals under each group showing the total price of the cats supplied by that breeder.

6 Add a Grand Total at the end to show the total amount of all Prices.

7 Add today's date and your name in a footer. Do not insert a page number.

Save your work as **Cat4Rpt.** Print this report.

Figure 3.11 Second Level database assignment 4

Did you remember to:

- use Table 2 on which to base the report?
- insert the heading?
- use only the 6 field headings to classify the data?
- divide the cats into groups based on the breeders?
- sort the groups from A–Z?
- align the data with the field headings?
- make sure the columns are wide enough to show all the data?
- increase the font size and where necessary embolden the data so that the report can be read more easily?
- calculate the sub-total and the grand total on the **Price** field?

Good. Now check your printout with the worked assignment which appears in Figure 3.28 on page 100.

HELPFUL HINTS

- If you should find that you have made a complete mess of setting up the database initially, do not panic! Scrap this work. It is often easier to start again from scratch than to try to revise and correct mistakes. Much of the later work is based on how the initial tables and queries are set up, so accurate design and data entry is essential.

- As suggested in the First Level hints, make a copy of the original database file when you have set it up. This acts as a safety net should you encounter any difficulties later which would mean having to enter all the data again. You can use the copy. This can save you valuable examination time.

- Remember, too, to make a copy of the amended database file. This can then be used should you have to return to the amended file instead of the file you first set up.

- Does all your work fit on the one printout? If not try using landscape orientation instead of portrait or ticking the "Fit on one page" option, which is usually found in modern packages.

- If you have printed in landscape and the work still does not fit the page consider altering the point size. However, remember your work must still be readable.

Third Level

For success in a Third Level Database assignment, you should be able to perform the functions tested at First Level:

1 *Manage files by creating, sorting and retrieving data;*

2 *Set up a simple database table;*

3 *Add data to a table;*

4 *Edit data in a table;*

5 *Delete data from a table;*

6 *Re-order or sort the data in a table;*

7 *Search a table and retrieve information;*

8 *Print lists;*

9 *Format and print reports.*

(continued)

You should also be able to carry out the functions tested at Second Level:

1 *Set up a more complex database with fields and records;*

2 *Change the structure of the table;*

3 *Create a data entry screen;*

4 *Retrieve complex information;*

5 *Use multiple fields;*

6 *Prepare a report on grouped data.*

In addition you should also be able to carry out the functions tested at Third Level, namely:

1 *Create a primary and a secondary table from given data;*

2 *Link or join the data in the two tables;*

3 *Create data entry screens;*

4 *Create data checking mechanisms;*

5 *Create report templates;*

6 *Produce a sample database;*

7 *Produce printouts.*

Check that you can perform all these basic functions before you continue.

Before attempting this assignment, consider the following points:

- You will need to set up headers, footers, margins and page orientation.
- You will need to set up a primary database table with fields and allocate correct properties to each field.
- You must also set up a secondary database table with fields and allocate correct properties to each field.
- These tables will have to be linked to create a relationship using referential integrity.
- Based on data for the above two tables, two data entry screens must be set up.
- At least two reports, which may group the data, must be set up with font sizes and line spacing altered to present the reports in the best manner.
- There will be a simple calculation on one field and you must insert sub-totals and a grand total overall.

The **Third Level** database assessment consists of four assignments which you must complete within 2 hours and 30 minutes. There will be seven printouts to show that you have accurately completed the tasks. Always check to make sure that you have printed all seven for marking.

Background

The background for the **Third Level** is important as it gives you essential details you will need to know in order to carry out all the tasks. You are expected to read this background carefully and then, unlike the other assignments, work through the instructions prior to starting to produce work in Assignment 1. When necessary refer to it to help you with any extra details you must take into consideration. You do not need to print anything at this stage, but you will need to carry out the instructions to set up the two template tables and to save your work.

Do not forget to:

- set up structures for two separate tables
- check which fields are specified for which table
- give each table its correct name
- save each table under the given reference.

Background information for the **Third Level** Database assignment is given in Figure 3.12.

> **BACKGROUND**
>
> You work for Athena House – Builders. This company has now produced plans for 5 new housing estates which are about to be developed in England. Today you are asked to use your database package to help the company's staff to manage these new developments by setting up a database in accordance with the following specifications.
>
> Two tables will be required, the **Estate** table and the **House Details** table.
>
> 1 Set up the **Estate** table for each of the new estates to be developed, with the following 10 fields: **Estate Ref** (set the primary key on this field), **Estate Name, Town, Year Started, Site Manager, Telephone No, Building Type,** whether **Incentives?** to buy are offered (this can be a Yes/No type of field or a check box) and the actual **Offer** (make this a Memo field). The tenth field is called **Clerk** and is for your initials. When you have set up this table save your work as **EstTab1**
>
> 2 Set up the **House Details** table with 9 fields which will have details of the types of houses to be built on the estate. These fields are the **House Ref** as the primary key, **Start Date, House Name, Detached, Bedrooms, Receptions, Garage** and **Price.** (The **Detached** and **Garage** fields are a Yes/No or check box type of field). The ninth field to be added is the **Estate Ref** (ie the primary key from the **Estate** table). This shows on which estate the house is being built.
>
> 3 In the **House Details** table **Estate Ref** field add a 3 column x 5 lines lookup box. Enter the **Estate Ref, Town** and **Estate Name** from the **Estate** table for each of the 5 new estates. This should enable you to link the **House Details** table to the **Estate** table. When you have set up this table save your work as **HseTab1**
>
> 4 Set up a relationship of one-to-many from the **Estate** table to the **House Details** table using referential integrity.
>
> 5 You do not need to print anything at this stage.

Figure 3.12 Background information for Third Level databases

Did you remember to:

- set up the two table structures?
- set up the lookup box in the **House Details** table?
- avoid entering any records at this stage?

ASSIGNMENT 1

Once you have read the Background information for the **Third Level**, read the first assignment below. In this assignment two templates have to be designed, one for each of two tables, the primary and the secondary tables, prior to actually entering any data. The fields and some of their properties are specified in the instructions. In the secondary table you must set up a lookup box on one of the fields. This must be linked in some way to a field or fields in the primary table. You must establish a one-to-many relationship between the two tables and link the two tables through a common field.

Do not forget to:

- set up two separate data entry screens based on the two tables

- check which fields are specified for which table
- give each screen its correct name
- enlarge font sizes for clarity
- only enter the first record in each screen.

The first assignment for the Third Level is given in Figure 3.13.

ASSIGNMENT 1

To enable staff to enter data more easily in the 2 tables, prepare 2 data entry forms, one for each table. You should first set up the field headings for the table and then create the appropriate data entry screen form ready for entering the data which appears on the following pages.

1 For the **Estate** data entry screen attach a property to the **Estate Name** field and the **Town** field so that these all appear in capital letters on the form and are saved to the table in the same format. Attach properties to most of the fields so that data is always entered in the correct manner and only valid data is accepted.

2 In the entry screen for the **House Details** table, providing you have set up the lookup box properly, when the **Estate Ref** box is selected it will automatically show a list of the 5 estate references, names, and towns. By checking which town and estate name is on the house record card staff can use this to enter the appropriate reference for the estate.

3 Add suitable headings to the data entry screens and your name and today's date in a footer for each of the two entry screens. Enter the first record for each entry screen to test the entry form. The first record for the **Estate** entry screen should be entered from the Supplied Data list shown below. Enter the first record for the **House Details** entry screen from the 16 records which appear after the Supplied Data overleaf.

4 Once you have entered the first record on each screen, save the **Estate** entry screen as **EstScrn1** and the **House Details** screen as **HseScrn1.**

5 Now print a copy of each screen in Form view.

Figure 3.13 Third Level database assignment 1

SUPPLIED DATA

Estate Table.

All estates are offering incentives.

RUN65, Runway Farm, Gatwick, Year started – 1998, John Piloter, Telephone number 01293 005 622, BuildingType – houses, Offer – mortgages, £1,000 discount.

FLO23, Floodgate Meadows, Northampton, Year started – 1997, Helen Diverson, Telephone 01604 505 802. Building Type – houses, Offer – mortgages, £200 holiday voucher.

CAN41, Canal View Valley, Manchester, Year started – 1998, Billy Shipper, Telephone 0161 429 0193, Building Type – houses and flats, Offer – 1% cashback and free carpets.

JUN16, Junction Square, Clapham, Year started – 1999, Bob Signalman, Telephone 0181 0022 163, Building Type – houses and flats, Offer – mortgages, 1% cashback.

DOC78, Dockland Ponds, London, Year started – 1999, Carol Fisher, Telephone 0181 004 3761, Building Type – flats and houses, Offer – mortgages, free carpets.

House Types

There are 16 record cards giving house details to be entered on the database. These appear on the next four pages.

Figure 3.13a   Supplied data for assignment 1 – Third Level databases

ATHENA HOUSE – BUILDERS

House Ref   GC1   Start Date   1 June 1998

House Name   Claridges   Detached   ✓

Bedrooms   4
Garage   ✓   Receptions   3

                         Price
Town   GATWICK   £200,000

ATHENA HOUSE – BUILDERS

House Ref   NS1   Start Date   7/3/97

House Name   Savoy   Detached   No

Bedrooms   3
Garage   No   Receptions   2
                         Price
Town   NORTHAMPTON   £125000

ATHENA HOUSE – BUILDERS

House Ref   MW1   Start Date   9 April 98

House Name   Waldorf   Detached   Yes

Bedrooms   3
Garage   ✓   Receptions   2
                         Price
Town   MANCHESTER   £130,000

ATHENA HOUSE – BUILDERS

House Ref   MG1   Start Date   21 May 98

House Name   Grosvenor   Detached   ✓

Bedrooms   4
Garage   ✓   Receptions   2
                         Price
Town   MANCHESTER   150000

Figure 3.13b   Record cards for assignment 1 – Third Level databases

---

ATHENA HOUSE – BUILDERS

House Ref GW2   Start Date 19 July 1998

House Name Waldorf   Detached ✓

Bedrooms 3   Receptions 2
Garage Yes   Price

Town GATWICK   £170 000

ATHENA HOUSE – BUILDERS

House Ref CR1   Start Date 22 May 99

House Name Ritz   Detached ✓

Bedrooms 5   Receptions 3
Garage ✓   Price

Town CLAPHAM   £330,000

ATHENA HOUSE – BUILDERS

House Ref CC1   Start Date 2nd May 99

House Name Clavidges   Detached ✓

Bedrooms 4   Receptions 3
Garage ✓   Price

Town CLAPHAM   295000

ATHENA HOUSE – BUILDERS

House Ref NS2   Start Date 4 March 97

House Name Savoy   Detached No

Bedrooms 3   Receptions 2
Garage No   Price

Town NORTHAMPTON   £125,000

Figure 3.13b (continued)

ATHENA HOUSE – BUILDERS

House Ref GG1   Start Date 25 May 1998

House Name Grosvenor   Detached ✓

Bedrooms 4   Receptions 2
Garage Yes   Price

Town GATWICK   £190,000

ATHENA HOUSE – BUILDERS

House Ref NW1   Start Date 12 June 97

House Name Waldorf   Detached ✓

Bedrooms 3   Receptions 2
Garage ✓   Price

Town NORTHAMPTON   £130,000

ATHENA HOUSE – BUILDERS

House Ref LC1   Start Date 18 April 99

House Name Claridges   Detached ✓

Bedrooms 4   Receptions 3
Garage ✓   Price

Town LONDON   £300,000

ATHENA HOUSE – BUILDERS

House Ref SG2   Start Date 14 April 98

House Name Savoy   Detached No

Bedrooms 3   Receptions 2
Garage No   Price

Town MANCHESTER   £145,000

Figure 3.13b (continued)

ATHENA HOUSE – BUILDERS

House Ref   GW1   Start Date   10 July 1998

House Name   Waldorf   Detached   ✓

Bedrooms   3   Receptions   2
Garage   ✓   Price

Town   GATWICK   £165 000

ATHENA HOUSE – BUILDERS

House Ref   SM1   Start Date   22/4/98

House Name   Savoy   Detached   No

Bedrooms   3   Receptions   2
Garage   No   Price

Town   MANCHESTER   145 000

ATHENA HOUSE – BUILDERS

House Ref   CR2   Start Date   27 March '99

House Name   Ritz   Detached   ✓

Bedrooms   5   Receptions   3
Garage   ✓   Price

Town   CLAPHAM   £350,000

ATHENA HOUSE – BUILDERS

House Ref   LG1   Start Date   30 April 99

House Name   Grosvenor   Detached   ✓

Bedrooms   4   Receptions   2
Garage   ✓   Price

Town   LONDON   285 000

Figure 3.13b (continued)

How did you get on with this assignment? Did you remember to:

- prepare the **Estate** data entry screen so that the **Estate Name** and the **Town** are converted to capital letters even if you had entered this data initially in initial capitals and lower case letters?

- add a **Clerk** field with space for your initials?

- select a clear font in bold for the headings and data?

- align the fields and the data boxes to make a neat entry form?

- widen the data boxes to take all the data which may have altered in size when you altered the point size, or do you still need to adjust them so that all the data appears?

- add labels for the current date and your name in the form's footer?

- try out your form by entering the **first** record only?

- immediately print this form with this first record entered, so that the header and the footer show on this printout?

Did you remember to:

- do all the above (apart from entering the Clerk's initials) but this time for the **House Details** Entry Screen?

- format the **Price** field for currency but with no decimal places? In large sums such as those for house prices, decimal places are not necessary.

- add a lookup box to the **Estate Ref** field in the **House Details** table? As the data record cards do not show the **Estate Ref**, only the town where the estate is situated, it is essential that you attach a lookup box to the **Estate Ref** field in the **House Details** table.

- print this **House Details** Entry Screen using just the one record so that the header and footer appear on this printout?

- set up a relationship from the **Estate** table to the **House Details** table on a "one-to-many basis" by using the **Estate Ref** field to link both tables together? This is essential for both data entry work and report work.

Check your work against the worked assignments which appear in Figures 3.29 and 3.30 on page 101.

USEFUL TIP

Make copies of the Estate Data Entry Screen and one of the House Details Entry Screen with only the one record entered on each screen. Should you have to add further labels or other information at a later date to these screens and have to still print the screen showing only the one record, then these copies will be invaluable.

ASSIGNMENT 2

In Assignment 2 you are asked to input all the data into the two tables using the appropriate data entry screen and then to sort the data. You are then asked to print all the records in table format.

Do not forget to:

- use the correct records for each entry screen
- sort the records for each table when you have finished entering the data
- save your work
- print the two tables in table format.

Your next set of instructions for Assignment 2 is given in Figure 3.14.

ASSIGNMENT 2

1 Using the data screens you have just set up, input the rest of the records in the appropriate tables. Enter the remaining 4 records for the **Estate** screen. (Use the Supplied Data for the **Estate** screen.) Then enter the remaining 15 records for the **House Details** screen. (Use the record cards for the **House Details** screen.) As different clerks have entered the details on the record cards, ensure you enter your data consistently on the data entry forms.

2 Once all the data has been entered into the **Estate** table, sort this table on the **Estate Ref** field.

3 Save this table as **EstTab2.**

4 Print a copy in table format.

5 Once all the data has been entered into the **House Details** table, sort this table in **House Ref** order.

6 Save this table as **HseTab2.**

7 Print a copy in table format.

Figure 3.14 Third Level database assignment 2

Did you remember to:

- enter the details of the 5 housing estates from the 5 records?
- sort the records in **Estate Ref** order in table format?
- widen the columns to take all the data, whether this is in the field headings or in the data details? By checking the column width you can avoid foreshortening the columns and losing some of the information.
- sort the **Estate** table?
- save the sorted table?
- print the **Estate** table?

Did you remember to:

- do all the above but this time in connection with the **House Details** table?
- enter the 16 records which make up the **House Details** table? As already mentioned above, are the columns wide enough?
- enter the actual reference from the lookup box for the estate concerned in the **Estate Ref** field, or did you set up the lookup box to enter the town by mistake?
- sort the **House Details** table on the **House Ref**?
- save this sorted table?
- print the **House Details** table?

Check your work against the worked assignments which appear in Figures 3.31 and 3.32 on pages 102 and 103.

ASSIGNMENT 3

In Assignment 3 you are asked to create a simple report based on only one of the tables. You will be asked to set up the report and carry out a primary sort on one of the fields, and a secondary sort on another. You will need to calculate a grand total based on one of the fields for insertion at the end of the report. A simple report is as acceptable as a more complicated one where field headings are automatically printed at the head of each and every group.

In this particular set of assignments you are not asked to select records to be printed in the report. However, this does not preclude your being asked to present a selection of records and field headings in report format. This would mean that you would have to prepare a query form first and then base your report on the query form rather than on the main table.

USEFUL TIP

Scrap your first attempt at the report if it appears not to be set out in the manner you expected. It is easier to start again if you have imported wrong fields or wrong data by mistake.

Do not forget to:

- specify the table on which you wish to base your report
- start the report with the primary sort field
- use clear fonts and enlarge point sizes where necessary to present the data as clearly as possible
- know how to calculate on a field to produce the grand total.

The instructions for Assignment 3 are given in Figure 3.15.

ASSIGNMENT 3

1   Create a simple tabular report headed **ATHENA HOUSE – BUILDERS, PRICE SUMMARY.** This report should start with the **Estate Ref** based on the <u>House Details</u> table, followed by the **House Ref** field, and show a summary of all new houses for each of the estates forming part of Athena House – Builders. Do not list each individual estate's name. The **Estate Ref** from the <u>House Details</u> table together with all the other fields from that table will identify on which estate the house is being built.

2   Sort the summary alphabetically on the **Estate Ref.**

3   Next sort the summary in **House Name** order within each estate.

4   At the end of the report, summarise the **Price** field to show the **Grand Total** of all house prices on the 5 estates.

5   Insert today's date in a footer together with your name. A page number will not be needed so do not insert one.

6   Save your work as **Report1.**

7   Print this report.

Figure 3.15 Third Level database assignment 3

Did you remember to:

- choose the correct table for this report? It should be based on the **House Details** table.

- sort the data? The first sort should be on the **Estate Ref** field and the secondary sort on the **House Name**.

- alter the font point size so that the data is well displayed? Larger font size and bold formatting help to display the summary report.

- format the **Price** field for currency?

- insert the words **Grand Total**, together with the actual amount?

- increase the point size and format the **Grand Total** field for currency with no decimals?

- alter the height of the **Grand Total** box so that the commas inserted to show "thousands" do not appear as full stops? If you find that the "thousands" separator appears to be a full stop instead of a comma, extend the control box upwards so it is high enough to show the tails of the commas so that they do not appear as full stops.

- adjust the width of the fields so that all data and field headings are visible?

- add the date and your name to the footers?

- delete the page number if the database application has inserted it by default?

- even up the ends of the lines which enclose the field headings so that they match the lines above?

- count the records to check that all have been entered on the one page and there is nothing on pages 2 or 3?
- check that the **Grand Total** is still on the first page together with all the data after any adjustments you may have made to the report? Or has it somehow found its way on to the next page. If this has happened, you will need to make very fine adjustments in the report's design view so everything appears on the one page.

Check your printout against the worked assignments which appear in Figures 3.33 and 3.34 on pages 104 to 105.

ASSIGNMENT 4

In this assignment you will make use of the relationship which you set up between the two tables. You are again asked to prepare a report but this time some fields and associated data will be taken from the **Estate** table, and other fields with their data will be used from the **House Detail** table. You may be asked to use all the fields from one of the tables, or only certain specified fields. Primary and secondary sorts will also be needed.

You must know how to divide the data into groups – in this case, the groups are the different estates on which the houses are to be built. Under each group you are required to insert a sub-total showing the total price for each group. You are then asked to give a grand total for the price of all the houses on all the estates. A simple report format is as acceptable as a more complicated one that selects and prints the field headings at the head of every group.

Do not forget to:

- choose the correct fields from the correct tables to include in your report. Fields from both tables will be needed, which is why the relationship between the tables was set up in the first place.
- scrap your first attempt if the report is not as you expected. It saves valuable examination time.
- set up the groups and use the correct fields for the headings and data for each group
- choose as simple a presentation for the report as you can. Though some automatic report formats show field headings every time for each group, one set of field headings for all the groups' data is just as acceptable.
- include sorting and grouping as you set up the report
- add the sub-totals for each group and the final grand total for the **Price** field
- increase font point size for better display, including sub-totals and grand total
- add the date and name footers to the report.

Your next assignment is given in Figure 3.16.

ASSIGNMENT 4

1   Making use of the one-to-many relationship between the two tables from Assignments 1 and 2, create a further report entitled **ATHENA HOUSE – BUILDERS, ESTATE ANALYSIS.** In this report group the houses under their respective estates. For this purpose, use the **Estate Ref, Estate Name** and **Town** from the **Estate Table**. For each group show only the field heading and data for the **House Name, Start Date, Bedrooms, Receptions** and **Price** fields taken from the **House Details** table. The field headings may appear every time for each group, or they may be set out at the head of the report once only, and only the actual data will appear in each group under the field headings at the head of the report. Either type of report is acceptable.

2   Sort the groups alphabetically on **Estate Ref.**

3   Within each group sort in **Start Date** order starting with the oldest date.

4   Add a **Sub-total** under each group based on the **Price** for each house in that group, and at the bottom of the report give the **Grand Total** showing the total value of the housing stock.

5   Insert today's date and your name as footers but do not insert a page number.

6   Save your work as **Report2.**

7   Print this report.

Figure 3.16   Third Level database assignment 4

You need to look at the checklist for all the items in Assignment 3 and apply these to Assignment 4. In addition, did you remember to:

- insert the sub-total figures for **Price** at the end of each group so that this gives a summary of the prices for each group?
- insert the actual word **Sub-total** under each group at the side of the **Price** figures?
- format these figures for currency with no decimal places?
- enlarge the point size of these figures, and the Sub-total label?
- line up the figures under the **Price** field?

Check your printout against the worked assignments which appear in Figures 3.35 and 3.36 on pages 106 and 107.

HELPFUL HINTS

- At this level, read and refer to the background notes frequently.

- Carefully follow the instructions to set up the data screens. In business the first file's data entry screen together with the records would probably be set up first before designing and entering the second screen's data. In the artificial conditions of the classroom, different instructions need to be given to check if an entry screen has been set up correctly.

- Use the simplest report format you can for Assignments 3 and 4.

- Make use of highlighting several boxes together at the same time in order to change a font or increase the point size for all the data.

- Use the format commands to align all the highlighted boxes together.

- Use text boxes for entering sub-totals, grand totals, footers etc.

- Your work may appear different from the marking guide because of font and style differences. This is not penalised providing you conform to the specified instructions within the assignment.

- Always check your work in preview to see what it looks like.

- Do not forget to use a Page Set Up command to set margins and page orientation.

Worked assignments

On the following pages you will find worked versions to the Database assignments at **First, Second** and **Third Levels**.

Check your work carefully against these worked versions.

Kit Ref	Item	Manufacturer	Usual Price	Sale Price
BA2	African Bead Kit	Ringold Bead Co plc	£26.99	£19.99
BN1	Naranja Indian Bead Kit	Ringold Bead Co plc	£28.99	£22.99
BS3	Sioux Indian Bead Kit	Ringold Bead Co plc	£27.99	£21.99
DB1	Sailor Teddy Bear Kit	Diana's Miniature Bears	£24.50	£19.50
DB2	Cricketer Teddy Bear Kit	Diana's Miniature Bears	£19.50	£24.50
MB1	Model Boat Kit	Mariposa Model Co	£35.00	£30.50
MH2	Model House Kit	Mariposa Model Co	£37.50	£32.50
PC1	Alice Porcelain Doll Kit	Annette's Unique Dolls	£50.00	£40.00
PC2	Emma Porcelain Doll Kit	Annette's Unique Dolls	£55.00	£47.99
TA3	Apron Cross Stitch Kit	Cassandra Crafts	£23.50	£19.00
TC1	Cushion Tapestry Kit	Cassandra Crafts	£37.25	£27.00
TS2	Stool Tapestry Kit	Cassandra Crafts	£29.99	£21.00

Figure 3.17 Worked assignment 1 – First Level database

Kit Ref	Item	Manufacturer	Usual Price	Sale Price
XPC4	Tosca Porcelain Doll Kit	Annette's Unique Dolls	£60.00	£50.00
XPC3	Carmen Porcelain Doll Kit	Annette's Unique Dolls	£60.00	£52.00
PC2	Emma Porcelain Doll Kit	Annette's Unique Dolls	£55.00	£47.99
TC1	Cushion Tapestry Kit	Cassandra Crafts	£37.25	£27.00
TS2	Stool Tapestry Kit	Cassandra Crafts	£29.99	£21.00
TA3	Apron Cross Stitch Kit	Cassandra Crafts	£23.50	£19.00
DB2	Cricketer Teddy Bear Kit	Diana's Miniature Bears	£24.50	£19.50
XDB3	Footballer Teddy Bear Kit	Diana's Miniature Bears	£28.00	£23.00
XDB4	Lawyer Teddy Bear Kit	Diana's Miniature Bears	£29.50	£25.00
DB1	Sailor Teddy Bear Kit	Diana's Miniature Bears	£24.50	£19.50
MB1	Model Boat Kit	Mariposa Model Co	£35.00	£30.50
MH2	Model House Kit	Mariposa Model Co	£37.50	£32.50
XMC3	Model Car Kit	Mariposa Model Co	£33.50	£28.50
BN1	Navajo Indian Bead Kit	Ringold Bead Co plc	£28.99	£22.99
BA2	African Bead Kit	Ringold Bead Co plc	£26.99	£19.99
BS3	Sioux Indian Bead Kit	Ringold Bead Co plc	£27.99	£21.99

Figure 3.18 Worked assignment 2 – First Level database

Kit Ref	Item	Manufacturer	Usual Price	Sale Price
XPC4	Tosca Porcelain Doll Kit	Annette's Unique Dolls	£60.00	£50.00
XPC3	Carmen Porcelain Doll Kit	Annette's Unique Dolls	£60.00	£52.00
PC2	Emma Porcelain Doll Kit	Annette's Unique Dolls	£55.00	£47.99
MH2	Model House Kit	Mariposa Model Co	£37.50	£32.50
TC1	Cushion Tapestry Kit	Cassandra Crafts	£37.25	£27.00
MB1	Model Boat Kit	Mariposa Model Co	£35.00	£30.50
XMC3	Model Car Kit	Mariposa Model Co	£33.50	£28.50
TS2	Stool Tapestry Kit	Cassandra Crafts	£29.99	£21.00
XDB4	Lawyer Teddy Bear Kit	Diana's Miniature Bears	£29.50	£25.00
BN1	Navajo Indian Bead Kit	Ringold Bead Co plc	£28.99	£22.99
XDB3	Footballer Teddy Bear Kit	Diana's Miniature Bears	£28.00	£23.00
BS3	Sioux Indian Bead Kit	Ringold Bead Co plc	£27.99	£21.99
BA2	African Bead Kit	Ringold Bead Co plc	£26.99	£19.99
DB1	Sailor Teddy Bear Kit	Diana's Miniature Bears	£24.50	£19.50
DB2	Cricketer Teddy Bear Kit	Diana's Miniature Bears	£24.50	£19.50
TA3	Apron Cross Stitch Kit	Cassandra Crafts	£23.50	£19.00

Figure 3.19 Worked assignment 3 – First Level database

Kit Ref	Item	Manufacturer	Usual Price	Sale Price
DB1	Sailor Teddy Bear Kit	Diana's Miniature Bears	£24.50	£19.50
XDB4	Lawyer Teddy Bear Kit	Diana's Miniature Bears	£29.50	£25.00
XDB3	Footballer Teddy Bear Kit	Diana's Miniature Bears	£28.00	£23.00
DB2	Cricketer Teddy Bear Kit	Diana's Miniature Bears	£24.50	£19.50

Figure 3.20 Worked assignment 4 – First Level database

Item	Manufacturer	Date
Model Boat Kit	Mariposa Model Co	3/4/98
Cricketer Teddy Bear Kit	Diana's Miniature Bears	19/4/98
Cushion Tapestry Kit	Cassandra Crafts	19/4/98
Apron Cross Stitch Kit	Cassandra Crafts	19/4/98
Sailor Teddy Bear Kit	Diana's Miniature Bears	19/4/98
Stool Tapestry Kit	Cassandra Crafts	27/4/98
Navajo Indian Bead Kit	Ringold Bead Co plc	12/6/98
African Bead Kit	Ringold Bead Co plc	12/6/98
Sioux Indian Bead Kit	Ringold Bead Co plc	12/6/98
Emma Porcelain Doll Kit	Annette's Unique Dolls	4/7/98
Lawyer Teddy Bear Kit	Diana's Miniature Bears	31/8/98
Footballer Teddy Bear Kit	Diana's Miniature Bears	31/8/98
Carmen Porcelain Doll Kit	Annette's Unique Dolls	15/9/98
Tosca Porcelain Doll Kit	Annette's Unique Dolls	15/9/98
Model Car Kit	Mariposa Model Co	15/9/98
Model House Kit	Mariposa Model Co	15/9/98

Figure 3.21 Worked assignment 5 – First Level database

ATHENA HOUSE TEDDY BEAR KITS

Date

REFERENCE	NAME OF ITEM	DISCOUNT SALE PRICE
DB2	Cricketer Teddy Bear Kit	£19.50
XDB3	Footballer Teddy Bear Kit	£23.00
XDB4	Lawyer Teddy Bear Kit	£25.00
DB1	Sailor Teddy Bear Kit	£19.50
	GRAND TOTAL:	£87.00

Figure 3.22 Worked assignment 6 – First Level database

COMLON CATTERY DATA ENTRY SCREEN

Cat Ref	601
Cat Type	Tortoiseshell
Cat Name	Felicity
Birth Date	15/10/98
Breed	Tortoiseshell
Colour Details	Red/Black
Gender	Female
Breeder	Tamara's Exotic Felines
Address	Brixton, London
Price	£255

Figure 3.23 Entry screen – Second Level database assignment 1

Cat Ref	Cat Type	Cat Name	Birth Date	Breed	Colour Details	Gender	Breeder	Address	Price
601	Tortoiseshell	Felicity	15/10/98	Tortoiseshell	Red/Black	Female	Tamara's Exotic Felines	Brixton, London	£255
602	Siamese	Beauty	16/2/99	Siamese	Seal Point	Female	Jaswinder's Topcats	Ashton, Somerset	£350
603	Angora	Zara	22/1/99	Angora	Lilac/White	Female	Barset Cat Breeders	Framley, Barset	£395
604	Ocicat	Nanamay	14/4/99	Ocicat	White	Female	Barset Cat Breeders	Framley, Barset	£340
605	Tortie Tabby	Dumpling	17/3/99	Tortie Tabby	Blue/Silver	Female	Cuddly Cats plc	Stockport, Cheshire	£345
608	Manx	Pushkin	31/3/99	Manx	White	Male	Jaswinder's Topcats	Ashton, Somerset	£320
612	Tabby	Shamus	6/2/99	Tabby	Red	Male	Barset Cat Breeders	Framley, Barset	£345
614	Burmese	King John	14/2/99	Burmese	Brown	Male	Tamara's Exotic Felines	Brixton, London	£385
615	Tortoiseshell	Gingerbread	3/2/99	Tortoiseshell	Red/Black/White	Female	Tamara's Exotic Felines	Brixton, London	£295
616	Persian	Vanilla	27/1/99	Persian	White	Female	Pat Cloggs Moggies	Leeds, Yorkshire	£315
617	Persian	Bella	21/2/99	Persian	Black Smoke	Female	Cuddly Cats plc	Stockport, Cheshire	£325
618	Siamese	Milor	23/2/99	Siamese	Cream Point	Female	Jaswinder's Topcats	Ashton, Somerset	£298
619	Maine Coon	Whiskey	17/1/99	Maine Coon	Brown/White	Male	Pat Cloggs Moggies	Leeds, Yorkshire	£220
625	Tortie Tabby	Candyrue	1/3/99	Tortie Tabby	Blue/Silver	Female	Cuddly Cats plc	Stockport, Cheshire	£355
627	Siamese	Torquil	16/4/99	Siamese	Cream Point	Male	Jaswinder's Topcats	Ashton, Somerset	£325
644	Persian	Xanadu	13/4/99	Persian	Black	Male	Pat Cloggs Moggies	Leeds, Yorkshire	£350
666	Somali	Little Caesar	19/3/99	Somali	Lilac	Male	Cuddly Cats plc	Stockport, Cheshire	£305

Figure 3.24 Worked assignment 1 – Second Level database

Cat Ref	Cat Name	Birth Date	Breed	Colour Details	Long Hair?	Gender	Breeder	Address	Price
601	Felicity	15/10/98	Tortoiseshell	Red/Black	No	Female	Tamara's Exotic Felines	Brixton, London	£255
619	Whiskey	17/1/99	Maine Coon	Brown/White	Yes	Male	Pat Cloggs Moggies	Leeds, Yorkshire	£220
603	Zara	22/1/99	Angora	Lilac/White	No	Female	Barset Cat Breeders	Framley, Barset	£395
616	Vanilla	27/1/99	Persian	White	Yes	Female	Pat Cloggs Moggies	Leeds, Yorkshire	£315
615	Gingerbread	3/2/99	Tortoiseshell	Red/Black/White	No	Female	Tamara's Exotic Felines	Brixton, London	£295
614	King John	14/2/99	Burmese	Brown	No	Male	Tamara's Exotic Felines	Brixton, London	£385
602	Beauty	16/2/99	Siamese	Seal Point	No	Female	Jaswinder's Topcats	Ashton, Somerset	£350
617	Bella	21/2/99	Persian	Black Smoke	Yes	Female	Cuddly Cats plc	Stockport, Cheshire	£325
618	Milor	23/2/99	Siamese	Cream Point	No	Male	Jaswinder's Topcats	Ashton, Somerset	£298
625	Candyrue	1/3/99	Tortie Tabby	Blue/Silver	Yes	Female	Cuddly Cats plc	Stockport, Cheshire	£355
671	Sultana	5/3/99	Turkish Van	Auburn	No	Female	Tamara's Exotic Felines	Brixton, London	£340
605	Dumpling	17/3/99	Tortie Tabby	Blue/Silver	Yes	Female	Cuddly Cats plc	Stockport, Cheshire	£345
666	Little Caesar	19/3/99	Somali	Lilac	Yes	Male	Cuddly Cats plc	Stockport, Cheshire	£305
677	Caramba	24/3/99	Tortoiseshell	Red/Black	No	Female	Jaswinder's Topcats	Ashton, Somerset	£310
673	Rolypoly	31/3/99	Persian	Cream/White	Yes	Male	Pat Cloggs Moggies	Leeds, Yorkshire	£300
608	Pushkin	31/3/99	Manx	White	No	Male	Jaswinder's Topcats	Ashton, Somerset	£320
672	Cookienet	3/4/99	Angora	Chocolate	No	Female	Barset Cat Breeders	Framley, Barset	£325
676	Sterlingworth	3/4/99	Tabby	Silver	Yes	Male	Cuddly Cats plc	Stockport, Cheshire	£350
678	Saroola	4/4/99	Singapura	Sable Brown	No	Male	Barset Cat Breeders	Framley, Barset	£325
644	Xanadu	13/4/99	Persian	Black	Yes	Male	Pat Cloggs Moggies	Leeds, Yorkshire	£350
679	Frisky	13/4/99	Siamese	Red Point	No	Male	Jaswinder's Topcats	Ashton, Somerset	£330
680	Martina Babbage	14/4/99	Persian	Blue	No	Female	Tamara's Exotic Felines	Brixton, London	£340
604	Nanamay	14/4/99	Ocicat	Chocolate	No	Female	Barset Cat Breeders	Framley, Barset	£340
627	Torquil	16/4/99	Siamese	Cream Point	No	Male	Jaswinder's Topcats	Ashton, Somerset	£325

Figure 3.25 Amended table – worked assignment 2 – Second Level database

Cat Ref	Cat Name	Gender	Birth Date
605	Dumpling	Female	17/3/99

Figure 3.26 Worked assignment 3(1) – Second Level database

Cat Ref	Cat Name	Birth Date	Gender	Breeder	Price
619	Whiskey	17/1/99	Male	Pat Cloggs Moggies	£220
673	Rolypoly	31/3/99	Male	Pat Cloggs Moggies	£300
666	Little Caesar	19/3/99	Male	Cuddly Cats plc	£305
616	Vanilla	27/1/99	Female	Pat Cloggs Moggies	£315
617	Bella	21/2/99	Female	Cuddly Cats plc	£325
605	Dumpling	17/3/99	Female	Cuddly Cats plc	£345
625	Candyrue	1/3/99	Female	Cuddly Cats plc	£355

Figure 3.27 Worked assignment 3(2) – Second Level database

COMLON CATTERY - BREEDERS

Cat Ref	Birth Date	Cat Name	Breed	Gender	Price
Barset Cat Breeders		**Framley, Barset**			
603	22/1/99	Zara	Angora	Female	£395
672	3/4/99	Cookienet	Angora	Female	£325
678	4/4/99	Saroola	Singapura	Male	£325
604	14/4/99	Nanamay	Ocicat	Female	£340
			Sub Total		**£1,385**
Cuddly Cats plc		**Stockport, Cheshire**			
617	21/2/99	Bella	Persian	Female	£325
625	1/3/99	Candyrue	Tortie Tabby	Female	£355
605	17/3/99	Dumpling	Tortie Tabby	Female	£345
666	19/3/99	Little Caesar	Somali	Male	£305
676	3/4/99	Sterlingworth	Tabby	Male	£350
			Sub Total		**£1,680**
Jaswinder's Topcats		**Ashton, Somerset**			
602	16/2/99	Beauty	Siamese	Female	£350
618	23/2/99	Milor	Siamese	Male	£298
677	24/3/99	Caramba	Tortoiseshell	Female	£310
608	31/3/99	Pushkin	Manx	Male	£320
679	13/4/99	Frisky	Siamese	Male	£330
627	16/4/99	Torquil	Siamese	Male	£325
			Sub Total		**£1,933**
Pat Cloggs Moggies		**Leeds, Yorkshire**			
619	17/1/99	Whiskey	Maine Coon	Male	£220
616	27/1/99	Vanilla	Persian	Female	£315
673	31/3/99	Rolypoly	Persian	Male	£300
644	13/4/99	Xanadu	Persian	Male	£350
			Sub Total		**£1,185**
Tamara's Exotic Felines		**Brixton, London**			
601	15/10/98	Felicity	Tortoiseshell	Female	£255
615	3/2/99	Gingerbread	Tortoiseshell	Female	£295
614	14/2/99	King John	Burmese	Male	£385
671	5/3/99	Sultana	Turkish Van	Female	£340
680	14/4/99	Martina Babbage	Persian	Female	£340
			Sub Total		**£1,615**
			Grand Total		**£7,798**

Date   **Name**

Figure 3.28 Worked assignment 4 – Second Level database

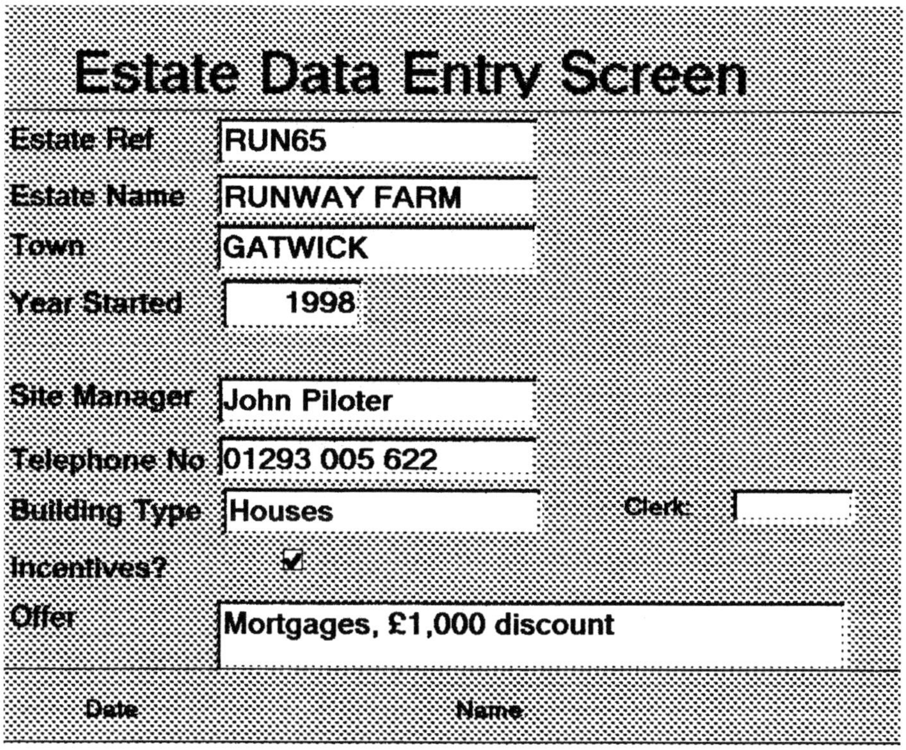

Estate Data Entry Screen

Estate Ref	RUN65
Estate Name	RUNWAY FARM
Town	GATWICK
Year Started	1998
Site Manager	John Piloter
Telephone No	01293 005 622
Building Type	Houses
Incentives?	☑
Offer	Mortgages, £1,000 discount

Clerk: [   ]

Date   Name

Figure 3.29 Estate screen for worked assignment 1 – Third Level database

HOUSE DETAILS DATA ENTRY SCREEN

House Ref	GC1
House Name	Claridges
Detached	☑
Bedrooms	4
Receptions	3
Garage	☑
Price	£200,000
Estate Ref	RUN65

Start Date   1/6/98

Date   Name

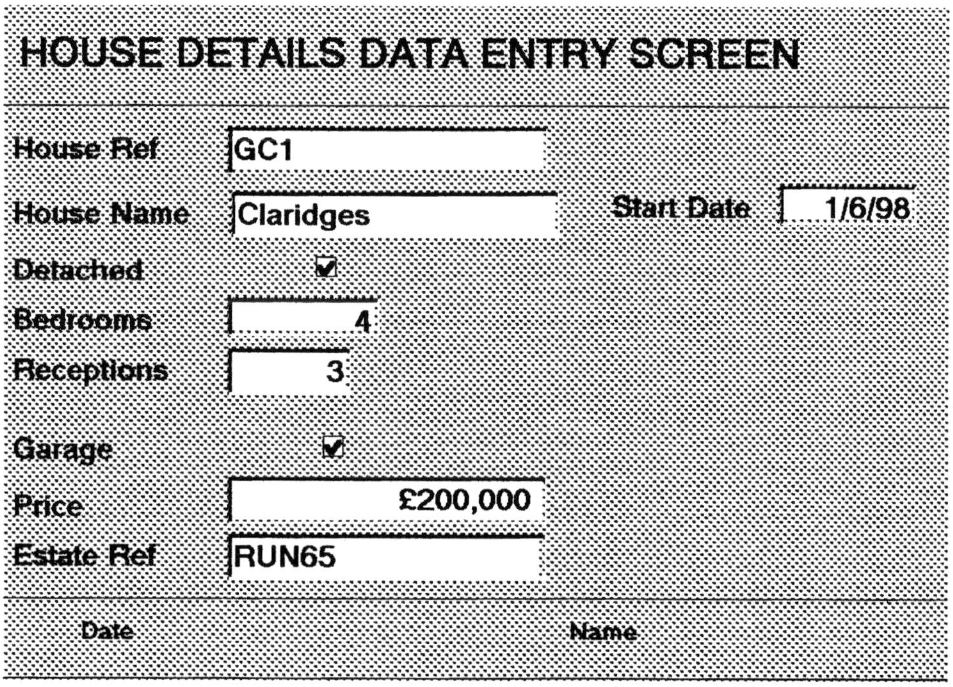

Figure 3.30 House details screen for worked assignment 1 – Third Level database

Estate Ref	Estate Name	Town	Year Started	Site Manager	Telephone No	Building Type	Incentives?	Offer
CAN41	CANAL VIEW VALLEY	MANCHESTER	1998	Billy Shipper	0161 429 0193	Houses, Flats	☑	1% cashback, free carpets
DOC78	DOCKLAND PONDS	LONDON	1999	Carol Fisher	0181 004 3761	Houses, Flats	☑	Mortgages, free carpets
FLO23	FLOODGATE MEADOWS	NORTHAMPTON	1997	Helen Diverson	01604 505 802	Houses	☑	Mortgages, £200 holiday voucher
JUN16	JUNCTION SQUARE	CLAPHAM	1999	Bob Signalman	0181 0022 163	Houses, Flats	☑	Mortgages, 1% cashback
RUN65	RUNWAY FARM	GATWICK	1998	John Piloter	01293 005 622	Houses	☑	Mortgages, £1,000 discount

Figure 3.31 Estate table – Third Level database assignment 2

House Ref	Start Date	House Name	Detached	Bedrooms	Receptions	Garage	Price	Estate Ref
CC1	2/5/99	Claridges	✓	4	3	✓	£295,000	JUN16
CR1	22/5/99	Ritz	✓	5	3	✓	£330,000	JUN16
CR2	27/3/99	Ritz	✓	5	3	✓	£350,000	JUN16
GC1	1/6/98	Claridges	✓	4	3	✓	£200,000	RUN65
GG1	25/5/98	Grosvenor	✓	4	2	✓	£190,000	RUN65
GW1	10/7/98	Waldorf	✓	3	2	✓	£165,000	RUN65
GW2	19/7/98	Waldorf	✓	3	2	✓	£170,000	RUN65
LC1	18/4/99	Claridges	✓	4	3	✓	£300,000	DOC78
LG1	30/4/99	Grosvenor	✓	4	2	✓	£285,000	DOC78
MG1	21/5/98	Grosvenor	✓	4	2	✓	£150,000	CAN41
MW1	9/4/98	Waldorf	✓	3	2	✓	£130,000	CAN41
NS1	7/3/97	Savoy	☐	3	2	☐	£125,000	FLO23
NS2	4/3/97	Savoy	☐	3	2	☐	£125,000	FLO23
NW1	12/6/97	Waldorf	✓	3	2	✓	£130,000	FLO23
SG2	14/4/98	Savoy	☐	3	2	☐	£145,000	CAN41
SM1	22/4/98	Savoy	☐	3	2	☐	£145,000	CAN41

Figure 3.32 House details table – Third Level database assignment 2

ATHENA HOUSE - BUILDERS, PRICE SUMMARY

Estate Ref	House Ref	Start Date	House Name	Detached	Bedrooms	Receptions	Garage	Price
CAN41	MG1	21/5/98	Grosvenor	☑	4	2	☑	£150.000
CAN41	SM1	22/4/98	Savoy	☐	3	2	☑	£145.000
CAN41	SG2	14/4/98	Savoy	☐	3	2	☐	£145.000
CAN41	MW1	9/4/98	Waldorf	☑	3	2	☑	£130.000
DOC78	LC1	18/4/99	Claridges	☑	4	3	☑	£300.000
DOC78	LG1	30/4/99	Grosvenor	☑	4	2	☑	£285.000
FLO23	NS1	7/3/97	Savoy	☐	3	2	☐	£125.000
FLO23	NS2	4/3/97	Savoy	☐	3	2	☐	£125.000
FLO23	NW1	12/6/97	Waldorf	☑	3	2	☑	£130.000
JUN16	CC1	2/5/99	Claridges	☑	4	3	☑	£295.000
JUN16	CR1	22/5/99	Ritz	☑	5	3	☑	£330.000
JUN16	CR2	27/3/99	Ritz	☑	5	3	☑	£350.000
RUN65	GC1	1/6/98	Claridges	☑	4	3	☑	£200.000
RUN65	GG1	25/5/98	Grosvenor	☑	4	2	☑	£190.000
RUN65	GW1	10/7/98	Waldorf	☑	3	2	☑	£165.000
RUN65	GW2	19/7/98	Waldorf	☑	3	2	☑	£170.000
							Grand Total	**£3,235,000**

Date   Candidate's Name

Figure 3.33 Worked assignment 3 – Third Level database

Athena House - Builders, Price Summary

Estate Ref   CAN41

House Ref	Start Date	House Name	Detached	Bedrooms	Receptions	Garage	Price
MG1	21/5/98	Grosvenor	☑	4	2	☑	£150,000
SM1	22/4/98	Savoy	☐	3	2	☐	£145,000
SG2	14/4/98	Savoy	☐	3	2	☐	£145,000
MW1	9/4/98	Waldorf	☑	3	2	☑	£130,000

Estate Ref   DOC78

House Ref	Start Date	House Name	Detached	Bedrooms	Receptions	Garage	Price
LC1	18/4/99	Claridges	☑	4	3	☑	£300,000
LG1	30/4/99	Grosvenor	☑	4	2	☑	£285,000

Estate Ref   FLO23

House Ref	Start Date	House Name	Detached	Bedrooms	Receptions	Garage	Price
NS1	7/3/97	Savoy	☐	3	2	☐	£125,000
NS2	4/3/97	Savoy	☐	3	2	☐	£125,000
NW1	12/6/97	Waldorf	☑	3	2	☑	£130,000

Estate Ref   JUN16

House Ref	Start Date	House Name	Detached	Bedrooms	Receptions	Garage	Price
CC1	2/5/99	Claridges	☑	4	3	☑	£295,000
CR1	22/5/99	Ritz	☑	5	3	☑	£330,000
CR2	27/3/99	Ritz	☑	5	3	☑	£350,000

Estate Ref   RUN65

House Ref	Start Date	House Name	Detached	Bedrooms	Receptions	Garage	Price
GC1	1/6/98	Claridges	☑	4	3	☑	£200,000
GG1	25/5/98	Grosvenor	☑	4	2	☑	£190,000
GW1	10/7/98	Waldorf	☑	3	2	☑	£165,000
GW2	19/7/98	Waldorf	☑	3	2	☑	£170,000

Grand Total: £3,235,000

Date   Name

Figure 3.34 Alternative worked assignment 3 – Third Level database

Athena House - Builders, Estate Analysis

Estate Ref   CAN41   CANAL VIEW VALLEY   MANCHESTER

House Name	Start Date	Bedrooms	Receptions	Price
WALDORF	9/4/98	3	2	£130,000
SAVOY	14/4/98	3	2	£145,000
SAVOY	22/4/98	3	2	£145,000
GROSVENOR	21/5/98	4	2	£150,000
			Sub Total:	£570,000

Estate Ref   DOC78   DOCKLAND PONDS   LONDON

House Name	Start Date	Bedrooms	Receptions	Price
CLARIDGES	18/4/99	4	3	£300,000
GROSVENOR	30/4/99	4	2	£285,000
			Sub Total:	£585,000

Estate Ref   FLO23   FLOODGATE MEADOWS   NORTHAMPTON

House Name	Start Date	Bedrooms	Receptions	Price
SAVOY	4/3/97	3	2	£125,000
SAVOY	7/3/97	3	2	£125,000
WALDORF	12/6/97	3	2	£130,000
			Sub Total:	£380,000

Estate Ref   JUN16   JUNCTION SQUARE   CLAPHAM

House Name	Start Date	Bedrooms	Receptions	Price
RITZ	27/3/99	5	3	£350,000
CLARIDGES	2/5/99	4	3	£295,000
RITZ	22/5/99	5	3	£330,000
			Sub Total:	£975,000

Estate Ref   RUN65   RUNWAY FARM   GATWICK

House Name	Start Date	Bedrooms	Receptions	Price
GROSVENOR	25/5/98	4	2	£190,000
CLARIDGES	1/6/98	4	3	£200,000
WALDORF	10/7/98	3	2	£165,000
WALDORF	19/7/98	3	2	£170,000
			Sub Total:	£725,000
			Grand Total:	£3,235,000

Date: Name:

Figure 3.35 Worked assignment 4 – Third Level database

ATHENA HOUSE - BUILDERS, ESTATE ANALYSIS

Start Date	House Name	Bedrooms	Receptions	Price

Estate Ref `CAN41` **Estate Name** `CANAL VIEW VALLEY` **Town** `MANCHESTER`

Start Date	House Name	Bedrooms	Receptions	Price
9/4/98	Waldorf	3	2	£130,000
14/4/98	Savoy	3	2	£145,000
22/4/98	Savoy	3	2	£145,000
21/5/98	Grosvenor	4	2	£150,000
		Sub Total		£570.000

Estate Ref `DOC78` **Estate Name** `DOCKLAND PONDS` **Town** `LONDON`

Start Date	House Name	Bedrooms	Receptions	Price
18/4/99	Claridges	4	3	£300,000
30/4/99	Grosvenor	4	2	£285,000
		Sub Total		£585.000

Estate Ref `FLO23` **Estate Name** `FLOODGATE MEADOWS` **Town** `NORTHAMPTON`

Start Date	House Name	Bedrooms	Receptions	Price
4/3/97	Savoy	3	2	£125,000
7/3/97	Savoy	3	2	£125,000
12/6/97	Waldorf	3	2	£130,000
		Sub Total		£380.000

Estate Ref `JUN16` **Estate Name** `JUNCTION SQUARE` **Town** `CLAPHAM`

Start Date	House Name	Bedrooms	Receptions	Price
27/3/99	Ritz	5	3	£350,000
2/5/99	Claridges	4	3	£295,000
22/5/99	Ritz	5	3	£330,000
		Sub Total		£975.000

Estate Ref `RUN65` **Estate Name** `RUNWAY FARM` **Town** `GATWICK`

Start Date	House Name	Bedrooms	Receptions	Price
25/5/98	Grosvenor	4	2	£190,000
1/6/98	Claridges	4	3	£200,000
10/7/98	Waldorf	3	2	£165,000
19/7/98	Waldorf	3	2	£170,000
		Sub Total		£725.000
		Grand Total		£3.235.000

Date   Name

Figure 3.36 Alternative worked assignment 4 – Third Level database

4

Word processing

Introduction

A word processing software package enables the user to enter text, save it to disk and then print out a hard copy on paper. Whilst the text is showing on screen, the user can make amendments by adding and deleting words and phrases. This is known as text amendment. The user can also change the appearance of the text by altering the line spacing and the margins. This is known as formatting. All the changes can be saved so that the appearance of the final document may be very different from the original version which was keyed in by the user.

In addition, text can be arranged in columns, pages can be automatically numbered and a wide range of functions can be performed to transform a document quickly and easily.

Documents which have been stored on disk may be recalled to screen and printed out when needed.

This section of the workbook will guide you through the LCCIEB's three levels of Word Processing assignments. On the following pages you will find typical **First, Second** and **Third Level** Word Processing assignments. Each assignment is broken down into its composite parts and guidance is given as to how to approach the tasks.

This is what you should do:

1 First of all, check that you can perform all the functions that are listed for each level.
2 Read the accompanying text and follow the instructions carefully.
3 Work through each assignment at your own speed.
4 When you have completed the assignment, check your work with the specimen answer which appears at the end of this section.
5 When you feel confident that you can competently perform all the functions for the next level, continue through the workbook.

A full version of each assignment appears in Chapter 7.

First Level

For success in a **First Level** Word Processing assignment, you should be able to:

1 *Create a new document and input text;*
2 *Proofread and correct errors;*
3 *Save to disk and print a single copy;*
4 *Open an existing document;*
5 *Amend text by inserting and deleting words;*
6 *Enhance text by using bold, underline and italic commands;*
7 *Format text by using the centre, right align and fully justified commands;*
8 *Change left and right margins;*
9 *Change line spacing from single to double spacing;*
10 *Copy and move blocks of text;*
11 *Use a three-column table.*

Check that you can perform all these basic functions before you continue.

The **First Level** assignment set comprises six assignments which you must complete within the time allowance of 1 hour and 30 minutes. You will need to produce a printout for each assignment, making a total of six printouts. It is a good idea to print your work as you proceed through the six assignments so that if you find any errors, you can correct them and print out a further copy within the time allowance. You can print out as many versions of your work as you wish, but clearly it is not wise to waste paper. You are not allowed to make any changes to your work once the time allowance has elapsed.

ASSIGNMENT I

The first assignment in the set is a simple keyboarding exercise in which you are asked to input a short piece of continuous text, proofread it for errors and print out a copy. The text will be in simple English and there will be no abbreviations or unusual words. You should use the default margins on your computer and single line spacing. All instructions are given at the top of the assignment. Follow them carefully and save the document under the filename given in the instructions.

Do not forget to:

- input the text carefully, trying to avoid making keyboarding errors
- be consistent when leaving spaces after a full stop – it is customary to leave two spaces, but you may leave only one, provided you do so consistently

- leave one clear line space between paragraphs
- proofread your work carefully, both manually and using the on-line spellchecker
- add your name at the bottom of the document
- save your work and print out a copy.

Figure 4.1 gives your first assignment.

ASSIGNMENT 1

1   Key in the text below in single line spacing, using the default margins.

2   Key in your name at the bottom of the document.

3   Proofread your work carefully.

4   Save the document as [WP1ASS1].

5   Print a copy.

It is generally believed that the purchase of a good bed is one of the best investments a person can make. We spend, on average, a third of our life in bed and so it is important that these hours are spent in an environment which is comfortable and healthy.

We need a good night's sleep to recharge our batteries, both mentally and physically. If we sleep badly, our daily life can be adversely affected. We make more mistakes, lose our temper more easily and generally enjoy life less.

A suitable bed, which gives the comfort and support we need for a good night's sleep, can be a vital factor in our happiness. It should be comfortable and large enough to allow us to move freely. It should be purchased from a reputable retailer and changed every eight or ten years.

Choose your bed wisely, or your body will suffer!

Figure 4.1   First Level word processing assignment 1

Did you remember to:

- check your work carefully for errors?
- leave one or two spaces, consistently, after full stops?
- leave a clear line space between paragraphs?
- save your work under the appropriate filename?
- print out a perfect copy?

If so, check your printout with the worked assignment which appears in Figure 4.15 on page 151.

ASSIGNMENT 2

Assignment 2 is a short memorandum which you must key in from handwritten copy. The handwriting will always be clear and there will be no abbreviations or deliberate mistakes to confuse you. You should just copy what you see. However, you must remember to include today's date, which will not be given in the assignment. The date should appear above the reference. You are also asked to add your initials to the reference. This means that you simply key in your initials after the oblique [/], ie RM/PS. Once again the document must be in single line spacing. However, this time you must use fully justified margins (ie, the left and right margins should be straight). Be sure to save the document under the appropriate filename because you will need to recall this assignment to screen later and make amendments to it.

Do not forget to:

- type the memorandum heading in capital letters, as on the copy
- use the [TAB] key to leave a space after the To, From, Date and Ref headings
- leave a clear line space between the To, From, Date and Ref headings
- use initial capitals where shown (Sales Supervisor, Marketing Manager, etc)
- insert your initials after the reference
- leave a clear line space before and after the main heading
- leave a clear line space between paragraphs
- proofread your work carefully and correct any errors
- save your work under the filename as instructed.

Assignment 2 is shown in Figure 4.2.

ASSIGNMENT 2

1   Key in the text below in single line spacing, using fully justified margins.

2   Insert today's date.

3   Add your initials at the end of the reference.

4   Key in your name at the bottom of the document.

5   Proofread your work carefully.

6   Save the document as [WP1ASS2].

7   Print a copy.

MEMORANDUM

To   Sheila Conway
         Sales Supervisor

From   Robert Malloy
         Marketing Manager

Ref   RM/

HOME INTERIORS EXHIBITION, OLYMPIA

Please note that our attendance at this exhibition has now been confirmed. We have been allocated Stand Number 240 which is on the first floor of the exhibition hall. This is a prime location and should enable us to show our products to a large number of visitors.

We shall need a sales team of ten people to cover the four-day event in shifts. Please prepare a list of staff from your department who would be willing to attend. The exhibition is open from 1000 to 2000 each day. It will be necessary, therefore, for some members of staff to increase their working hours for the exhibition period. Please tell them that they will be paid for the extra hours worked.

The space available to us will accommodate three double beds and one single, in addition to glass shelves on which we can display our range of bedlinen and matching accessories.

I look forward to receiving your list by Friday.

Figure 4.2   First Level word processing assignment 2

Did you remember to:

- key in the word MEMORANDUM in closed capitals?
- leave enough space between the headings and the information so that all the information starts at the same position?
- leave a clear line space between the headings?

- insert the date?
- add your initials to the reference?
- key in the remainder of the document exactly as on the copy?
- proofread your work carefully and correct any errors?
- save your work as [WP1ASS2]?

Turn to page 152 and check your memorandum against the worked assignment shown in Figure 4.16.

ASSIGNMENT 3

Assignment 3 is a short manuscript exercise which you must key in and save under the appropriate filename. For this assignment, you must be able to centre and embolden text and change the left and right hand margin settings. If you are unable to do this, you should not attempt this assignment just yet.

It is a good idea to change the margins *before* keying in all the text exactly as shown.

Do not forget to:

- change both margins to 5 cm (2 inches)
- key in the text exactly as shown
- use fully justified margins (both margins straight)
- centre and embolden the heading
- leave two clear line spaces between the paragraphs
- add your name at the bottom of the document
- proofread your work carefully and correct any errors
- save the document under the filename given.

Assignment 3 is shown in Figure 4.3.

ASSIGNMENT 3

1   Key in the text below, in single line spacing, using left and right margins of 5 cm (2 inches).

2   Leave two clear line spaces between paragraphs.

3   Use fully justified margins.

4   Make the necessary changes as shown.

5   Key in your name at the bottom of the document.

6   Proofread your work carefully.

7   Save the document as [WP1ASS3].

8   Print a copy.

CHOOSING A NEW BED? — centre and bold

When choosing a new bed, always buy the largest you can afford. Buy the mattress and base together and select a protective cover for the mattress.

It's unhygienic to buy a second-hand bed — so don't be tempted!

Figure 4.3   First Level word processing assignment 3

Did you remember to:

- make the margin changes?
- leave two clear lines between the paragraphs?
- check your work carefully and correct any errors?
- leave one space either side of the dash [–] in the second paragraph?
- centre and embolden the heading?
- use fully justified margins?
- add your name at the bottom of the document?
- save your work under the appropriate filename?

If so, turn to page 153 and check your printout against the worked assignment in Figure 4.17.

ASSIGNMENT 4

This assignment is a recall exercise in which you are asked to recall the memo from Assignment 2 and make changes to it. It is vital, therefore, that you have saved Assignment 2 under the correct filename so that you can find the document easily. The changes to be made include the insertion and deletion of text, a line-spacing change and the movement of a paragraph. It is a good idea to make the textual changes (ie the insertion and deletion of words) before making the formatting changes (bold, line-spacing and paragraph move).

Do not forget to:

- check that you have made all the textual amendments
- leave one clear line space consistently between paragraphs
- change the line spacing for the first paragraph only
- move the third paragraph to its correct location
- proofread the document and correct any errors
- save your work under a new filename, as given
- print out a copy of the updated memorandum.

Assignment 4 is given in Figure 4.4.

ASSIGNMENT 4

1   Recall your document saved as [WP1ASS2].

2   Make the changes to the text as shown below.

3   Proofread your work carefully.

4   Save the document as [WP1ASS4].

5   Print a copy.

MEMORANDUM

To   Sheila Conway
                Sales Supervisor

From   Robert Malloy
                Marketing Manager

Date

Ref

double line spacing for this paragraph

HOME INTERIORS EXHIBITION, OLYMPIA   — bold

demonstrate Please note that our attendance at this exhibition has now been confirmed. We have been allocated Stand Number 240 which is on the first floor of the exhibition hall. This is a prime location and should enable us to show our products to a large number of visitors.

experienced
We shall need a sales team of ten people to cover the four-day event in shifts. Please prepare a list of staff from your department who would be willing to attend. The exhibition is open from 1000 until 2000 each day. It will be necessary, therefore, for some members of staff to increase their working hours for the exhibition period. Please tell them that they will be paid for the extra hours worked. *Travel expenses can also be claimed.*

The space available to us will accommodate three double beds and one single, in addition to glass shelves on which we can display our range of bedlinen and matching accessories.

draft I look forward to receiving your list by ~~Friday~~ next Monday.

Figure 4.4   First Level word processing assignment 4

Did you remember to:

- embolden the heading as instructed?
- change the line spacing for the first paragraph?
- move the third paragraph to its new position?
- ensure consistency of spacing between paragraphs?
- make all the textual changes accurately?
- save your document as [WP1ASS4]?

To see if your printout is accurate, check your memo against the worked assignment which appears in Figure 4.18 on page 154.

ASSIGNMENT 5

This assignment also makes amendments to an earlier assignment, namely Assignment 3. In this case, you must add some extra text at the end of the original document and then key in a simple table. The table will have a maximum of three columns and five rows. You do not have to arrange the table so that there is equal spacing between columns, although it will look better if you do. If you choose not to do so, you will not be penalised.

The table will be shown without gridlines and without a border. It is suggested that you produce a table which looks like the one in the assignment. However, if you choose to add gridlines and a border, you will not be penalised provided the contents of the table are accurate.

Do not forget to:

- recall the correct assignment (Assignment 3)
- add the additional text exactly as shown
- leave two clear line spaces between paragraphs for consistency
- leave at least one clear line space before the table
- follow the capitalisation used within the table
- proofread your work carefully and correct any errors
- save the work under a new filename as instructed
- print out a copy of the amended document.

Assignment 5 is given in Figure 4.5.

ASSIGNMENT 5

1   Recall your document saved as [WP1ASS3].

2   Make the necessary additions to the document as shown.

3   Proofread your work carefully.

4   Save the document as [WP1ASS5].

5   Print a copy.

CHOOSING A NEW BED?

When choosing a new bed, always buy the largest you can afford. Buy the mattress and base together and select a protective cover for the mattress.

It's unhygienic to buy a second-hand bed – so don't be tempted! Always throw away your old bed.

There are many types of bed to choose from. These are our most popular lines:

Range	Mattress Type	Covering
Prestige	Continuous springs	Diamond quilting
Emperor	Open springs	Micro quilting
Ambassador	Pocket springs	Tufting

Figure 4.5   First Level word processing assignment 5

Did you remember to:

- make all the textual additions?
- leave two clear line spaces between paragraphs?
- leave at least one clear line space before the table?
- produce the table exactly as shown?
- proofread your work carefully and correct any errors?

Figures 4.19 and 4.20 on pages 155 and 156 show two versions of this assignment. The first one shows the table without gridlines or border, as the original document suggests. The second one shows the table with printed gridlines and a border. Both versions are correct.

ASSIGNMENT 6

Assignment 6 at **First Level** is always a display exercise, which asks you to produce an attractive notice or advertisement using bold, underline and italics. You are also asked to centre each line horizontally. You must follow the line spacing exactly, so that if the assignment shows two clear line spaces between the text, you must do the same, or incur a penalty.

You are *not* required to centre the task vertically on the page. You may wish to do so, but you will not incur any penalty if you do not.

Do not forget to:

- key in all the text exactly as on the copy
- follow the exact line spacing
- use capitalisation exactly as shown
- make the necessary formatting changes (bold, underline, italics)
- add your name to the bottom of the document (preferably against the left margin)
- proofread your work carefully and correct any errors
- save your work.

Figure 4.6 shows Assignment 6.

ASSIGNMENT 6

1   Key in the text below following line spacing exactly.

2   Centre each line horizontally.

3   Make the necessary formatting changes.

4   Key in your name at the bottom of the document.

5   Proofread your work carefully.

6   Save the document as [WP1ASS6].

7   Print a copy.

DECORATING YOUR BEDROOM?   } *bold*

BUYING A NEW BED?

If you're thinking about making changes to your bedroom,
come along and see our exciting new range of beds and bedlinen.

You can find us on

<u>Stand Number 240</u>   — *bold and underline*

at the

HOME INTERIORS EXHIBITION   — *bold*

at Olympia

next month!

<u>We look forward to seeing you!</u>   — *bold and underline*

Athena Bedrooms, 4 Grove Gardens, Bexley   } *italics*
0181 302 0261

Figure 4.6   First Level word processing assignment 6

Did you remember to:

- follow the line spacing exactly?
- make the necessary formatting changes?
- add your name at the bottom?
- save your work as [WP1ASS6]?

There is a worked version of this assignment shown in Figure 4.21 on page 157. Check your printout carefully against this version.

If you have managed to successfully complete the six assignments at **First Level**, you may be ready for a formal assessment. You must discuss this with your tutor, who will advise you regarding the date and time of the assessment.

It would be a good idea to do some further practice on past assignments at **First Level**. These may be available in your centre or they can be purchased from the LCCI Examinations Board.

Always be certain that you can competently satisfy all the syllabus requirements before attempting a formal assessment. It is wiser to wait until you are more experienced than enter an examination before you are ready.

Whatever your decision, good luck!

HELPFUL HINTS

- **Always check your work carefully and correct any errors that occur.**

- **Follow all instructions at the top of the assignment carefully.**

- **Enter the text first before making any formatting changes.**

- **Always leave at least one clear line space consistently between paragraphs.**

- **Always leave at least one space consistently after full stops.**

- **Follow the assignment regarding the use of capitals and lower case letters.**

- **Be sure to insert the date on letters and memoranda.**

- **Check that any margin changes are exact by measuring your printout.**

- **Save your work carefully under the filenames given.**

- **Add your name at the bottom of each document.**

- **Print out one copy of each document to hand to your tutor for marking.**

Second Level

For success in a Second Level Word Processing assignment, you should be able to perform the functions tested at First Level:

1 *Create a new document and input text;*

2 *Proofread and correct errors;*

3 *Save to disk and print a single copy;*

4 *Open an existing document;*

5 *Amend text by inserting and deleting words;*

6 *Enhance text by using bold, underline and italic commands;*

7 *Format text by using the centre, right align and fully justified commands;*

8 *Change left and right margins;*

9 *Change line spacing from single to double spacing;*

10 *Copy and move blocks of text;*

11 *Use a three-column table.*

You should also be able to:

1 *Indent sections of text;*

2 *Insert and delete hard page breaks;*

3 *Number all pages of a multi-page document;*

4 *Insert headers and footers;*

5 *Use search and replace;*

6 *Insert bullets and/or numbered points;*

7 *Create vertical spaces;*

8 *Use a four-column table;*

9 *Use standard manuscript corrections;*

10 *Expand abbreviations;*

11 *Change font size.*

Check that you can perform all these basic functions before you continue.

The **Second Level** set of assignments comprises four assignments which must be completed within the time allowance of 2 hours. You will need to produce a printout for each of the four assignments. Assignments 2 and 4 will fit on to one sheet of A4 paper, but Assignments 1 and 3 are multi-page documents comprising two and three pages respectively. The assignments are longer than those at **First Level**, so you will need to key in the text more quickly. Once again, however, the handwriting will always be legible and every effort is made to make the instructions as clear as possible. Some abbreviations are used at **Second Level**. They must be expanded accurately. A full list of abbreviations appears in Chapter 1, pages 8–9 of this workbook. No other abbreviations will be used and they will only be tested in Assignment 1. You must learn this list because you will not be allowed to take a copy of it into the assessment room.

ASSIGNMENT 1

Assignment 1 is a two-page letter which you must key in from a mixture of typescript and handwritten text. The letter will include abbreviations which must be expanded. You must also make your own decision about where to insert the hard page break to begin page 2. It is a good idea to key in the entire letter first and then make your decision. Never split a paragraph and be sure to take at least one complete paragraph and the complimentary close over to the second page. If you follow these guidelines, you will not be penalised for your decision. However, you must not decrease the font size so that the letter fits on one sheet of A4.

Do not forget to:

- key in the text carefully, making sure that all errors are corrected
- expand all abbreviations, including those in the address
- insert today's date in the appropriate position
- follow copy regarding the use of capitals and initial capitals
- make any formatting changes as instructed (increased font size for the main letter heading and double line spacing for the final paragraph)
- number the second page at the top left (just 2 will be sufficient)
- key in your name at the bottom of the document (or, if you wish, in the footer zone)
- save your work under the appropriate filename.

Assignment 1 is given in Figure 4.7. Time yourself to see how long it takes to produce the letter. You should aim to produce a perfect letter within 25 minutes.

ASSIGNMENT 1

1   Key in the text below and edit as shown.

2   Insert today's date.

3   Expand abbreviations.

4   Insert a hard page break at an appropriate point in the text.

5   Key in your name at the bottom of the document.

6   Proofread your work carefully.

7   Save the document as [WP2ASS1].

8   Print out a copy.

ATHENA TOURS   — *increase font size*   *bold and centre*

Voyager House
24-28 Rodney Place
LONDON EC4A 3PG

Mr James Kildare
152 Hurstwood Rd
CROYDON
CR2 9KM

Dr Mr Kildare

Chief Executive
Your letter, addressed to our ~~Managing Director~~, has been passed to me. I am sorry to hear
that you were dissatisfied with your recent Athena Tours coach trip to Austria.

CHANNEL CROSSING

complain
You ~~say~~ that the timing of the Channel crossing was delayed by approx 90 minutes. I am
reliably informed that on that particular day all trains were running late. ~~due to an earlier
emergency.~~ I ~~can only~~ apologise for this inconvenience *but wd point out that
our brochure does state that 'we reserve the right to substitute
alternative crossings if necessary without liability.'*

Figure 4.7   Second Level word processing assignment 1

COACH SEATS

I am sorry that you were not able to be seated in row 3 as you requested. Unfortunately, seat allocations are made on a first come, first served basis and row 3 had already been reserved when yr booking was made.

run on

All seats offer panoramic views and we trust/ *that* yr seat in row 5 was comfortable.

HOTEL ACCOMMODATION IN VIENNA

You state that the Hotel Imperial in Vienna was, in yr opinion, not a 4-star hotel as described in the brochure. You mention low standards of hygiene and poor quality food. The Hotel Imperial has an official 4-star rating and is a popular choice amongst our regular clients.

I am sorry that yr holiday was spoilt by these misunderstandings. Although this co bears no responsibility for the changes, please accept the enclosed voucher which entitles you to free holiday insurance when you next book with Athena Tours.

double line spacing here

Yrs sncly

Rose Weston
Public Relations Officer

Enc

Figure 4.7 (continued)

Did you remember to:

- increase the font size for the main heading (four point sizes larger than the normal text is a good guide)?
- centre and embolden the main heading?
- insert the date (ideally against the left margin)?
- expand all abbreviations?
- leave one clear line space above and below each shoulder heading?

- include a page number at the top of the second page?
- proofread your work carefully and correct any errors?

Check your letter against the worked version that appears in Figure 4.22 on pages 158 and 159. Make a mental note of any errors made and try to avoid them next time.

ASSIGNMENT 2

Assignment 2 is a short document which is entirely handwritten. The handwriting is clear and there are no abbreviations. You must key in the text exactly as it appears on the assignment. You must include bullet points as shown in the copy, but you may make your own decision as to the type of bullet chosen. Do not spend a long time deciding on the type of bullet. You should aim to complete this document within 20 minutes.

Do not forget to:

- follow the instructions relating to the heading
- leave at least one clear line space consistently between paragraphs
- leave at least one clear line space before the section with bullet points
- change the order of the bulleted points as indicated
- indent the final paragraph 2.5 cm (1 inch) from both margins
- use fully justified margins (both margins straight)
- add your name at the bottom of the document
- proofread your work carefully and correct any errors.

Assignment 2 is shown in Figure 4.8.

ASSIGNMENT 2

1   Key in the text below and edit as shown.

2   Key in your name at the bottom of the document.

3   Proofread your work carefully.

4   Save the document as [WP2ASS2].

5   Print out a copy with justified right and left margins.

ATHENA TOURS

HELPFUL HINTS FOR COACH TRAVELLERS ⎫ bold

Thank you for booking your coach travel with Athena Tours. You can be confident of receiving professional service from our experienced staff.

Before you depart, please spend a few ~~minutes~~ moments studying the following information:

- please arrive at your pick-up point at least 30 minutes prior to the scheduled departure time
- check that you have all necessary documentation to hand
- please do not exceed the stated limit of one medium-sized suitcase per person (weight limit — 20 kilos)
- ensure that all baggage is clearly labelled
- please do not ask your driver to make unscheduled stops

trs [arrow]

indent 2.5 cm (1 inch) from both margins

All hotels listed on the itinerary will be located centrally. All rooms will have private facilities. Colour television and air conditioning are standard. Most hotels have restaurant facilities; in exceptional cases, a local restaurant will have been designated for the exclusive use of our clients.

Figure 4.8   Second Level word processing assignment 2

Did you remember to:

- centre, underline and embolden the main headings, as shown?
- key in the text exactly as shown?
- leave a consistent number of clear line spaces between paragraphs?
- insert bullet points at the appropriate places?

- transpose bullet points 3 and 4?
- indent the final paragraph 2.5 cm (1 inch) from both margins?
- use fully justified margins for the document?
- ensure that there are no errors in your work?
- save the document under the filename [WP2ASS2]?

Check your printout with the worked version that appears in Figure 4.23 on page 160.

ASSIGNMENT 3

This assignment is the longest and most complicated assignment at **Second Level**. It comprises three pages and includes text movement, the allocation of vertical and horizontal space and the use of a header and page numbering. There is a long list of instructions at the top of the assignment and you must make sure that you do everything on this list. It is a good idea to tick off each instruction in pencil as you do it. In this way, you can check that all instructions have been carried out before you produce your final printout.

You should aim to complete this assignment within 45 minutes. It may take you longer the first time you attempt the assignment, but you will find that your speed will increase as you become more familiar with the changes you have to make.

Do not forget to:

- centre and embolden the headings
- key in all the text and check it before making any formatting changes
- use double line spacing except for the second paragraph, which is in single line spacing
- start pages 2 and 3 where instructed
- produce the four-column table with gridlines and a border
- leave at least 2.5 cm (1 inch) consistently between sections
- number each page at the bottom centre
- include a header at the top right of each page
- use fully justified margins
- add your name at the bottom of the document
- check your work through very carefully and make any amendments
- save your document under the filename given.

Assignment 3 is shown in Figure 4.9. Key in the text carefully and check it against the original before making the changes. It is easier to check if the text is in its original position on the page.

ASSIGNMENT 3

1   Key in the text below and edit as shown.

2   Insert hard page breaks where shown and number each page at the bottom centre.

3   Insert a header AT/125 at the top right of each page.

4   Use double line spacing except where indicated.

5   Leave a space of at least 2.5 cm (1 inch) consistently between sections.

6   Use justified right and left margins.

7   Key in your name at the bottom of the document.

8   Proofread your work carefully.

9   Save the document as [WP2ASS3] and print out a copy.

ATHENA TOURS   } *Centre and bold*

HOLIDAYS WITH A DIFFERENCE!

Thank you for enquiring about Athena Tours. We hope that you will enjoy reading our latest brochure. Here are a few of the features ~~which~~ we ~~are pleased to~~ offer to all our clients ...

ACCOMMODATION ONLY

perhaps
If you prefer to make your own travel plans, ~~maybe~~ taking advantage of points gained through a Frequent Flyer programme, we can arrange your accommodation in any of the hotels listed *in the brochure at preferential rates.*

CREATE YOUR OWN HOLIDAY

leave a space at least 7.5 cm (3 inches) wide by 5 cm (2 inches) deep for a photograph

Although our brochure offers a wide range of holidays, we can arrange a customised holiday for you and your family. You can extend the length of your stay at the hotel of your choice, or you can combine two destinations for a two-centre holiday. Let us know your preference and we will quote an all-inclusive price.

single line spacing here

Figure 4.9   Second Level word processing assignment 3

PAGE 2 STARTS HERE

Ⓐ

                    COACH
ESCORTED TOURS

We offer a wide range of escorted coach tours to most European countries. Numbers on board our luxury air-conditioned coaches are restricted to 36, allowing for greater convenience and comfort.

trs   convenience[3] and[2] comfort[1].

SPECIALLY SELECTED REPRESENTATIVES

All our holidays include the services of one of our a specially selected representatives who has have an excellent working knowledge of the language and local area. A representative will escort you on coach tours or, in the case of holidays by air, collect you from the airport and visit you at your hotel.

MOTORING HOLIDAYS   INSERT AT Ⓐ

If you choose wish to take your own car with you, we can arrange your Channel crossings by ferry or train. Our special car insurance is also available with this service.

Figure 4.9 (continued)

PAGE 3 STARTS HERE

ALL-INCLUSIVE PRICES

Check the table below to see what is included in the price of your holiday:

Type of Holiday	Transportation	Accommodation	Insurance
Accommodation only	No	Yes	Yes
Coach tour	Yes	Yes	No
Motoring holiday	Yes	No	Yes
Two-centre holiday	Yes	Yes	No

Figure 4.9 (continued)

Did you remember to:

- include the header at the top right of each page?
- include the page number at the bottom centre of each page?
- use fully justified margins throughout?
- use double line spacing except for the second paragraph?
- leave at least 2.5 cm (1 inch) consistently between sections?
- leave a space of at least 7.5 cm (3 inches) wide by 5 cm (2 inches) deep next to the second paragraph? You need not be exact but your space must meet the minimum measurements
- format the table for gridlines and a border?
- check your work carefully and correct any errors?
- include your name at the bottom of the document?
- save your document as [WP2ASS3]?
- print a perfect copy?

Did you manage to complete it within the suggested time allowance of 45 minutes? If you were successful, then this is the speed you should maintain during your final assessment. If not, do not worry. A little more practice and your speed should quickly improve!

Check your document against the worked version that appears in Figure 4.24 on pages 161–163.

ASSIGNMENT 4

The final assignment in the **Second Level** set is a recall exercise in which you are asked to recall Assignment 2 to screen and make some changes to it. Check that you can find Assignment 2 on your disk. If you saved it under the correct filename, you should be able to locate it easily. This assignment gives you a printout of Assignment 2, to which handwritten amendments have been added. You must make all the amendments and use the search and replace facility to amend the text as required. You should aim to spend no more than 15 minutes on this assignment.

Do not forget to:

- check that all text to be deleted is removed before new text is added
- insert the new text in the correct position
- use the default margin settings for the final paragraph
- change coach to air wherever it occurs, making sure that you keep the capital letters where applicable
- proofread the revised document very carefully before saving it under its new filename.

Figure 4.10 gives Assignment 4.

ASSIGNMENT 4

1   Recall your document saved as [WP2ASS2].

2   Change coach to air wherever it occurs.

3   Make the necessary changes to the text as shown below.

4   Proofread your work carefully.

5   Save the document as [WP2ASS4].

6   Print out a copy.

<u>ATHENA TOURS</u>

HELPFUL HINTS FOR COACH TRAVELLERS

Thank you for booking your coach travel with Athena Tours. You can be confident of receiving professional service from our experienced staff.

Before you depart, please spend a few moments studying the following information:

- • identify yourself to the Athena Tours Representative as soon as possible
- please arrive at ~~your pick-up point~~ the airport at least ~~30 minutes~~ 2 hours prior to the scheduled departure time
- check that you have all necessary documentation to hand
- ensure that all baggage is clearly labelled using Athena Tours labels
- please do not exceed the stated limit of one medium-sized suitcase per person (weight limit – 20 kilos)
- ~~please do not ask your driver to make unscheduled stops~~
- only take one piece of hand luggage on to the plane
- let us know if you have any special dietary requirements

All hotels listed on the itinerary will be located centrally. All rooms will have private facilities. Colour television and air conditioning are standard. ~~Most hotels have restaurant facilities; in exceptional cases, a local restaurant will have been designated for the exclusive use of our clients.~~ All hotels have restaurant facilities; most offer 24-hour room service.

Clients who have booked a two-centre holiday should check that the Athena Tours Representative knows of your second destination at least two days prior to your onward travel. Appropriate arrangements can then be made locally.

Figure 4.10 Second Level word processing assignment 4

Did you remember to:

- change coach to air on two occasions?
- follow capitalisation as shown?
- insert the new text in the correct position?

- add three more bullet points?
- ensure that you left no space before or after the hyphen in words like 24-hour and two-centre?
- make sure that the final paragraph is formatted for fully justified margins?
- save your work under the new filename?
- proofread the revised document carefully and correct any errors?

The worked version appears in Figure 4.25 on page 164. Check your document carefully and make a note of any errors.

If you have managed to complete all these assignments within the suggested time allowance, and if you feel confident that you can perform all the functions without error, you may be ready for a formal assessment. You must discuss this with your tutor who will advise you as to your next step.

However, practice on past assignments is vital for speed and confidence, so always try to work through some past assignments before attempting the formal assessment.

When you take your formal assessment, always aim to produce perfect work. Good luck!

HELPFUL HINTS

- **Expand all abbreviations in Assignment 1.**

- **Insert today's date on all letters.**

- **Number the second page of a letter at the top left margin.**

- **Choose bullet points which fit in with the subject matter of the document.**

- **Ensure consistency between paragraphs by leaving the same amount of space between each.**

- **Format tables with gridlines and a border, as on the copy.**

- **Ensure that the header and footer information is correctly positioned.**

- **Save your documents under the appropriate filename so that they can be easily recalled to screen.**

- **Manually check that search and replace has been effectively performed.**

- **Always proofread carefully and correct any errors.**

- **Produce four documents for marking by your tutor.**

Third Level

For success in a Third Level Word Processing assignment, you should be able to perform the functions tested at First Level:

1 *Create a new document and input text;*

2 *Proofread and correct errors;*

3 *Save to disk and print a single copy;*

4 *Open an existing document;*

5 *Amend text by inserting and deleting words;*

6 *Enhance text by using bold, underline and italic commands;*

7 *Format text by using the centre, right align and fully justified commands;*

8 *Change left and right margins;*

9 *Change line spacing from single to double spacing;*

10 *Copy and move blocks of text;*

11 *Use a three-column table.*

You should also be able to carry out the functions tested at Second Level:

1 *Indent sections of text;*

2 *Insert and delete hard page breaks;*

3 *Number all pages of a multi-page document;*

4 *Insert headers and footers;*

5 *Use search and replace;*

6 *Insert bullets and/or numbered points;*

7 *Create vertical spaces;*

8 *Use a four-column table;*

9 *Use standard manuscript corrections;*

10 *Expand abbreviations;*

11 *Change font size.*

(continued)

You should also be able to:

1 *Use special characters;*

2 *Use mailmerge;*

3 *Design a form from notes;*

4 *Use display facilities including borders and shading;*

5 *Change top and/or bottom margins;*

6 *Change paper orientation;*

7 *Use vertical columns.*

Check that you can perform all these functions before you continue.

Third Level assignments must be completed within the time allowance of 2 hours and 30 minutes. There are four assignments in total. Assignment 1 will require five printouts and the remaining three assignments will require one copy each. However, Assignment 2 is a 3-page document, so a total of ten printouts will be needed for **Third Level**. Assignment 4 must be printed on A4 landscape (long side at the top) so check that you can do this before starting the assignments. You may also be asked to insert special characters within the text of Assignment 2. As at **Second Level**, all abbreviations must be expanded. However, words which do not appear on the list (see Chapter 1, pages 8–9) will not be included.

ASSIGNMENT I

The first assignment in the set is a mailmerge exercise, in which you must produce a standard letter and a datafile from the manuscript copy supplied. You are asked to key in a letter, print a copy to show where the variable information is to be inserted, and then produce a datafile which includes data relating to eight people. A printout of the datafile is also required. You must then merge the two documents to produce complete letters for three people. The criteria on which the merge is based are listed in the instructions.

Do not forget to:

- expand all abbreviations in the letter and the datafile
- insert today's date
- insert appropriate prompt words at the locations marked with an X to enable the merge to take place
- leave equal space consistently between paragraphs

- print a copy of the standard letter and save it carefully (at **Third Level** no filenames will be supplied, so use a sensible filename that you can easily retrieve)
- input the variable information in the appropriate format for a datafile
- use the same prompts as in the standard letter
- print a copy of the datafile and save it carefully
- merge the two files and print out only the letters that relate to the criteria given in Instruction 5 (three in total)
- check all the documents very carefully.

Assignment 1 is given in Figure 4.11. Take your time to read through the instructions carefully before beginning the assignment. You should aim to complete this assignment within 30 minutes. Test yourself and make a note of how long it takes you to produce five perfect printouts!

ASSIGNMENT 1

1   Key in this standard letter with a ragged right margin.

2   Insert merge points at the places shown with an X to take the information shown on page 2.

3   Print one copy of the standard letter.

4   Key in the information given on page 2 as a datafile and print one copy of the file.

5   Merge the datafile with the standard letter and print copies of the letters for those people who have registered as Full Members.

6   Ensure that your name appears on all documents.

ATHENA HEALTH CLUB   — enlarge font size

Riverside Gardens
BROMLEY
BR7 4SF   centre and bold

Telephone: 0181 302 0261   ] reduce font size
Fax: 0181 302 0263

Today's date

X
X
X
X

Dr X

With ref to yr recent letter, I have pleasure in confirming yr registration as a X Member of our Club.

I enclose yr membership card, which you shd sign immed and use each time you visit the Club. I also enclose a voucher entitling you to a complimentary X in our

Figure 4.11 Third Level word processing assignment 1

Treatment Suite.

I look forward to welcoming you to the Athena Health Club very soon.

Yrs sncly

Joanna Turner
Membership Manager

Encs

Mrs G Stone
5 City Rd
Petts Wood
BR9 6FS
Full
manicure

Mrs W Harris
4 Bartley Pk
Sevenoaks
BR 11 1AL
Senior
pedicure

Mr J Wilson
38 London Rd
Sevenoaks
BR11 4LB
Student
pedicure

Mr F Hollis
10 Park Ave
Bromley
BR1 2AL
Senior
massage

Mr K Leavis
67 Arndale Rd
Dartford
DA2 3HM
Full
massage

Mrs D Caswell
126 The Cedars
Dartford
DA1 9PM
Senior
facial

Miss R Timms
103 Manor Rd
Crayford
DA4 6CM
Student
facial

Ms S Boyd
14 Lark Rise
Bromley
BR4 8JW
Full
manicure

Figure 4.11 (continued)

Did you remember to:

- make the necessary changes to the letter headings?
- set up the infill points with suitable prompt words?
- expand all abbreviations and follow copy for capitalisation?
- check the letter carefully before printing a copy?
- key in all the client information in a form suitable for use as a datafile?
- expand abbreviations within the addresses?
- check the datafile carefully before printing a copy?
- give the two documents sensible filenames?
- merge the two documents so that the variable information fits neatly into the standard letter?
- produce three printouts (letters to Mrs Stone, Mr Leavis and Ms Boyd who are Full members of the Club)?

Now check your work against the worked versions which appear in Figures 4.26 to 4.28c on pages 165–169. Did you manage to complete this assignment within the suggested time allowance? If you took slightly longer, you will find that further practice will help you to increase your speed.

ASSIGNMENT 2

Assignment 2 is a three-page document which tests a range of functions, including the use of headers and footers, the allocation of vertical space, the rearrangement of text into alphabetical or numerical order, changes to margins and line spacing and the insertion of bullets and special characters. It is a challenging assignment which demands a high level of concentration and a good standard of accuracy. It is vital that you check your work very carefully to ensure that you have not omitted words or sentences from the document.

Because the document is quite long, it is a good idea to key in the text in the order that it appears on the assignment, making sure that you check it carefully before making the necessary alterations. In this way, you can be sure that nothing has been overlooked before you begin to make the formatting changes. As at **Second Level**, you may choose to tick off the instructions as you complete them. This acts as a simple checklist so that you do not forget any important instruction.

A suggested time allowance for this assignment is 50 minutes. See if you can produce a perfect three-page document within the time limit!

Do not forget to:

- read through the whole assignment before you begin
- key in the text using the default margin and line spacing settings

- insert appropriate bullets on page 3
- ignore page breaks until later
- check the text carefully and correct any errors before making formatting changes
- change the order of the paragraphs (alphabetical order)
- insert at least 2.5 cm (1 inch) between each section consistently (use a ruler to check that you have been accurate in the amount of space inserted)
- make changes to line spacing and margins
- insert the header and footer text in the correct position
- use fully justified margins
- add your name at the bottom and save under a sensible filename.

Assignment 2 is shown in Figure 4.12.

ASSIGNMENT 2

1 Key in the text below and edit as shown.

2 Use double line spacing unless otherwise instructed.

3 Insert hard page breaks at appropriate points to produce a 3-page document.

4 Insert a header with FACILITIES at the right margin and a page number at the bottom right of the page.

5 Use justified right and left margins.

6 Reorganise the text into alphabetical order of headings.

7 Leave at least 2.5 cm (1 inch) consistently between sections.

8 Key in your name at the bottom of the document.

9 Save the document under a meaningful filename.

10 Print a copy of your work.

Single spacing here

ATHENA HOUSE HEALTH CLUB   — *bold and centre*

We believe that a healthy lifestyle is of paramount importance to our members. We work hard to provide them with all the facilities they need to keep fit and healthy. Here is a brief outline of some of the ways in which we can make exercise more enjoyable ....

GYMNASIUM   — *bold*

Our superbly-equipped gymnasium offers *all* the equipment you need to keep in shape including a range of treadmills, *low impact* climbers and computerised weight machines.

, located close to the treatment rooms,

Therapy Pool   — *capitals and bold*

Our therapy pool is *only* open to members with a specific appointment. The clear blue water is maintained at a therapeutic 90° F to allow the full benefit of the pool to take effect. *Around the pool, lush vegetation grows in the tropical heat. Book now for a treatment in the therapy pool – it's an unforgettable experience!*

Figure 4.12 Third Level word processing assignment 2

PATIO AND

SUN TERRACE — **bold**

patio
Come outside and enjoy a light snack on the ~~terrace~~. This secluded area offers members an opportunity to spend a quiet moment over a cup of coffee or a soft drink. ~~The food served is healthy and fresh~~. Light lunches are served from 1130 until 1430 daily.

AEROBIC STUDIO — **bold**

trs This spacious studio has fully-mirrored walls and a maple wood sprung floor. Used for low and high impact sessions, circuit training and dance classes, the studio is ~~very~~ popular with all our members.

EXERCISE POOL — **bold**

Ideal for the serious swimmer as well as for those who wish to take some gentle exercise,

Thursday
our experienced staff offer free swimming lessons at 0930 and 1230 every ~~Tuesday~~.

Our full-sized swimming pool is open from 0700 until 2300 every day of the week.

RESTAURANT — **bold**

indent 5 cm (2 inches) from left margin only

but low-calorie
Our spacious restaurant serves food all day and specialises in appetizing meals for those

wide
who are watching their weight. A selection of freshly-made sandwiches and salads is always

available.

Figure 4.12 (continued)

Rooms

TREATMENT ~~SUITE~~ — *bold*

experienced

Our treatment rooms are staffed by ~~a team of~~ beauty therapists who offer a caring *and*

trs professional service to non-members and members. [Due to the popularity of the treatments,

it is advisable to make a telephone booking prior to your visit.

IF YOU WOULD LIKE TO BECOME A MEMBER OF THE ATHENA HEALTH] *single*
CLUB, THIS IS WHAT YOU ~~MUST~~ *SHOULD DO:* *spacing*
and bold

trs
→ *telephone 0181 302 0261 for an application form*
→ *enclose yr cheque made payable to Athena Health Club*
→ *complete the form clearly in capital letters*
→ *return the above in the pre-paid envelope supplied*

We will contact you by return. Your membership card will be enclosed and you should] *single*
spacing
uc use this whenever you visit the club.

ATHENA HEALTH CLUB] *centre these lines*
Riverside Gardens
BROMLEY BR7 4SF

INSERT AT ✗ ABOVE

The full range of treatments includes
aromatherapy, full and part-body
massage, facial and body treatments
and manicures and pedicures.

Figure 4.12 (continued)

Did you remember to:

- check your document very carefully and correct any errors?
- make the headings bold as instructed?
- rearrange the order of the paragraphs?
- change the line spacing and margins as requested?
- leave the same amount of space between each section and check it with a ruler?
- insert the header and footer on each page?
- insert hard page breaks at the appropriate places?
- add your name at the bottom
- print out a perfect copy for marking?

Now check your document with the worked version that appears in Figure 4.29 on pages 170–172. Make a note of any mistakes you might have made for future reference.

ASSIGNMENT 3

Assignment 3 is the shortest of the **Third Level** assignments and fits neatly on one sheet of A4 paper. It is a form which is to be keyed in from a mixture of typescript and handwritten copy. The address and telephone number at the top of the form must be taken from Assignment 1. You can do this by copying the text from Assignment 1 and importing it into Assignment 3, or you can simply look at the address and key it in manually. You must remember to leave sufficient space for the form to filled in by hand, so double line spacing should be used. You should aim to complete this assignment within 30 minutes.

Do not forget to:

- make the necessary formatting changes to the headings
- leave one line of dots for the name and two lines for the address – you can include the telephone number and the date of birth on one line
- leave at least one space consistently between words and dots
- arrange the list of treatments as attractively as possible
- follow copy regarding capitalisation
- transpose the last two headings on the form
- check your work very carefully and correct any errors
- add your name at the bottom and save under a meaningful filename
- print out one copy for marking.

Assignment 3 is given in Figure 4.13.

ASSIGNMENT 3

1   Create a form from the information given below.

2   Ensure that sufficient space is left for completion by hand.

3   Key in your name at the bottom of the document.

4   Save the document under a meaningful filename.

5   Print a copy of your work.

ATHENA HEALTH CLUB   *—bold and centre*

insert address and telephone/fax numbers from Assignment 1

TREATMENT BOOKING FORM   *— bold, underline and centre*

Please complete this form and return it to Julia Stevens, Treatment Room Manager.

CLIENT DETAILS *— bold*

insert space for Full Name, Address, Telephone and Date of Birth

Any health problems *(please give details)*

~~SELECTED~~ TREATMENTS *— bold*

Aromatherapy	Manicure	
Body Scrub and Shower	Massage – Full Body	
Facial Treatments	Massage – Part Body	
Make Up Lesson	Pedicure	

Additional Treatments *(please give details)*

CLIENT APPOINTMENT MADE FOR

CLIENT SIGNATURE

Figure 4.13 Third Level word processing assignment 3

Did you remember to:

- include the correct address and telephone number from Assignment 1?
- make formatting changes to the headings?
- leave sufficient space for entries on the form?
- display the list of treatments attractively?
- check that all rows of dots end at the same point at the right margin (using a right tab will help you to do this quickly and easily)?
- add your name at the bottom?

Check your form with a suggested version that appears in Figure 4.30 on page 173. Did you manage to complete this assignment within 30 minutes? Keep practising until you increase your speed, but retain your accuracy.

ASSIGNMENT 4

Assignment 4, the final assignment at **Third Level**, is designed to test your use of the column function in your word processing software. You must produce a document which consists of three columns of text, with fully justified margins. The document must be printed on A4 landscape and you must also make changes to the top margin to allow space for a photograph. Use a ruler to check that you have left at least 5 cm (2 inches). A border must also be positioned around the main heading.

You should try to complete this assignment within a time allowance of 30 minutes. Try to see if you can achieve this target.

Do not forget to:

- read through the assignment carefully before you begin
- change the page orientation to landscape before you start to key in the text – in this way you know exactly how much space is available to you
- check that there is 1.2 cm (0.5 inches) between each of the three columns
- leave at least 5 cm (2 inches) at the top of the document for a photograph
- increase the font size of the main heading – but not too large or you may have difficulty in fitting the assignment on to one page
- key in the text carefully, correcting any errors
- check that all margins are fully justified
- add your name to the bottom of the document.

Assignment 4, the final assignment at **Third Level**, is given in Figure 4.14.

ASSIGNMENT 4

1   Key in the text below, using justified left and right margins.

2   Use a landscape page orientation (wide edge at the top).

3   Display the text in 3 columns of equal width with 1.2 cm (0.5 inches) between each column.

4   Leave a top margin of at least 5 cm (2 inches) for a photograph.

5   Key in your name at the bottom of the document.

6   Print a copy of your work.

ATHENA HEALTH CLUB PACKAGE DEALS

create a border and increase font size. Centre this heading.

Athena Health Club is ~~pleased~~ delighted to offer the following Treatment Packages to both members and non-members. To avoid disappointment, please telephone to check availability before sending us a cheque for the full amount.

centre these lines

SHEER INDULGENCE
£120

bold

Come and be pampered by our team of ~~professional~~ experienced therapists. [Start your day with an invigorating swim and sauna. Follow this with a relaxing full-body massage to relieve muscular tension. ~~and stress~~ After a light lunch, enjoy a luxurious facial. To complete the package, you will be given a manicure and pedicure.

Figure 4.14 Third Level word processing assignment 4

TOP-TO-TOE SPECIAL ⌐ bold
£90

Take a day off to treat yourself to a complete body overhaul.

Begin your visit with a body scrub and shower. ~~Then~~ Follow this with a one-hour reflexology/foot massage to eliminate the toxins in the body. Then enjoy a facial to cleanse and moisturise your skin.

run on
A hairwash and style completes your day.

HEALTH AND FITNESS ⌐ bold
£75

NP Combine fitness training with some treatments for maximum benefit. [Spend an hour with one of our fitness consultants to plan your exercise routine. Then visit the steam room to cleanse your body.

run on
A part-body massage follows, after which you may choose a manicure, pedicure or facial.

Figure 4.14 (continued)

Did you remember to:

- change the page orientation to A4 landscape?
- measure the top margin to ensure at least 5 cm (2 inches)?
- increase the font size of the main heading and surround it with a border?
- centre the following three lines?

- set up three columns of equal width with a space of 1.2 cm (0.5 inches) between each?
- check the text carefully and correct any errors?
- print a copy on one sheet of A4 paper?

Now check your version of the assignment with the worked copy that appears in Figure 4.31 on page 174.

If you managed to complete all these assignments within the suggested time allowance, you may be ready for a formal assessment. Discuss your progress with your tutor and try to practise on some past assignments before attempting the actual **Third Level** assessment.

Always be certain that you can competently perform all the syllabus functions within the time allowance before taking a formal assessment. For **Third Level** assignments, speed and accuracy are a vital part of the assessment process, so be sure that you can complete all assignments within 2 hours and 30 minutes.

Good luck!

HELPFUL HINTS

- **Expand all abbreviations.**

- **Insert today's date on all letters.**

- **Use appropriate prompt words for the variable information in the standard letter.**

- **Use the same prompts as column headings in the datafile.**

- **Ensure that you include five printouts in total for Assignment 1.**

- **Leave the required amount of space consistently between sections.**

- **Insert headers and footers as requested.**

- **Always follow copy regarding capitalisation.**

- **Leave sufficient space on the form for it to be completed by hand.**

- **Ensure that sufficient space is left consistently between columns in Assignment 4.**

- **Check that your top margin is deep enough on Assignment 4.**

- **Print out Assignment 4 on one sheet of A4 landscape.**

- **Always proofread carefully and correct any errors.**

- **Always ensure that your work includes your name.**

Worked assignments

On the following pages, you will find worked versions of the Word Processing assignments at **First, Second** and **Third Levels**.

Check your work carefully against these correct versions.

ASSIGNMENT 1

It is generally believed that the purchase of a good bed is one of the best investments a person can make. We spend, on average, a third of our life in bed and so it is important that these hours are spent in an environment which is comfortable and healthy.

We need a good night's sleep to recharge our batteries, both mentally and physically. If we sleep badly, our daily life can be adversely affected. We make more mistakes, lose our temper more easily and generally enjoy life less.

A suitable bed, which gives the comfort and support we need for a good night's sleep, can be a vital factor in our happiness. It should be comfortable and large enough to allow us to move freely. It should be purchased from a reputable retailer and changed every eight or ten years.

Choose your bed wisely, or your body will suffer!

Candidate's name

Figure 4.15 Worked version of First Level word processing assignment 1

ASSIGNMENT 2

MEMORANDUM

To   Sheila Conway
            Sales Supervisor

From   Robert Malloy
            Marketing Manager

Date   Today's

Ref   RM/candidate's initials

HOME INTERIORS EXHIBITION, OLYMPIA

Please note that our attendance at this exhibition has now been confirmed. We have been allocated Stand Number 240 which is on the first floor of the exhibition hall. This is a prime location and should enable us to show our products to a large number of visitors.

We shall need a sales team of ten people to cover the four-day event in shifts. Please prepare a list of staff from your department who would be willing to attend. The exhibition is open from 1000 until 2000 each day. It will be necessary, therefore, for some members of staff to increase their working hours for the exhibition period. Please tell them that they will be paid for the extra hours worked.

The space available to us will accommodate three double beds and one single, in addition to glass shelves on which we can display our range of bedlinen and matching accessories.

I look forward to receiving your list by Friday.

Candidate's name

Figure 4.16 Worked version of First Level word processing assignment 2

ASSIGNMENT 3

CHOOSING A NEW BED?

When choosing a new bed, always buy the largest you can afford.   Buy the mattress and base together and select a protective cover for the mattress.

It's unhygienic to buy a second-hand bed – so don't be tempted!

Candidate's name

Figure 4.17 Worked version of First Level word processing assignment 3

ASSIGNMENT 4

MEMORANDUM

To   Sheila Conway
               Sales Supervisor

From   Robert Malloy
               Marketing Manager

Date   Today's

Ref   RM/candidate's initials

HOME INTERIORS EXHIBITION, OLYMPIA

Please note that our attendance at this exhibition has now been confirmed. We have been

allocated Stand Number 240 which is on the first floor of the exhibition hall. This is a prime

location and should enable us to demonstrate our products to a large number of visitors.

The space available to us will accommodate three double beds and one single, in addition to glass shelves on which we can display our range of bedlinen and matching accessories.

We shall need a sales team of ten experienced people to cover the four-day event in shifts. Please prepare a list of staff from your department who would be willing to attend. The exhibition is open from 1000 until 2000 each day. It will be necessary, therefore, for some members of staff to increase their working hours for the exhibition period. Please tell them that they will be paid for the extra hours worked. Travel expenses can also be claimed.

I look forward to receiving your draft list by next Monday.

Candidate's name

Figure 4.18 Worked version of First Level word processing assignment 4

ASSIGNMENT 5

155

CHOOSING A NEW BED?

When choosing a new bed, always buy the largest you can afford. Buy the mattress and base together and select a protective cover for the mattress.

It's unhygienic to buy a second-hand bed – so don't be tempted! Always throw away your old bed.

There are many types of bed to choose from. These are our most popular lines:

Range	Mattress Type	Covering
Prestige	Continuous springs	Diamond quilting
Emperor	Open springs	Micro quilting
Ambassador	Pocket springs	Tufting

Candidate's name

Figure 4.19 Worked version of First Level word processing assignment 5

ASSIGNMENT 5

CHOOSING A NEW BED?

When choosing a new bed, always buy the largest you can afford.   Buy the mattress and base together and select a protective cover for the mattress.

It's unhygienic to buy a second-hand bed — so don't be tempted! Always throw away your old bed.

There are many types of bed to choose from.   These are our most popular lines:

Range	Mattress Type	Covering
Prestige	Continuous springs	Diamond quilting
Emperor	Open springs	Micro quilting
Ambassador	Pocket springs	Tufting

Candidate's name

Figure 4.20 Alternative version of First Level word processing assignment 5

ASSIGNMENT 6

DECORATING YOUR BEDROOM?

BUYING A NEW BED?

If you're thinking about making changes to your bedroom,
come along and see our exciting new range of beds and bedlinen.

You can find us on

Stand Number 240

at the

HOME INTERIORS EXHIBITION

at Olympia

next month!

We look forward to seeing you!

Athena Bedrooms, 4 Grove Gardens, Bexley
0181 302 0261

Candidate's name

Figure 4.21 Worked version of First Level word processing assignment 6

ASSIGNMENT 1

ATHENA TOURS

Voyager House
24-28 Rodney Place
LONDON EC4A 3PG

Today's date

Mr James Kildare
152 Hurstwood Road
CROYDON
CR2 9KM

Dear Mr Kildare

Your letter, addressed to our Chief Executive, has been passed to me. I am sorry to hear that you were dissatisfied with your recent Athena Tours coach trip to Austria.

CHANNEL CROSSING

You complain that the timing of the Channel crossing was delayed by approximately 90 minutes. I am reliably informed that on that particular day all trains were running late. I apologise for this inconvenience but would point out that our brochure does state that 'we reserve the right to substitute alternative crossings if necessary without liability'.

COACH SEATS

I am sorry that you were not able to be seated in row 3 as you requested. Unfortunately, seat allocations are made on a first come, first served basis and row 3 had already been reserved when your booking was made. All seats offer panoramic views and we trust that your seat in row 5 was comfortable.

HOTEL ACCOMMODATION IN VIENNA

You state that the Hotel Imperial in Vienna was, in your opinion, not a 4-star hotel as described in the brochure. You mention low standards of hygiene and poor quality food. The Hotel Imperial has an official 4-star rating and is a popular choice amongst our regular clients.

Figure 4.22 Worked version of Second Level word processing assignment 1

2

I am sorry that your holiday was spoilt by these misunderstandings. Although this company bears no responsibility for the changes, please accept the enclosed voucher which entitles you to free holiday insurance when you next book with Athena Tours.

Yours sincerely

Rose Weston
Public Relations Officer

Enc

Figure 4.22 (continued)

ASSIGNMENT 2

<u>ATHENA TOURS</u>

HELPFUL HINTS FOR COACH TRAVELLERS

Thank you for booking your coach travel with Athena Tours. You can be confident of receiving professional service from our experienced staff.

Before you depart, please spend a few moments studying the following information:

- please arrive at your pick-up point at least 30 minutes prior to the scheduled departure time
- check that you have all necessary documentation to hand
- ensure that all baggage is clearly labelled
- please do not exceed the stated limit of one medium-sized suitcase per person (weight limit – 20 kilos)
- please do not ask your driver to make unscheduled stops

> All hotels listed on the itinerary will be located centrally. All rooms will have private facilities. Colour television and air conditioning are standard. Most hotels have restaurant facilities; in exceptional cases, a local restaurant will have been designated for the exclusive use of our clients.

Figure 4.23 Worked version of Second Level word processing assignment 2

ASSIGNMENT 3

AT/125

ATHENA TOURS

HOLIDAYS WITH A DIFFERENCE!

Thank you for enquiring about Athena Tours. We hope that you will enjoy reading our latest

brochure. Here are a few of the features we offer to all our clients ...

CREATE YOUR OWN HOLIDAY

Although our brochure offers a wide range of holidays, we can arrange a customised holiday for you and your family. You can extend the length of your stay at the hotel of your choice, or you can combine two destinations for a two-centre holiday. Let us know your preference and we will quote an all-inclusive price.

ACCOMMODATION ONLY

If you prefer to make your own travel plans, perhaps taking advantage of points gained

through a Frequent Flyer programme, we can arrange your accommodation in any of the

hotels listed in the brochure at preferential rates.

-1-

Figure 4.24 Worked version of Second Level word processing assignment 3

AT/125

162

MOTORING HOLIDAYS

If you wish to take your own car with you, we can arrange your Channel crossings by ferry or train. Our special car insurance is also available with this service.

ESCORTED COACH TOURS

We offer a wide range of escorted coach tours to most European countries. Numbers on board our luxury air-conditioned coaches are restricted to 36, allowing for greater comfort and convenience.

SPECIALLY SELECTED REPRESENTATIVES

All holidays include the services of a specially selected representative who has an excellent knowledge of the language and local area. A representative will escort you on coach tours or, in the case of holidays by air, collect you from the airport and visit you at your hotel.

-2-

Figure 4.24 (continued)

AT/125

ALL-INCLUSIVE PRICES

Check the table below to see what is included in the price of your holiday:

Type of Holiday	Transportation	Accommodation	Insurance
Accommodation only	No	Yes	Yes
Coach tour	Yes	Yes	No
Motoring holiday	Yes	No	Yes
Two-centre holiday	Yes	Yes	No

-3-

Figure 4.24 (continued)

ASSIGNMENT 4

<u>ATHENA TOURS</u>

HELPFUL HINTS FOR AIR TRAVELLERS

Thank you for booking your air travel with Athena Tours. You can be confident of receiving professional service from our experienced staff.

Before you depart, please spend a few moments studying the following information:

- please arrive at the airport at least 2 hours prior to the scheduled departure time
- identify yourself to the Athena Tours Representative as soon as possible
- check that you have all necessary documentation to hand
- ensure that all baggage is clearly labelled using Athena Tours labels
- please do not exceed the stated limit of one medium-sized suitcase per person (weight limit – 20 kilos)
- only take one piece of hand luggage on to the plane
- let us know if you have any special dietary requirements

All hotels listed on the itinerary will be located centrally. All rooms will have private facilities. Colour television and air conditioning are standard. All hotels have restaurant facilities; most offer 24-hour room service.

Clients who have booked a two-centre holiday should check that the Athena Tours Representative knows of your second destination at least two days prior to your onward travel. Appropriate arrangements can then be made locally.

Figure 4.25 Worked version of Second Level word processing assignment 4

ASSIGNMENT 1

ATHENA HEALTH CLUB

Riverside Gardens
BROMLEY
BR7 4SF

Telephone: 0181 302 0261
Fax: 0181 302 0263

(Date)

[Name]
[Address1]
[Address2]
[Address3]

Dear [Salutation]

With reference to your recent letter, I have pleasure in confirming your registration as a [Category] Member of our Club.

I enclose your membership card, which you should sign immediately and use each time you visit the Club. I also enclose a voucher entitling you to a complimentary [Treatment] in our Treatment Suite.

I look forward to welcoming you to the Athena Health Club very soon.

Yours sincerely

Joanna Turner
Membership Manager

Encs

Figure 4.26 Third Level word processing assignment 1 – standard letter

DATAFILE

Name	Address1	Address2	Address3	Salutation	Category	Treatment
Mrs G Stone	5 City Road	Petts Wood	BR9 6FS	Mrs Stone	Full	manicure
Mr F Hollis	10 Park Avenue	Bromley	BR1 2AL	Mr Hollis	Senior	massage
Miss R Timms	103 Manor Road	Crayford	DA4 6CM	Miss Timms	Student	facial
Mrs W Harris	4 Bartley Park	Sevenoaks	BR11 1AL	Mrs Harris	Senior	pedicure
Mr K Leavis	67 Arndale Road	Dartford	DA2 3HM	Mr Leavis	Full	massage
Ms S Boyd	14 Lark Rise	Bromley	BR4 8JW	Ms Boyd	Full	manicure
Mr J Wilson	38 London Road	Sevenoaks	BR11 4LB	Mr Wilson	Student	pedicure
Mrs D Caswell	126 The Cedars	Dartford	DA1 9PM	Mrs Caswell	Senior	facial

Figure 4.27 Third Level word processing assignment 1 – datafile

ATHENA HEALTH CLUB

Riverside Gardens
BROMLEY
BR7 4SF

Telephone: 0181 302 0261
Fax: 0181 302 0263

(Date)

Mrs G Stone
5 City Road
Petts Wood
BR9 6FS

Dear Mrs Stone

With reference to your recent letter, I have pleasure in confirming your registration as a Full Member of our Club.

I enclose your membership card, which you should sign immediately and use each time you visit the Club. I also enclose a voucher entitling you to a complimentary manicure in our Treatment Suite.

I look forward to welcoming you to the Athena Health Club very soon.

Yours sincerely

Joanna Turner
Membership Manager

Encs

Figure 4.28a   Third Level word processing assignment 1 – personalised letter

167

ATHENA HEALTH CLUB

Riverside Gardens
BROMLEY
BR7 4SF

Telephone: 0181 302 0261
Fax: 0181 302 0263

(Date)

Mr K Leavis
67 Arndale Road
Dartford
DA2 3HM

Dear Mr Leavis

With reference to your recent letter, I have pleasure in confirming your registration as a Full Member of our Club.

I enclose your membership card, which you should sign immediately and use each time you visit the Club. I also enclose a voucher entitling you to a complimentary massage in our Treatment Suite.

I look forward to welcoming you to the Athena Health Club very soon.

Yours sincerely

Joanna Turner
Membership Manager

Encs

Figure 4.28b   Third Level word processing assignment 1 – second personalised letter

ATHENA HEALTH CLUB

Riverside Gardens
BROMLEY
BR7 4SF

Telephone: 0181 302 0261
Fax: 0181 302 0263

(Date)

Ms S Boyd
14 Lark Rise
Bromley
BR4 8JW

Dear Ms Boyd

With reference to your recent letter, I have pleasure in confirming your registration as a Full Member of our Club.

I enclose your membership card, which you should sign immediately and use each time you visit the Club. I also enclose a voucher entitling you to a complimentary manicure in our Treatment Suite.

I look forward to welcoming you to the Athena Health Club very soon.

Yours sincerely

Joanna Turner
Membership Manager

Encs

Figure 4.28c   Third Level word processing assignment 1 – third personalised letter

ASSIGNMENT 2

FACILITIES

ATHENA HOUSE HEALTH CLUB

We believe that a healthy lifestyle is of paramount importance to our members. We work hard to provide them with all the facilities they need to keep fit and healthy. Here is a brief outline of some of the ways in which we can make exercise more enjoyable ...

AEROBIC STUDIO

This spacious studio has fully-mirrored walls and a maple wood sprung floor. Used for high and low impact sessions, circuit training and dance classes, the studio is popular with all our members.

EXERCISE POOL

Our full-sized swimming pool is open from 0700 until 2300 every day of the week. Ideal for the serious swimmer as well as for those who wish to take some gentle exercise, our experienced staff offer free swimming lessons at 0930 and 1230 every Thursday.

GYMNASIUM

Our superbly equipped gymnasium offers all the equipment you need to keep in shape including a range of treadmills, low impact climbers and computerised weight machines.

1

Figure 4.29 Worked version of Third Level word processing assignment 2

FACILITIES

PATIO AND SUN TERRACE

Come outside and enjoy a light snack on the patio. This secluded area offers members an opportunity to spend a quiet moment over a cup of coffee or a soft drink. Light lunches are served from 1130 until 1430 daily.

RESTAURANT

Our spacious restaurant serves food all day and specialises in appetizing but low-calorie meals for those who are watching their weight. A wide selection of freshly-made sandwiches and salads is always available.

THERAPY POOL

Our therapy pool, located close to the treatment rooms, is only open to members with a specific appointment. The clear blue water is maintained at a therapeutic 90° F to allow the full benefit of the pool to take effect. Around the pool, lush vegetation grows in the tropical heat. Book now for a treatment in the therapy pool – it's an unforgettable experience!

2

Figure 4.29 (continued)

FACILITIES

TREATMENT ROOMS

Our treatment rooms are staffed by experienced beauty therapists who offer a caring and professional service to members and non-members. The full range of treatments includes aromatherapy, full and part-body massage, facial and body treatments and manicures and pedicures. Due to the popularity of the treatments, it is advisable to make a telephone booking prior to your visit.

IF YOU WOULD LIKE TO BECOME A MEMBER OF THE ATHENA HEALTH CLUB, THIS IS WHAT YOU SHOULD DO:

- telephone 0181 302 0261 for an application form
- complete the form clearly in capital letters
- enclose your cheque made payable to Athena Health Club
- return the above in the pre-paid envelope supplied

We will contact you by return. Your membership card will be enclosed and you should Use this whenever you visit the Club.

ATHENA HEALTH CLUB
Riverside Gardens
BROMLEY BR7 4SF

3

Figure 4.29 (continued)

ASSIGNMENT 3

ATHENA HEALTH CLUB

Riverside Gardens
BROMLEY
BR7 4SF

Telephone: 0181 302 0261
Fax: 0181 302 0263

TREATMENT BOOKING FORM

Please complete this form and return it to Julia Stevens, Treatment Room Manager.

CLIENT DETAILS

Full Name ....

Address ....

....

Telephone ....   Date of Birth ....

Any Health Problems (please give details)

....

....

TREATMENTS

Aromatherapy	....	Manicure	....
Body Scrub and Shower	....	Massage – Full Body	....
Facial Treatments	....	Massage – Part Body	....
Make Up Lesson	....	Pedicure	....

Additional Treatments (please give details)

....

....

CLIENT SIGNATURE ....

CLIENT APPOINTMENT MADE FOR ....

Figure 4.30 Worked version of Third Level word processing assignment 3

ATHENA HEALTH CLUB PACKAGE DEALS

Athena Health Club is pleased to offer the following Treatment Packages to both members and non-members.
To avoid disappointment, please telephone to check availability
before sending us a cheque for the full amount.

SHEER INDULGENCE
£120

Come and be pampered by our team of experienced therapists.

Start your day with an invigorating swim and sauna. Follow this with a relaxing full-body massage to relieve muscular tension. After a light lunch, enjoy a luxurious facial. To complete the package, you will be given a manicure and pedicure.

TOP-TO-TOE SPECIAL
£90

Take a day off to treat yourself to a complete body overhaul.

Begin your visit with a body scrub and shower. Follow this with a one-hour reflexology foot massage to eliminate the toxins in the body. Then enjoy a facial to cleanse and moisturise your skin. A hairwash and style completes your day.

HEALTH AND FITNESS
£75

Combine fitness training with some treatments for maximum benefit.

Spend an hour with one of our fitness consultants to plan your exercise routine. Then visit the steam room to cleanse your body. A part-body massage follows, after which you may choose a manicure, pedicure or facial.

Figure 4.31 Worked version of Third Level word processing assignment 4

5

Presentation graphics

Introduction

Graphics are everywhere. Wherever you look, in the papers, on buses, on hoardings, in the post, on television, you will see graphics. Firms need to impress you with their logo so that you are manipulated into thinking well of the company image and into thinking of that company first.

Any graphics presentation packages can be used, such as Microsoft PowerPoint, Lotus Freelance or Corel Presentation. Many word processing packages also offer you features which are normally found in a dedicated graphics package, such as drawing tools, or word art which allows you to manipulate text. Spreadsheet packages offer chart and graphic capabilities as specialist features.

Even though graphics are produced for serious purposes, they are fun to use and can be very effective. Using colour in presentations is an added feature as our perception of colour influences the way such graphic images can impress or repel us. However, you will not be penalised at any of the levels should your assignments not be in colour.

Graphics software allows the user to combine text, numbers, charts and images into a presentation. These can be coloured, or left in different shades of grey. The results can be saved and printed out. Data can be edited, images can be cropped or altered in other ways and charts can be formatted for best effects.

This section of the workbook will guide you through the LCCIEB's three levels of Presentation Graphics assignments. On the following pages you will find typical **First, Second** and **Third Level** sets of Presentation Graphics assignments. Each assignment is broken down into its composite parts and guidance is given as to how to approach the tasks.

This is what you should do:

1   First of all, check that you can perform all the functions that are listed for each level.
2   Read the accompanying text and follow the instructions carefully.
3   Work through each assignment at your own speed.

4 When you have completed the assignment, check your work with the worked version which appears at the end of this chapter. Even if your work is not exactly like this answer, as long as it conforms to what is specified in the assignment and there are no text errors it will probably be a valid answer.

5 When you feel confident that you can competently perform all the functions for the next level, continue through the section.

A full version of each assignment appears in Chapter 7.

First Level

For success in a First Level Presentation Graphics assignment, you should be able to:

1 *Manage files;*
2 *Produce graphical representation of data;*
3 *Import a graphic image;*
4 *Manipulate a graphic image;*
5 *Create graphic shapes;*
6 *Manipulate graphic shapes;*
7 *Print graphics.*

Check that you can perform all these basic functions before you continue.

The **First Level** set of assignments comprises six assignments (or tasks) which you must complete within 1 hour and 30 minutes. You are required to produce six printouts of your work, each one being proof that you have accurately completed the tasks. Always check that you have prepared and printed these six printouts for marking.

Background

This is an introductory section which gives you background information about the work to be done before you actually begin to work on your Presentation Graphics. You will be told the name of the company you are working for and the reason why you are required to produce the work.

Background information for the **First Level** Presentation Graphics assignment is given in Figure 5.1.

BACKGROUND

You work for Athena House Handicrafts where you help with the preparation of printed materials. Today you have been asked to use your graphics package to produce some graphic images for the firm's publications. Please carry out the following instructions.

Figure 5.1   Background information for First Level presentation graphics

ASSIGNMENT I

In this assignment you will be asked to create graphical representations based on the given data. You need to know how to create a graph or chart and you can choose whether you represent the data as a pie chart, bar chart or line graph. For this particular assignment you are asked to choose either a bar chart or a pie chart to illustrate the data. At this stage you do not need to insert the headings, nor even the figures unless your graphics application inserts them automatically. Create whichever graph or chart is the easiest or quickest for you to do.

Do not forget to:

- set up the chart so that the correct data is shown in the Y axis and the X axis, if you opt for the bar chart.

Your first assignment is given in Figure 5.2.

ASSIGNMENT 1

Using your computer, create a graphical representation of the following figures.

Section	Profit (£)
Sewing	40,930
Tapestries	44,650
Beadwork	48,160
Soft Toys	37,540

It can be in the form of:

    (a)   a pie chart

or   (b)   a bar chart.

Save your work as **Craft1**.

Print a copy of your work.

Figure 5.2   First Level presentation graphics assignment 1

Did you remember to:

- enter the Sections (Sewing, Tapestry and so on) on the X axis and the amounts on the Y axis, if you opted for a bar chart?
- enter the 4 headings? If they did not all appear on the X axis, try rotating the angle of the text (from horizontal to almost vertical) so that all 4 section headings fit on the chart.

Check your work with the worked assignments which appear in Figures 5.18 and 5.19 on pages 201 and 202.

ASSIGNMENT 2

In this assignment you are asked to recall the chart which you created in Assignment 1 and add titles and labels to show sections and figures.

Do not forget to:

- add clear titles and labels
- alter the fonts and the point sizes for clarity
- make sure that it is clear to which section the figures apply.

Instructions for Assignment 2 are given in Figure 5.3.

ASSIGNMENT 2

Retrieve the file you created, called **Craft1**. Add centrally over the chart the title **Athena House Handicrafts** in bold capitals and, on the next line, **Profit In 1999 for Each Section (£).** Use bold capitals for both titles. If the package has not added them automatically, add labels to show the sections and the figures associated with them.

Save your work as **Craft2.**

Print a copy of your work.

Figure 5.3   First Level presentation graphics assignment 2

Did you remember to:

- centre both titles above the graphic image?
- check that your chart shows the correct figures applied to the correct sections?
- use an attractive font and larger point size for a better display?
- choose a font and point size which has not dwarfed your image?
- centre your work to make it look attractive?

Check your work against the worked assignments which appear in Figures 5.20 and 5.21 on pages 203 and 204.

ASSIGNMENT 3

In this assignment you demonstrate your ability to choose an appropriate image to match the subject, to import this image into your document and then to manipulate it. You may have to reduce it in size and then place it in a suitable position in the document. You will also have to add text in the form of headings.

Do not forget to:

- choose a suitable image to import
- keep the ratio of width and height so that the graphic is not distorted
- use text boxes to position your text.

Instructions for Assignment 3 are detailed in Figure 5.4.

ASSIGNMENT 3

Import into a blank document a graphical image depicting a soft toy, a doll or another item associated with handicrafts. Centre the image on the page. Add the title **ATHENA HOUSE HANDICRAFTS** above the image and another caption **Enjoy Your Leisure Hours With Our Crafts** beneath the image. Use suitable fonts and point sizes for these captions and embolden them. Save your work as **Craft3** and print a copy. You may set out your work on A4 portrait or A4 landscape orientation.

Figure 5.4   First Level presentation graphics assignment 3

Did you remember to:

- import an image such as a soft toy or doll or other handicraft item?
- display the image centrally on the page?
- enlarge or reduce the image as appropriate but without distorting it?
- use upper case letters for the main title?
- use initial capitals and lower case letters for the second title?
- position the titles above and below the image as requested?
- check that your work looks right on the page? Presenting a good image is what Presentation Graphics is all about.

TWO USEFUL TIPS

Reduce your page size to 25% or 33% instead of 100%. This makes it easier to see exactly where the image is positioned on the page so that you can manipulate it more easily. It also allows you to see immediately what size the image actually is in relation to your page. Some images arrive on your page as a huge picture, others are the size of a postage stamp. By working with a reduced size page it becomes much easier to manipulate the image and find the sizing handles to make it smaller or bigger.

If you need to copy your image, or you wish to import a second image into your presentation sheet, do not be surprised if it appears immediately above the image already present, and in minuscule size. Just highlight the new image, move it, place it in position, and resize it according to your requirements.

Check your work against a worked version of this assignment which appears in Figure 5.22 on page 205.

ASSIGNMENT 4

In this assignment you are required to retrieve the image you imported into your work in the previous assignment and show your ability to manipulate the image and to remove titles if necessary. You will also be expected to add additional text to the document.

Do not forget to:

- resize the image according to the instructions
- place the image where you are instructed to do so
- place the text where it is required
- if you are using a word processing package for this part of the work use a page layout view which will show images as well as text.

Your instructions for Assignment 4 are detailed in Figure 5.5.

ASSIGNMENT 4

Retrieve the file **Craft3** (any image of handicrafts) and carry out the following changes:

1   Reduce the image to approximately 2.54 cm (1 inch) square and position it at the top left hand corner of a document. Remove the captions.

2   At the top right hand corner of the document, key in the address of the firm. Use a new line for each part of the address; centre and embolden each line:

　　　Honeypot Lane
　　　LULWORTH COVE
　　　Dorset
　　　DT5 4JR

3   Position the firm's name, Athena House Handicrafts, at the head of the letter in the centre between your reduced size image and the firm's address centred at the right hand side of the document. Use a large point size and fancy font for this heading and embolden it.

4   Save your work as **Craft4** and print a copy.

Figure 5.5   First Level presentation graphics assignment 4

Did you remember to:

- insert the image in the top left hand corner of the document?
- resize the image?
- insert the company address in the top right hand corner?
- position the company name centrally in between the image and the address?
- increase the point size and embolden the text to make the firm's name stand out?
- preview your work to get a better idea of how you have positioned both the image and the text?

Check your version with the worked assignment which appears in Figure 5.23 on page 206.

ASSIGNMENT 5

In this assignment you are required to use your applications package to produce 4 simple shapes. You can draw these freehand on the screen using tools from a draw toolbar, select them from an auto-shape menu, or import them from a clip art library. You are also asked to add simple text below each shape. Your image will appear in colour on the monitor screen, but you will not be penalised if your printout is printed in shades of grey!

Do not forget to:

- choose a sensible size for each of the images. Do not display 4 postage stamps in one small corner of an A4 size sheet of paper!

- choose a readable point size for your font so do not pick point size 6 or size 8.

Your instructions for Assignment 5 are given in Figure 5.6.

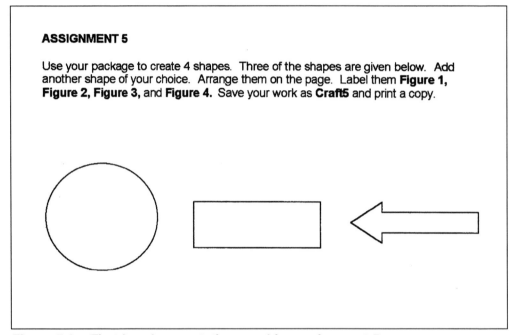

ASSIGNMENT 5

Use your package to create 4 shapes. Three of the shapes are given below. Add another shape of your choice. Arrange them on the page. Label them **Figure 1, Figure 2, Figure 3,** and **Figure 4.** Save your work as **Craft5** and print a copy.

Figure 5.6   First Level presentation graphics assignment 5

Did you remember to:

- make the page appear attractive by displaying your work in a medium size and in an appropriate manner?

- leave at least one line below the shape and your label?

- centre or consistently align each label under each shape?

Now check your version against the worked assignment which appears in Figure 5.24 on page 206.

ASSIGNMENT 6

This is the final assignment, and the object is to see if you can combine various shapes given in the previous assignment to make a picture given in this assignment.

Do not forget to:

- manipulate your shapes. The image or drawing may require a larger or smaller version of the shapes you used in Assignment 5. It is up to you to reduce or increase them in size and display them in the document.

Instructions for Assignment 6 are given in Figure 5.7.

ASSIGNMENT 6

Retrieve the file **Craft5** and re-arrange the circle, square and the arrow into a compass in the following manner:

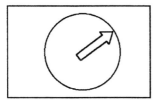

As appropriate, change the sizes and orientation of the shapes and centre the group. Increase the oblong shape to at least 10 cm (4") wide.

Add a heading under the picture, Which Way Up Is North? Embolden it, use a different font and a larger point size.

Save this new work as **Craft6** and print a copy.

Figure 5.7   First Level presentation graphics assignment 6

Did you remember to:

- resize the images and make them bigger?
- manipulate the shapes by using the sizing handles and the handle for rotating each image?
- add the emboldened text?
- use an attractive font for the work?

Check your work against the suggested version which appears in Figure 5.25 on page 207.

HELPFUL HINTS

- If you have difficulty in deciding which is the Y axis and which is the X axis, remember the X axis is the horizontal axis ("lying down" so X marks the spot).

- Every part of a chart can be formatted. By right clicking or double clicking the mouse on the part you wish to format, a menu appears showing adjustments which can be made to axes, chart labels, data labels, chart area, plot area, fonts etc.

- If your imported image arrives on the page with a frame, or you wish to remove a frame around text, try using the commands in your application which format text boxes, borders and frames and removes them. Alternatively, try clicking the frame edge when you format the plot area.

- Always lock the ratio of any image you have imported so that when you resize it, the image will still be in the same proportions as the original and the image will not be distorted.

Second Level

For success in a Second Level Presentation Graphics assignment, you should be able to perform the functions tested at First Level, namely:

1 *Manage files;*
2 *Produce graphical representation of data;*
3 *Import a graphic image;*
4 *Manipulate a graphic image;*
5 *Create graphic shapes;*
6 *Manipulate graphic shapes;*
7 *Print graphics.*

In addition you now need to carry out the functions specified for this level, namely:

1 *Extract figures from information to produce a graphical representation;*
2 *Use text to label the graphic;*
3 *Produce a logo to match a hand-drawn example;*
4 *Manipulate the logo;*
5 *Select and combine stored images;*
6 *Add text;*
7 *Alter attributes of images;*
8 *Print images.*

Check that you can perform all these basic functions before you continue.

On the following pages is a typical **Second Level** Presentation Graphics paper. This consists of four assignments which you must complete within 2 hours. You are required to produce six printouts, each one being proof that you have accurately completed the specified tasks. Always check that you have printed out these six tasks.

Before attempting this assignment you must be able to:

- combine text and an image
- manipulate text
- wrap text around an image or picture or logo.

Background

Again, some background is given to set the scene and to give you a brief idea of what is required. Background information to this **Second Level** Presentation Graphics assignment is given in Figure 5.8.

BACKGROUND

You work for the Athena House Hotels Group where you have been assigned to the Advertising Department to help with the preparation of printed materials. Today you have been asked to use your graphics package to produce some charts and graphic images relating to the group's business. Please carry out the following instructions:

Figure 5.8   Background information for Second Level presentation graphics

ASSIGNMENT 1

This assignment asks you to produce either a pie chart with an exploded slice, or a bar chart. Not only must you be capable of doing this but you are also asked to select the figures which are going to be used for your base data. In some papers you may also be asked to prepare a line graph instead of a pie chart or bar chart.

Do not forget to:

- choose only 4 sets of statistics from the 6 which are given
- leave out the 2 lowest sets of figures
- choose one graph only to represent the data
- explode a slice of the pie chart instead of leaving the slices grouped together.

Your first assignment is given in Figure 5.9.

ASSIGNMENT 1

The provisional balance sheet for 1999 shows the following turnover for the 6 main hotels belonging to the Group:

Hotel Name	(£ thousands)
Athena North	169.8
Athena Park	430.6
Athena South	254.7
Athena Ferry	301.2
Athena Winston	223.1
Athena Forest	369.4

EITHER

(a)　Create a pie chart to represent the highest 4 of the above figures. Explode the slice which represents the hotel with the highest turnover (to emphasise it). Add a title **Athena House Hotels Group** and a sub-title **Best Turnover in 1999 (£ thousands).** Label each slice showing the turnover figure for the hotel it represents and each hotel's name. You may also add a legend if you wish. Save your work under the filename **Hotel1** and print a copy.

OR

(b)　Create a bar chart based on the figures in (a) above, to display the turnover figures for the best 4 hotels (show the hotels in the Legend). Add the title **Athena House Hotels Group** and a sub-title **Best Turnover in 1999 (£ thousands).** Save your work under the filename **Hotel1** and print a copy.

Figure 5.9　Second Level presentation graphics assignment 1

Did you remember to:

- choose the highest figures and omit the figures for Athena North and Athena Winston?
- choose only 1 method of displaying the figures?
- add the title and sub-title?
- add the figure labels in a suitable place and alter the size to make them legible?
- add a legend where asked to, or explode a slice of the pie chart?
- show all the hotel names consistently, either the two parts of the name on one line, or with Athena on one line and the other name below?

Check your version against the worked assignments which appear in Figures 5.26 and 5.27 on pages 208 and 209.

ASSIGNMENT 2

This assignment asks you to import an image, a picture or clip art of a particular object. Once you have imported the image you will then be asked to key in text and set out your work in a similar manner to the sketch shown in Assignment 2.

USEFUL TIP

When you are satisfied with the appearance of your logo or image and any text you may have added, group these together so that they can be moved as one image keeping the positions and proportions which you have selected. This makes it much easier to move this new image and resize it without distorting it.

Do not forget to:

- choose a similar image
- size it according to the A4 sheet, keeping the ratios for the height and width so that the image does not get distorted
- position it centrally
- add text in the appropriate position.

Details for the second assignment are given in Figure 5.10.

ASSIGNMENT 2

The group needs a new logo. Import a picture into A4 landscape of a large building to use as the centre of the logo. Then key in **ATHENA HOUSE HOTELS GROUP** around it as in the design below. Save your work under the filename **Hotel2** and print a copy of it.

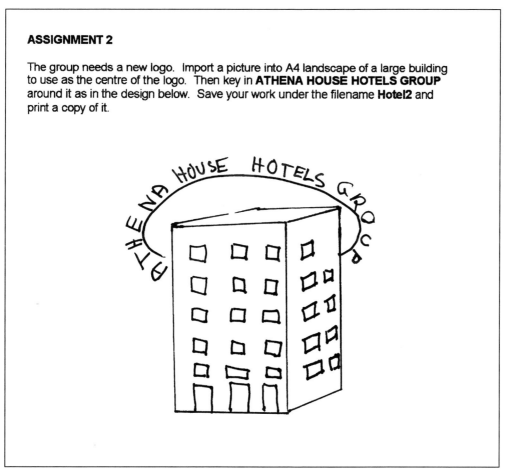

Figure 5.10 Second Level presentation graphics assignment 2

Did you remember to:

- size the picture appropriately?
- use an attractive font for the text?
- use an appropriate point size? Text should not be so big as to distract your attention from the picture nor yet so small as to be insignificant.
- manipulate the text in a similar manner to the hand drawn sketch?
- group the text and picture together so they can be moved as one group? This is useful for the next assignment.

Now check your version with the worked assignment which appears in Figure 5.28 on page 210.

ASSIGNMENT 3

In this assignment you are asked to produce a logo for new stationery. This could be headed paper, a compliments slip or an invoice heading. You will be expected to enter text, which may have to be positioned centrally or aligned in some other way on the paper.

Do not forget to:

- use a text box where text may have to be inserted in an unusual position
- lock the aspect ratio of the logo or image before you start to reduce it in size. This will keep the image in the same proportions as it was in Assignment 2, but in a smaller size.
- use page layout view when appropriate.

Details of the third assignment are given in Figure 5.11.

ASSIGNMENT 3

The group requires new stationery. Prepare a design for the letterhead which is to be on A4 portrait paper.

1   Position the group's name as a centred heading in bold at the top of the letter. Use a large fancy font and word or text art to embellish it.

2   Retrieve the logo with text which you created in ASSIGNMENT 2. Reduce its size to approximately 2.54 cm (1 inch) square and position it in the top left hand corner.

3   Leave approximately 2-3 clear line spaces under the logo then add the group's address in bold and on separate lines and left justified. The address is:

4 – 8 Portland Row   READING   Berkshire   RG1 3SL

4   Save your work under the filename **Hotel3** and print a copy.

Figure 5.11 Second Level presentation graphics assignment 3

Did you remember to:

- use a fancy font?
- try embellishing the heading by rotating it a little, using a wave form or a semi-circular form for the text?
- position the address lines exactly two or three clear line spaces under the logo and aligned with its left margin?

Now check your version with the worked assignment which appears in Figure 5.29 on page 211.

ASSIGNMENT 4

This assignment asks you to add additional features to the logo which you have already created. You will need to add text and then flow the text round the logo to form an attractive announcement.

Do not forget to:

- retrieve the logo you created in Assignment 2
- add further text to the logo
- group the additions and the logo together so they can be moved as one.

Details of Assignment 4 are given in Figure 5.12.

ASSIGNMENT 4

Open the building logo which you have already created and saved as **Hotel2**.

1   Import a banner shape or word or text art shape and position this under the logo. In the banner or shape add text to read **ATHENA MILLENNIUM.**

2   Group the logo and the banner (or word art) together. Print a copy of this new image.

3   Reduce this new image to approximately 2.54 cm (1 inch) in size and insert it into the following piece of text so that the text flows round it. Position the image approximately centrally for best effect.

4   This text should be keyed in with fully justified margins of approximately 5 cm (2 inches) on either side and centre the heading.

ATHENA HOUSE HOTELS LATEST HOTEL

Athena House Hotels Group is delighted to announce the opening of the Group's newest hotel. The hotel is the ATHENA MILLENNIUM. It is set in extensive grounds on a magnificent site by Southampton Water, not far from the chemical and other industrial plants in that area. It is ideally placed for visitors being near to the M27 and the Airport. There are 200 tastefully furnished bedrooms, all with en suite bathrooms, several restaurants and other public rooms. There are conference rooms which are fully equipped with all the facilities designed to make life easier for the many business visitors who are expected to book. However, the Group anticipates that this hotel will greatly appeal to both business visitors and holidaymakers alike. It fulfils an urgent need for a large conference hotel with all modern facilities set in this particularly attractive area of the UK.

5   Save your work under filename **Hotel4** and print a copy on A4 paper.

Figure 5.12 Second Level presentation graphics assignment 4

Did you remember to:

- wrap the text around the image so that it is well displayed?
- centre the heading?
- spell "MILLENNIUM" correctly with two "L"s and two "N"s?
- increase both margins to approximately 5 cm (2 inches)?
- fully justify the text?

Now check your version with the worked assignments which appear in Figures 5.30 and 5.31 on pages 211 and 212.

HELPFUL HINTS

- If a grey background appears when clicking on certain areas of the slide and you are unable to clear the background, the grey area will disappear when you return to a slide sorter view.

- It is worth repeating a hint from the First Level. Always lock the ratio of any image you have so that when you resize it, the image will still be in the same proportions as the original.

Third Level

For success in a Third Level Presentation Graphics assignment, you should be able to perform the functions tested at First Level, namely:

1 *Manage files;*

2 *Produce graphical representation of data;*

3 *Import a graphic image;*

4 *Manipulate a graphic image;*

5 *Create graphic shapes;*

6 *Manipulate graphic shapes;*

7 *Print graphics.*

In addition you need to carry out the functions tested at Second Level, namely:

1 *Extract figures from information to produce a graphical representation;*

2 *Use text to label the graphic;*

3 *Produce a logo to match a hand-drawn example;*

4 *Manipulate the logo;*

5 *Select and combine stored images;*

6 *Add text;*

7 *Alter attributes of images;*

8 *Print images.*

(continued)

> **Finally you should also be able to carry out the functions tested in Third Level, namely:**
>
> 1 *Use graphics/drawing package;*
>
> 2 *Create drawings;*
>
> 3 *Import images;*
>
> 4 *Create slides;*
>
> 5 *Combine slides;*
>
> 6 *Enable transitions;*
>
> 7 *Provide explanations.*

Check that you can perform all these basic functions before you continue.

On the following pages is a typical **Third Level** Presentation Graphics task. This consists of four assignments which you must complete within 2 hours and 30 minutes. You are required to produce nine printouts, each one being proof that you have accurately completed the tasks. Always check that you have printed out all the printouts for these four tasks.

Before attempting this assignment you must be able to:

- set up a master slide including footers and headers
- import images and combine them with text
- import additional matter to add to the original image
- know how to print the slides in different formats as you will be expected to print anything from 1–6 slides on one printout as well as printing single slides.

The background information for this paper at **Third Level** is given in Figure 5.13.

BACKGROUND

You work for Comlon's Cattery which sells cats to cat lovers. You have been asked to prepare promotional material and advertising matter to inform the general public and cat lovers in particular of the many cats which are available from Comlon's Cattery. Today you have been asked to use your software packages to produce a logo and a set of slides about various aspects of the business. Please carry out the following instructions.

Figure 5.13 Background information for Third Level presentation graphics

ASSIGNMENT I

In this assignment you will see a drawing or an example of clip art and you will be asked to import a similar image, or perhaps the same one, into your presentation. If you prefer, you may design a picture or image using the application package's facilities.

Do not forget to:

- reduce the page size when you are manipulating your image so as to make it easier to check the best position and size for the graphic which you import
- lock the ratio.

The first assignment is given in Figure 5.14.

ASSIGNMENT 1

Using your computer create a logo to represent the company. It should feature a picture of a cat or cats and have the words COMLON'S CATTERY as part of the logo. You may draw the picture of the cat or cats, or import it from any clip art available on your computer. The completed logo could be similar to this:

Entitle this logo **LOGO FOR INSERTION IN SLIDE MASTER.** Add the date and your name as a footer and save the image as **Comcat1**. Print a copy.

Figure 5.14 Third Level presentation graphics assignment 1

Did you remember to:

- position the image centrally on the page?
- arrange the title on one line under the image?
- group the image and logo together?

Now check your version with the worked assignment which appears in Figure 5.32 on page 213.

ASSIGNMENT 2

In this assignment you will create the master slide on which are based all the other slides belonging to this presentation. You will be asked to insert the logo you prepared earlier into this master slide and to add text, together with headers and footers, so these will appear on every slide based on this master slide.

Do not forget to:

- actually specify a master slide for this part of the assignment so you can set up the logo, master title and any headers and footers
- check the headers and footers view and alter font sizes where necessary.

Instructions for Assignment 2 are given in Figure 5.15.

ASSIGNMENT 2

For the slide presentation described further on in Assignment 3, create the master slide. This will feature the logo you have just created in the bottom left hand corner, and the heading all on one line **COMLON'S CATS WITH CHARACTER.** This logo and heading will appear on every slide. In point size 10, 12 or 14 add the following footers to the Master, the date (in full) and your name. At this stage no printout is required. Save this logo as **Comcat2.**

Figure 5.15 Third Level presentation graphics assignment 2

Did you remember to:

- position the logo in the correct place?
- prepare the footers?
- insert the overall heading?
- lock the ratio?

There is no worked version of this assignment.

ASSIGNMENT 3

This is an assignment which requires four printouts. It is a little complicated but if you follow the instructions it should not be too difficult. All the printouts are based on the master slide. You will be asked to produce at least one slide in an organisation chart format, though this will not necessarily be based on how a company is organised. You must also produce a slide in chart format and at least one slide as a display or poster type slide.

USEFUL TIPS

To make small adjustments to boxes in organisation charts some programs allow you to use the arrow keys to move them slightly.

In presentation graphics, bullets do not always appear in a size corresponding to the size of the text you choose, so enlarge them where necessary. You can alter and widen the space between the bullet and the start of your text. You can also choose a different style of bullet from the standard one if you think that this will make your presentation look more effective and eye-catching.

Do not forget to:

- use six slides, each one based on the master slide, for this assignment
- use the organisation charts (based on the master slide) where indicated
- make these charts bigger by highlighting them and dragging the handles (this may have to be done in slide view rather than in the organisation chart view)
- use a font which is clearly readable even though the text is inside a box
- use fancy fonts where you think they will create a better display.

The instructions for this assignment are given in Figure 5.16.

ASSIGNMENT 3

Based on the Master Slide which you have just prepared, create 6 slides to form the presentation. Use your own judgement regarding fonts and formatting for all the slides. **Slide 1** must show the main heading and logo as described in Assignment 2. Add a title WHY YOU SHOULD CHOOSE YOUR CAT FROM US followed by a bulleted list to include the following phrases: **we only supply cats from healthy stock; our cats are individuals; pedigree or non-pedigree kittens; it's your choice.**

Slide 2 must show the main heading and logo as in the Master Slide. Use an organisation chart to show **CAT FUR TYPES**. There are two main fur types, Long-haired cats and Short-haired cats. The Long-haired cats are subdivided into Persian, Angora and Main Coon. The Short-haired cats have 4 main sub divisions: American Wirehair, British Smooth, Devon Rex and the "Hairless" Sphynx. Below is a sketch of how the slide will appear.

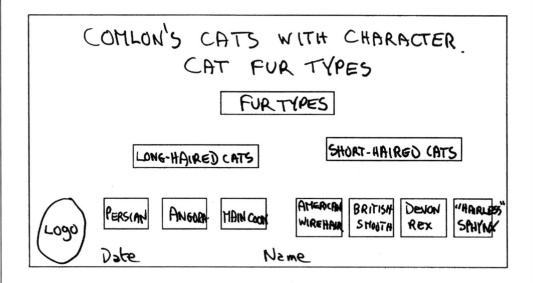

Slide 3 should show the **Cat Fur Colours**. Use an organisation chart for these. There are 5 types of colours: Ticked, Self, Tipped, Shaded and Smoke. The Smoke colour is often divided into two main colours, Blue Smoke and Black Smoke.

Slide 4 should show **Main Cat Face Shapes**. These are sub-divided into two categories: Long-haired and Short-haired cats, and each of these categories is further sub-divided into Round-faced, Intermediate-faced and Wedge-faced.

Figure 5.16 Third Level presentation graphics assignment 3

Slide 5 will be entitled **Popular Cats on our Register 1996 – 1998**. Incorporate a 3D bar chart in the slide, representing the following figures:

	1996	1997	1998
Persian	245	270	306
Tabby	310	329	350
Siamese	270	288	322

The bars should be clearly labelled with the figures.

Slide 6 should be based as usual on the master slide. Use the title CHAMPIONS EVERY ONE! Show this title as the heading for a bulleted list, giving the name and breed of Comlon's Cattery champion cats who have won top awards in regional and national cat shows throughout the country. These are Farida – a smoke blue Persian; Sherry Belinda – a tortie and white tortoiseshell; Bobby Bingo – a black and silver tabby.

Save your work as **Comcat3.**

Print the 6 slides on one printout as a handout with the date and your name as footers.

Print three full size printouts, namely **Slide 1** on "why you should choose your cat from us", **Slide 2** showing the Fur Types and **Slide 5** showing the chart.

Figure 5.16 (continued)

Did you remember to:

- base every slide on the Slide Master or master slide? This way, the overall heading and the cat logo will always appear, as will the footers and any headers.
- adapt the bullets in the ways suggested in Useful Tips?
- add a heading above the first box of the organisation chart, positioned between the master slide's heading and the first box?
- use the correct type of box to create a subordinate box for the organisation charts?
- widen and lengthen the overall organisation chart in presentation view and extend the joining lines so as to make the chart bigger?
- consider using a bar chart where the bars are 3-dimensional rather than flat?
- enlarge the bar chart for a better presentation?
- use different fonts, point sizes and emboldening for all the slides to produce attractive displays with maximum impact?

Now check your versions with the worked assignments that appear in Figures 5.33 and 5.34 (a–c) on pages 214–217. Your versions may not be identical to those in the figures, but if the wording and format are as instructed and the work is attractive then your versions will be just as correct as the suggested ones.

ASSIGNMENT 4

In this assignment you must prepare a Notes View slide which will incorporate all the details present in the master slide together with text which you will have prepared in another applications package. You may use your word processing package to do this and then import the text into the Notes View slide of your presentation graphics package.

Do not forget to:

- base this slide on the Master Slide
- alter the format of this slide to Notes Page View or Notes View
- prepare the text in a word processing program, alter fonts, margins, justify it etc, and then import the result into your Notes Page View. It is often easier to manipulate the text in a word processing program.

The last set of instructions is given in Figure 5.17.

ASSIGNMENT 4

Slide 7 must be a Notes Pages View slide. The top part must show the company's logo and a main heading as on the Master Slide, together with a heading **Rehearsing and Timing your Presentation.** Reduce the slide section in size as appropriate. Leave the footers in the slide section but remove them from the foot of the notes section.

The bottom part of the slide must show the following text. Use your word processing program to key in this text. Select suitable fonts, point size and formatting. Fully justify the margins then import this into the notes part of the Notes Pages View slide.

Prior to making an important presentation it is advisable to practise beforehand and time your Slide Show. At this stage you can correct any mistakes and set the timings for your slides. Most packages give you this option, thus allowing you to check all aspects of your presentation including any transitional, audio or animation effects, which you may have incorporated in your slides.

Timings can be set beforehand. All slides can be shown for exactly the same time, or you can vary the time for each and every slide. For instance, you may want your first slide to be on screen for 20 seconds and the others for 10 seconds only.

It is also wise to try out your presentation on the actual computer on which you are proposing to show it, as the computer may not be as fast as your own machine and may lack essential memory.

Rehearse in good time for a striking presentation.

Save your work as **Comcat4.**

Print this Notes Pages Slide 7.

Figure 5.17 Third Level presentation graphics assignment 4

Did you remember to:

- use the Note Page View slide format for your imported text?
- actually produce the printout in Note Page View format?
- justify the text?
- insert the heading in the upper part of the Note Page slide?
- follow the instructions regarding footers which applied to the two halves of the slide, ie leave the footers on the master part of the slide but remove them from the bottom half of the slide which contains the text?
- look at your presentation to see that you had displayed the text to the best advantage?

Now check your version with the worked assignment which appears in Figure 5.35 on page 218.

HELPFUL HINTS

- Know your fonts. Speed is essential in an examination so make sure you know which fonts and sizes are best suited to display. Arm yourself with this information in advance then practise altering and embellishing text quickly before you plan to do the assignments.

- There are more fonts and point sizes than Times New Roman 10 and Arial 10 or 11! So check what is on your system, choose what you think is best suited to presentation work and learn how to use them.

Worked assignments

On the following pages you will find worked versions of the
Presentation Graphics assignments at **First, Second** and **Third Levels**.

Check your work carefully against these versions.

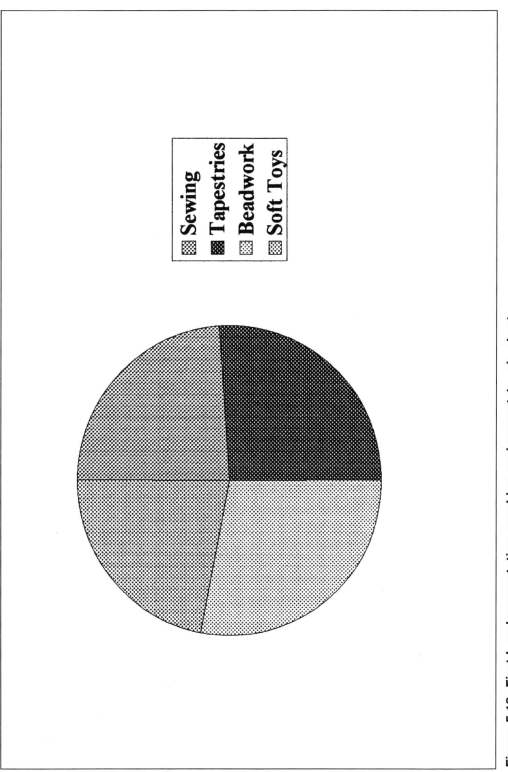

Figure 5.18 First Level presentation graphics assignment 1 – pie chart

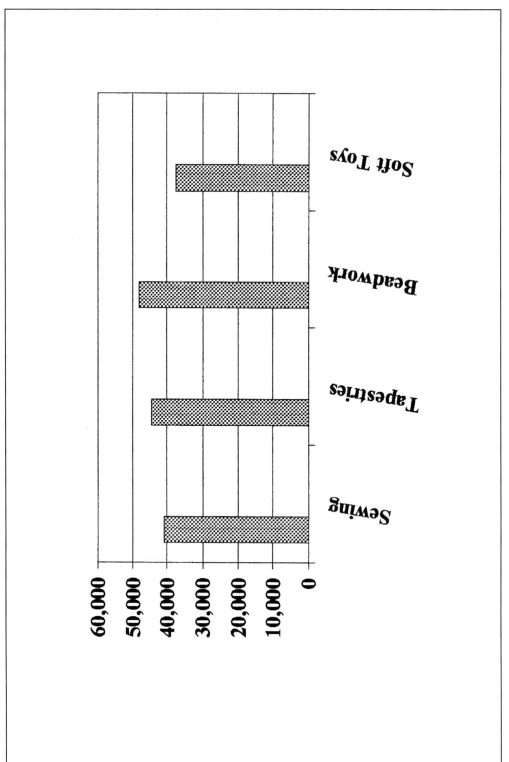

Figure 5.19 First Level presentation graphics assignment 1 – bar chart

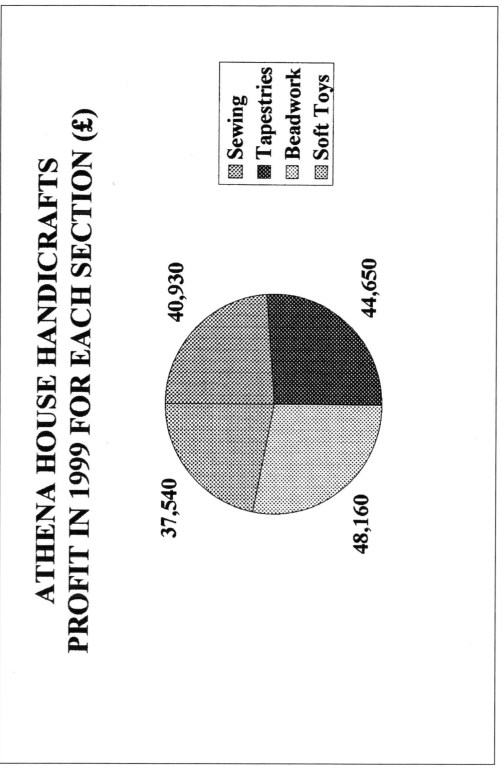

Figure 5.20 First Level presentation graphics assignment 2 – pie chart

203

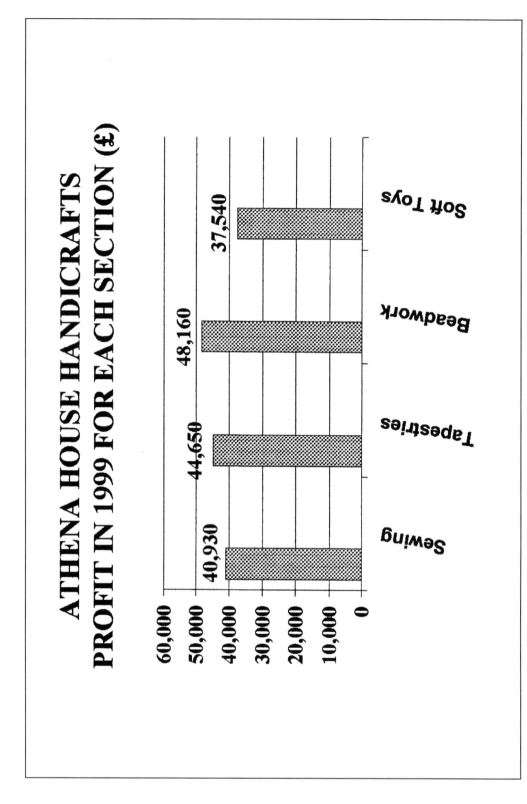

Figure 5.21 First Level presentation graphics assignment 2 – bar chart

ATHENA HOUSE HANDICRAFTS

Enjoy Your Leisure Hours With Our Crafts

Figure 5.22 Worked version of First Level presentation graphics assignment 3

Figure 5.23 Worked version of First Level presentation graphics assignment 4

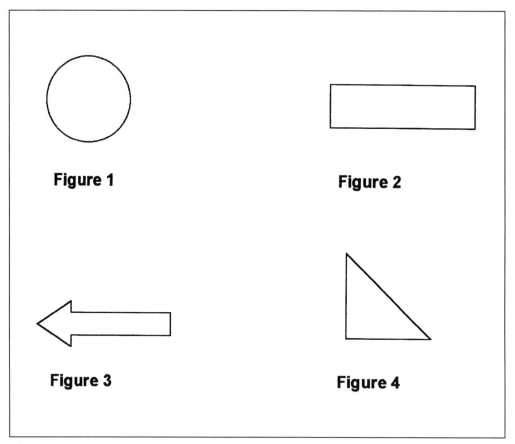

Figure 5.24 Worked version of First Level presentation graphics assignment 5

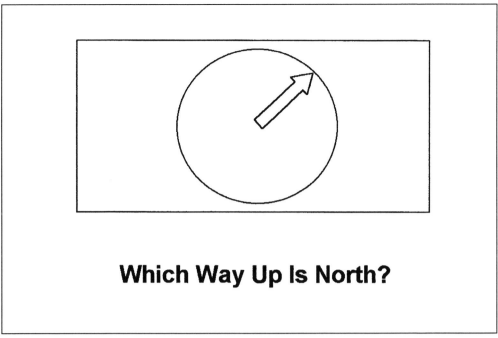

Which Way Up Is North?

Figure 5.25 Worked version of First Level presentation graphics assignment 6

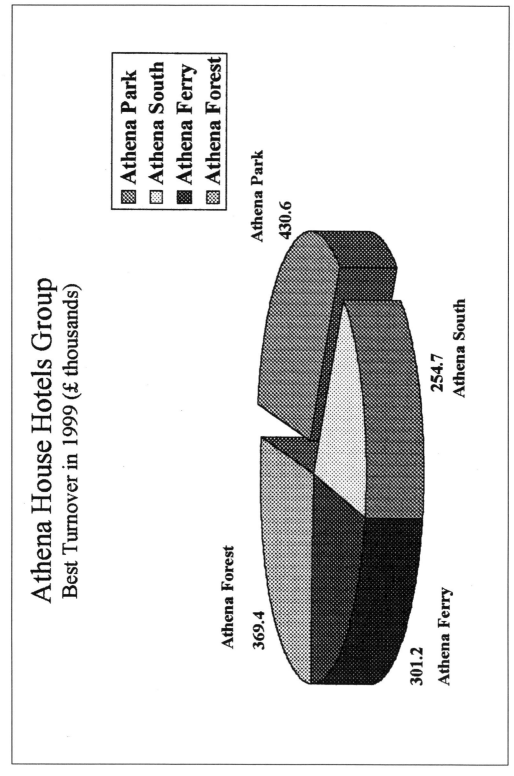

Figure 5.26 Second Level presentation graphics assignment 1 – pie chart

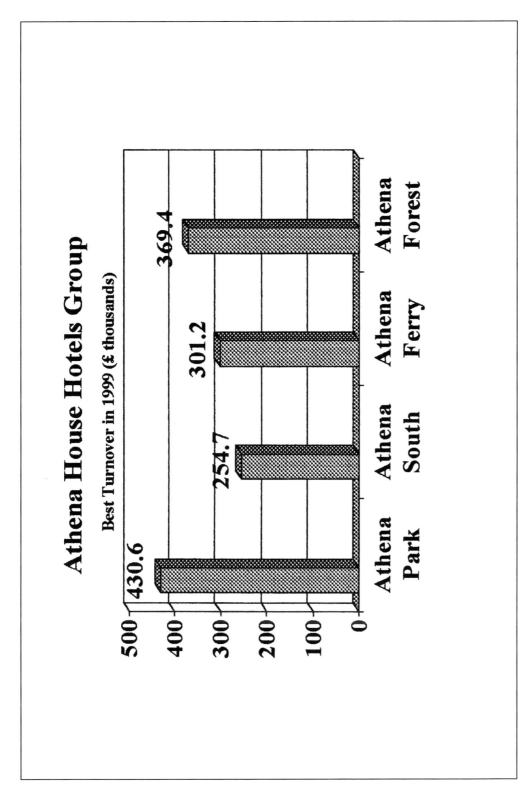

Figure 5.27 Second Level presentation graphics assignment 1 – bar chart

Figure 5.28 Worked version of Second Level presentation graphics assignment

4 – 8 Portland Row
READING
Berkshire
RG1 3SL

Figure 5.29 Worked version of Second Level presentation graphics assignment 3

Figure 5.30 Second Level presentation graphics assignment 4 – amended logo

ATHENA HOUSE HOTELS' LATEST HOTEL

Athena House Hotels Group is delighted to announce the opening of the Group's newest hotel. The hotel is the **ATHENA MILLENNIUM.** It is set in extensive grounds on a magnificent site by Southampton Water, not far from the chemical and other industrial plants in that area. It is ideally placed for visitors being near to the M27 and the Airport. There are 200 tastefully furnished bedrooms, all with en suite bathrooms, several restaurants and other public rooms. There are conference rooms which are fully equipped with all the facilities designed to make life easier for the many business visitors who are expected to book. However, the Group anticipates that this hotel will greatly appeal to both business visitors and holidaymakers alike. It fulfils an urgent need for a large conference hotel with all modern facilities set in this particularly attractive area of the UK.

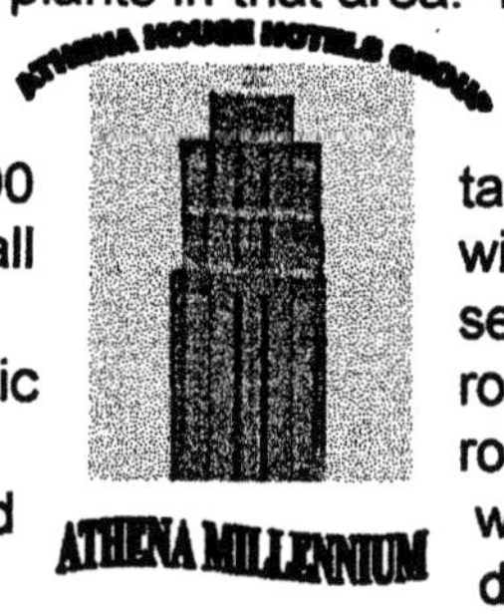

Figure 5.31   Worked version of Second Level presentation graphics assignment 4

Figure 5.32   Worked version of Third Level presentation graphics assignment 1

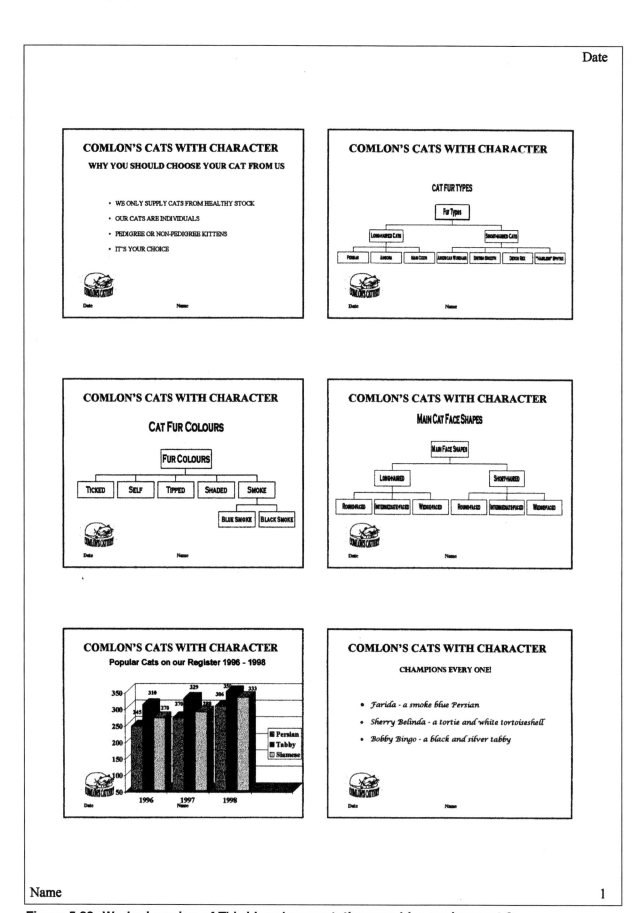

Figure 5.33 Worked version of Third Level presentation graphics assignment 3

COMLON'S CATS WITH CHARACTER

WHY YOU SHOULD CHOOSE YOUR CAT FROM US

- WE ONLY SUPPLY CATS FROM HEALTHY STOCK

- OUR CATS ARE INDIVIDUALS

- PEDIGREE OR NON-PEDIGREE KITTENS

- IT'S YOUR CHOICE

Date

Name

Figure 5.34a   Third Level presentation graphics assignment 3 – slide 1

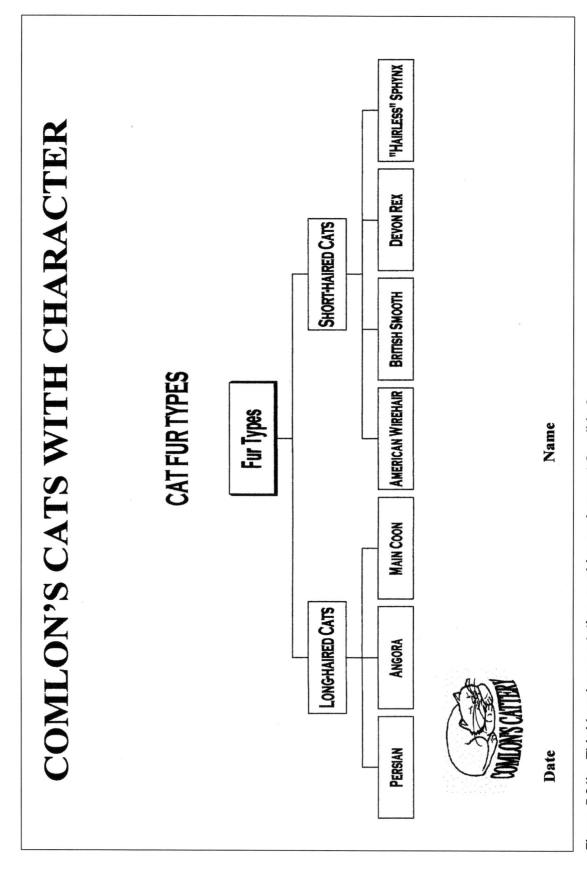

Figure 5.34b   Third Level presentation graphics assignment 3 – slide 2

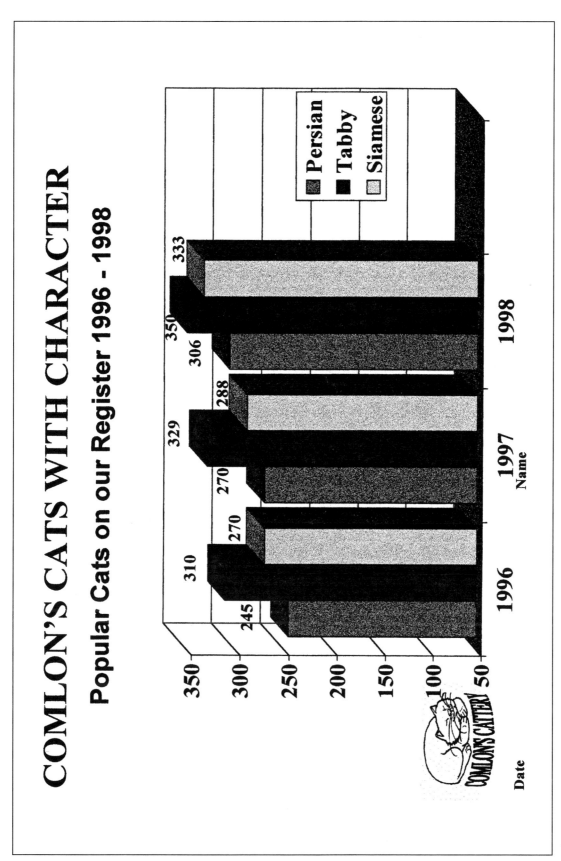

Figure 5.34c   Third Level presentation graphics assignment 3 – slide 5

217

COMLON'S CATS WITH CHARACTER

REHEARSING AND TIMING YOUR PRESENTATIONS

Date   **Name**

Prior to making an important presentation it is advisable to practise beforehand and time your Slide Show. At this stage you can correct any mistakes and set the timings for your slides. Most packages give you this option, thus allowing you to check all aspects of your presentation including any transitional, audio or animation effects, which you may have incorporated in your slides.

Timings can be set beforehand. All slides can be shown for exactly the same time, or you can vary the time for each and every slide. For instance, you may want your first slide to be on screen for 20 seconds and the others for 10 seconds only.

It is also wise to try out your presentation on the actual computer on which you are proposing to show it, as the computer may not be as fast as your own machine and may lack essential memory.

Rehearse in good time for a striking presentation.

Figure 5.35 Worked version of Third Level presentation graphics assignment 4

6

Marking criteria

By the end of this section you will be able to:

1 *understand how your work is marked;*

2 *understand what constitutes an error;*

3 *appreciate the need for careful proofreading;*

4 *avoid making the most common types of errors.*

How your work is marked

When your set of assignments is complete, it will be marked by your tutor. Each assignment is marked and graded separately. Your tutor will use a marking copy supplied by the LCCI Examinations Board. Your work will be compared with the correct version, much in the way that you have been comparing your printouts in the earlier sections of this book, and any errors will be circled. The grade allocated will depend upon the number of errors made. You should aim to produce perfect copy. You must pass every assignment in the set to gain an overall Pass grade.

What is an error?

An error is any uncorrected mistake that appears in your work. It could be:

- an incorrect word or number
- a faulty formula
- an omitted word
- an extra word
- failure to embolden, centre or underline a heading
- the incorrect positioning of a graphic
- the incorrect sizing of a graphic
- failure to follow an instruction, and so on.

It is impossible to list every type of error. Basically, if you have not followed all instructions or if you have failed to ensure consistency of formatting, etc, you will incur an error. Your tutor will circle the mistake in ink on your assignment and award you a grade for the work.

When all your work has been marked by your tutor, it will be sent to the LCCI Examinations Board where a moderator will re-mark your work. This process ensures that you will be awarded the correct grade for the work you have submitted.

Moderators do not usually change grades. This is because tutors have generally marked the candidates' work accurately and have awarded the correct grades. However, if a moderator feels that the work has not been marked according to the marking scheme, changes to a candidate's grades will be made.

Examples of marked work

On the following pages, you will see some sample assignments which have been marked by a tutor. The four candidates involved have produced work which contains errors; however, Candidates A and B achieve a good pass, Candidate C achieves a borderline pass and Candidate D fails the assignment.

These examples relate to Spreadsheet, Database, Word Processing and Presentation Graphics assignments.

Candidate A – Spreadsheet

Figure 6.1a is a copy of the **First Level** Spreadsheet assignment.

ASSIGNMENT 2

Unfortunately some of the information was not correct. Please make the following changes:

1   The April figure for Jewellers should be 35.52.

2   The June figure for Electrical Supplies should be 37.08.

3   Caterers are not considered appropriate for this survey; delete the record.

4   Grocers should be amended to Grocers and General Stores.

5   Five new records need to be added to the table, as follows:

Type of Shop	April	May	June	July	August
Record Shops	48.60	47.87	47.23	45.65	45.21
Pharmacies	59.08	58.43	57.70	57.46	57.61
Sandwich Shops	28.65	30.71	29.76	28.74	29.75
Travel Agents	85.45	86.90	80.98	83.21	85.87
Book Shops	56.76	57.03	55.42	58.75	56.43

Save the spreadsheet as SS2 and print a copy entitled ASSIGNMENT 2.

Figure 6.1a Example of a First Level spreadsheet assignment

Figure 6.1b shows the correct version as shown on the marking scheme.

ASSIGNMENT 2

	A	B	C	D	E	F
1	ATHENA MARKETING					
2						
3	MONTHLY TURNOVER (£000) OF HIGH STREET SHOPS					
4						
5	Type of Shop	April	May	June	July	August
6						
7	Grocers and General Stores	58.45	57.65	58.42	54.87	58.75
8	Florists	45.67	46.71	48.62	48.79	46.54
9	Bakers	34.55	35.67	36.41	34.69	35.63
10	Butchers	66.43	67.43	68.05	67.26	68.04
11	Electrical Supplies	38.76	37.65	37.08	38.77	39.05
12	Greengrocers	51.26	50.76	52.96	56.71	53.06
13	Ironmongers	39.56	40.42	36.81	37.85	38.15
14	Jewellers	35.52	35.98	36.75	34.76	33.05
15	Hairdressers	42.43	43.56	44.69	47.31	43.59
16	Wine Merchants	67.54	66.78	68.52	65.07	66.43
17	Photographers	19.76	20.54	21.45	20.06	21.32
18	Record Shops	48.60	47.87	47.23	45.65	45.21
19	Pharmacies	59.08	58.43	57.70	57.46	57.61
20	Sandwich Shops	28.65	30.71	29.76	28.74	29.75
21	Travel Agents	85.45	86.90	80.98	83.21	85.87
22	Book Shops	56.76	57.03	55.42	58.75	56.43

Figure 6.1b Correct version of First Level spreadsheet assignment

Finally Figure 6.1c shows what the candidate handed to the tutor for marking.

ATHENA MARKETING					
MONTHLY TURNOVER (£000) OF HIGH STREET SHOPS					
Type of Shop	April	May	June	July	August
Grocers & General Stores	58.45	57.65	58.42	54.87	58.75
Florists	45.67	46.71	48.62	48.79	46.54
Bakers	34.55	35.67	36.41	34.69	35.63
Butchers	66.43	67.43	68.05	67.26	68.04
Electrical Supplies	38.76	37.65	37.08	38.77	39.05
Greengrocers	51.26	50.76	52.96	56.71	53.06
Ironmongers	39.56	40.42	36.81	37.85	38.15
Jewellers	35.52	35.98	36.75	34.76	33.05
Hairdressers	42.43	43.56	44.69	47.31	43.59
Wine Merchants	67.54	66.78	68.52	65.07	66.43
Photographers	19.76	20.54	21.45	20.06	21.32
Record Shops	48.60	47.87	47.23	45.65	45.21
Pharmacies	59.08	58.43	57.70	57.46	57.61
Sandwich Shops	28.65	30.71	29.76	28.74	29.75
Travel Agents	85.45	86.9	80.98	83.21	85.87
Book Shops	56.76	57.03	55.42	58.75	56.43

ASSIGNMENT 2

Figure 6.1c Candidate's version of First Level spreadsheet assignment

As you can see, there are a few differences between the marking copy and the candidate's work. The candidate has not included the column and row headings, but this is not an error. There are no formulae in the spreadsheet and therefore it is not necessary to print out with the headings. The column headings have not been emboldened as in the marking copy. Once again, as there was no specific instruction to format the headings in bold, the candidate is not penalised. Within the spreadsheet, there are two main differences. Grocers and General Stores has been keyed in as Grocers & General Stores. This is not a major error, but would nevertheless be penalised. In cell C21 the number has not been formatted for two decimal places to correspond with the other numbers in the spreadsheet. This would also constitute an error. Therefore, Candidate A has incurred two errors, which would be a Pass grade.

Candidate B – Database

Candidate D's work is based on the **Second Level** Database assignment shown in Figure 6.2a.

ASSIGNMENT 3

1   The Managing Director wishes to know which staff joined the company between 1
     January 1992 and 1 January 1997. Search the database and when you have made
     your selection:

     i   save your work as Staff3Q1

     ii   print a list in table format showing only Last Name, First Name, Branch
             and Start Date.

2   The Personnel Director would like a list of all staff on the database who work in
     Leeds and Runcorn and earn in excess of £24,000 per annum. Search the database
     and when you have made your selection:

     i   sort the records in alphabetical order of office

     ii   save your work as Staff3Q2

     iii   print only the Last Name, First Name, Branch, Start Date and Salary fields.

Figure 6.2a Example of a Second Level database assignment

The marking scheme shows the correct version (Figure 6.2b).

Last Name	First Name	Branch	Start Date
Fielding	Sarah	Leeds	01/10/93
Morrison	Wendy	Runcorn	13/04/92
da Costa	Roberto	Runcorn	24/10/92
Lowry	Jill	Runcorn	30/05/95
Turner	Joanna	Bradford	31/03/94
Smith	Arthur	Runcorn	02/05/96

Last Name	First Name	Branch	Start Date	Salary
Andrews	William	Leeds	24/03/97	£35,850.00
Smith	Arthur	Runcorn	02/05/96	£25,450.00

Figure 6.2b Correct version of Second Level database assignment

Figure 6.2c shows what the candidate produced as a final printout.

X

Last Name	First Name	Branch	Salary	Start Date
Fielding	Sarah	Leeds	£15,250.00	01/10/93
Morrison	Wendy	Runcorn	£18,650.00	13/04/92
da Costa	Roberto	Runcorn	£10,675.00	24/10/92
Lowry	Jill	Runcorn	£15,950.00	30/05/95
Turner	Joanna	Bradford	£18,495.00	31/03/94
Smith	Arthur	Runcorn	£25,450.00	02/05/96

X

Last Name	First Name	Branch	Start Date	Salary
Smith	Arthur	Runcorn	02/05/96	£25,450.00
Andrews	William	Leeds	24/03/97	£35,850.00

Figure 6.2c Candidate's version of Second Level database assignment

In this case, the candidate incurred two errors. In the first query, the candidate printed the Salary field in addition to the four fields requested in the assignment. In the second query, the candidate failed to sort the records into alphabetical order of office. Leeds should have appeared above Runcorn. Two errors mean that this candidate passed the assignment.

Candidate C – Word Processing

Candidate C produced a **Third Level** Word Processing assignment for marking. Figure 6.3a shows a copy of the assignment.

ASSIGNMENT 3

1   Create a form from the information given below.

2   Ensure that sufficient space is left for completion by hand.

3   Key in your name at the bottom of the document.

4   Save the document under a meaningful filename.

5   Print a copy of your work.

ATHENA TRAINING   — *increase font size and bold*

      } insert address from Assignment 1 and bold

COURSE REGISTRATION FORM   — *bold, underline and centre*

Please complete this form and return it to Marianne Westbrook, Short Course Manager, as soon as possible. Thank you.

STUDENT DETAILS *– bold*

(insert space for Full Name, Address, Postcode, Telephone, Date of Birth and Nationality)

COURSE DETAILS *– bold*

Course Title _ . _ _ _ _ _ _ _ . _ . .

Course Length _ . _ . _ . _ _ . .

Preferred [Start Date _ . _ . _ _ _ _ _ _

Alternative Start Date _ . . . _ _ . .

SIGNATURE .... DATE ....

For College Use Only

Start Date . . . . . . *Date Confirmed* . . . . . .

Cost Of Course . . . . . – *Deposit Paid* . . . .

Figure 6.3a **Example of a Third Level word processing assignment**

The correct version as shown on the marking scheme is given in Figure 6.3b.

ATHENA TRAINING

Wellington Place
OXFORD
OX2 8KM

<u>COURSE REGISTRATION FORM</u>

Please complete this form and return it to Marianne Westbrook, Short Course Manager, as soon as possible. Thank you.

STUDENT DETAILS

Full Name ....

Address...

....

Postcode ....   Telephone ....

Date of Birth ....   Nationality ....

COURSE DETAILS

Course Title ....

Course Length ....

Preferred Start Date ....

Alternative Start Date ....

SIGNATURE ....   DATE ....

<u>For College Use Only</u>

Start Date ....   Date Confirmed ....

Cost of Course ....   Deposit Paid ....

Candidate's Name

Figure 6.3b Correct version of Third Level word processing assignment

Figure 6.3c shows what the candidate handed to the tutor for marking.

ATHENA TRAINING

Wellington Place
OXFORD
OX2 8KM

COURSE REGISTRATION FORM

✗

Please complete this form and return to Marianne Westbrook, Short Course
Manager, as soon as possible. Thank you.

STUDENT DETAILS

Full Name ....

Address... ✗

.... ✗

....

Postcode ....   Telephone ....

Date of Birth ....   Nationality ....✗

COURSE DETAILS

Course Title ....

Course Length ....

Preferred Start Date ....✗

Alternate Start Date ....

SIGNATURE ....   DATE ....

For College Use Only

Start Date ....   Date Confirmed ....

Cost of Course ....   Deposit Paid ....

MBK

Figure 6.3c Candidate's version of Third Level word processing assignment

This candidate produced a form as instructed, but unfortunately made several errors which were not corrected before printing. The first error is the omission of the word 'it' in the first sentence. When producing dotted lines on the form, the candidate did not finish at the same point for each line and therefore incurred one penalty for inconsistency. A further error, in which the candidate used the word 'alternate' instead of 'alternative', ensured that this candidate only achieved a borderline pass on this assignment.

Candidate D – Presentation Graphics

Candidate D's work relates to a **First Level** Presentation Graphics assignment. A copy of the assignment instruction sheet is shown in Figure 6.4a.

ASSIGNMENT 4

Retrieve the file TRAIN3 and carry out the following changes:

1   Reduce the image to approximately 2.5 cm (1 inch) square and position it at the top of the document in a central position.

2   At the top right of the document key in the address of the company, using a new line for each line of the address. Right align each line with the right margin:

        Athena House
        40-48 Basildon Road
        LEICESTER
        LE1 3DB

3   At the top left of the document, using three separate lines, key in Athena Training Group. Use capital letters and a large font size. Embolden the company name.

4   Save your work as TRAIN4 and print a copy.

Figure 6.4a Example of a First Level presentation graphics assignment

Figure 6.4b shows what the worked assignment should look like.

ATHENA
TRAINING
GROUP

Athena House
40-48 Basildon Road
LEICESTER
LE1 3DB

Figure 6.4b Correct version of First Level presentation graphics assignment

Unfortunately, Candidate D produced the version shown in Figure 6.4c.

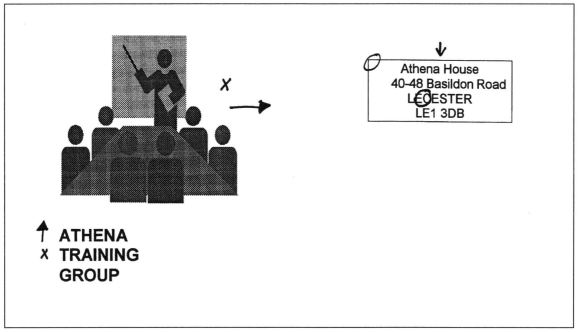

Figure 6.4c   Candidate's version of First Level presentation graphics assignment

This work is clearly not of a pass standard. The errors are numerous. The image has not been reduced to the appropriate size nor positioned correctly. The company name is positioned at the left margin, but should be at the top of the document. The company address is surrounded by a border (which was not requested) and is centred instead of right aligned. The spelling of the word 'Leicester' is also incorrect. This candidate has clearly failed. However, if this assignment is the only one that is not of a pass standard and, after additional practice, the candidate wishes to retake another set of assignments, this can be arranged with the tutor.

However, before undertaking a second set of assignments, do be confident that you are able to carry out all the functions listed in the syllabus.

How to be successful in your assignments

It is always disappointing to fail an assignment. Candidates are demotivated by failure, and tutors and moderators do not enjoy marking work which does not reach the required standard. To avoid this happening to you, let us consider why some candidates fail. Here are some simple steps which you can take to ensure your success.

1 Proofread your work very carefully and correct any errors

Many candidates simply do not check their work carefully enough. They rely too heavily on the spellcheck facility on their computer and do not spend time manually checking their work against the original Candidate

Instruction Sheet. Words which are repeated or missed out will not necessarily be identified by the spellchecker. In Database and Spreadsheet assignments, rows and columns of figures and dates can be particularly difficult to check. Do make sure, however, that all text and figures are checked carefully before printing a copy of your work for marking.

2 Practise the functions to be tested until you are fully competent

Many candidates attempt an assignment before they are sufficiently competent in the function to be tested. They may have practised the function once or twice, but have not had to produce an assignment within the specified time allowance. Therefore, when difficulties are encountered, they are too inexperienced to solve the problem.

Assignments should not be attempted under timed conditions until you are fully competent in all the functions to be tested. This may mean delaying the date of your assessment for a few weeks, but it is better to wait than to take an assessment and fail.

3 Read the instructions carefully

Many candidates fail an assignment simply because they have failed to carry out all the instructions contained within it. They may have forgotten to sort the database records alphabetically or they may have printed out more fields than they were instructed to. Always check carefully before sending your work to the printer. If necessary, tick off each instruction as you complete it successfully. Always check that what you have attempted to do has actually worked! Many candidates attempt to perform a particular function, assume it has happened and print out their document, in ignorance of the fact that nothing has happened.

4 Practise on past assignments

The best type of practice for an assessment is a set of old assignments. Ask your tutor to let you try a few assignments before you attempt an assessment. Many tutors prepare test material specifically for their candidates to get extra practice on similar types of tasks. In Chapter 7, the assignments which you have already worked through are printed out in their entirety so that you can see what a real set of assignments looks like.

5 Know your limitations

It is always disappointing for tutors and moderators to mark work which is clearly not up to the required standard purely because the candidate does not possess the skills necessary for the level of assignments undertaken.

First Level assignments are achievable by candidates with a basic knowledge of the software and a slow but accurate keyboarding skill. **Second Level** assignments require a faster keyboarding skill and the functions tested are more complicated. More text and figures must be keyed in within the time allowance. **Third Level** assignments are both demanding and complex and need a high level of expertise in the functions tested. The time allowance for **Third Level** assignments leaves little spare time to rectify errors.

It is important that you know your own limitations and only seek to progress as and when your knowledge and speed allow.

7

Assignments

On the following pages, you will find full Candidate Copies of the assignments which appear earlier in this workbook.

They are arranged as follows:

Spreadsheet	First Level
	Second Level
	Third Level
Database	First Level
	Second Level
	Third Level
Word Processing	First Level
	Second Level
	Third Level
Presentation Graphics	First Level
	Second Level
	Third Level

PRACTICAL COMPUTING – SPREADSHEET
FIRST LEVEL
CANDIDATE COPY

LONDON CHAMBER OF COMMERCE AND INDUSTRY EXAMINATIONS BOARD

PRACTICAL COMPUTING – FIRST LEVEL

SPREADSHEET – CANDIDATE'S COPY

PRACTICAL COMPUTING – SPREADSHEET
FIRST LEVEL
CANDIDATE COPY

Spreadsheet – First Level

PRACTICAL COMPUTING – SPREADSHEET
FIRST LEVEL
CANDIDATE COPY

234

TIME ALLOWANCE: **1 hour and 30 minutes**

PRACTICAL COMPUTING – SPREADSHEET
FIRST LEVEL
CANDIDATE COPY

PRACTICAL COMPUTING – FIRST LEVEL

SPREADSHEET – CANDIDATE'S COPY

BACKGROUND

You work for Athena Electrical PLC, a retail company selling electrical goods to the general public. You have been assigned to the Market Research Department to help with the preparation of reports and statistics. Today you have been asked to use your spreadsheet package to present information relating to sales of certain electrical items. Please carry out the following instructions:

ASSIGNMENT 1

Create a spreadsheet using the following layout (please format **Item Cost** figures to 2 decimal places):

ATHENA ELECTRICAL PLC

SALES FOR JANUARY – MARCH [YEAR]

Item Code	Item Description	Item Cost £	January	February	March
WM652	Washing Machine	349.99	219	230	264
WD438	Washer Dryer	620.20	124	100	145
DW871	Dishwasher	359.00	78	102	95
FR308	Larder Fridge	319.50	245	201	220
VC276	Upright Cleaner	69.50	145	202	164
MW283	Microwave Oven	249.99	213	302	265
VR994	Video Recorder	229.50	234	267	280
CC639	Camcorder	449.99	221	245	324
PR200	Deskjet Printer	145.00	456	403	387
TV880	Portable Television	199.50	521	530	568

Save this sheet as SS1 and print a copy entitled ASSIGNMENT 1.

PRACTICAL COMPUTING – SPREADSHEET
FIRST LEVEL
CANDIDATE COPY

ASSIGNMENT 2

Unfortunately some of the information was not correct. Please make the following changes:

1   The Washing Machine now sells at £359.99.

2   The January sales of Microwave Ovens was 241.

3   The Upright Cleaner should not appear on this list. Delete the record.

4   The Deskjet Printer should be called the Deskjet Colour Printer.

5   Five new records need to be added to the table, as follows:

Item Code	Item Description	Item Cost £	January	February	March
TD456	Tumble Dryer	189.50	300	286	265
CF294	Chest Freezer	110.00	402	459	521
CM113	Coffee Maker	54.50	78	61	89
UF667	Upright Freezer	149.50	145	120	210
HC312	Home Cinema	859.00	86	65	78

Save this sheet as SS2 and print a copy entitled ASSIGNMENT 2.

ASSIGNMENT 3

In the cell to the right of the March column, type **Total Sales**. In that column, create a suitable formula to show the value of sales for each product.

Save this sheet as SS3 and print a copy entitled ASSIGNMENT 3.

ASSIGNMENT 4

Sales for April are thought to be the same as those for March. Insert a new column between March and Total Sales, label it **April (Projected)** and enter the figures for each product. Ensure that the Total Sales column now shows the figures for the first four months of the year.

Insert a column between Item Code and Item Description and label it **Item Category**. Insert the word **Entertainment** alongside Video Recorder, Camcorder, Deskjet Colour Printer, Portable Television and Home Cinema. Insert the word **Domestic** alongside the other records.

Save this sheet as SS4 and print a copy entitled ASSIGNMENT 4.

ASSIGNMENT 5

Sort the table so that all the Domestic items are together and all the Entertainment items are under them. Within each grouping, the items should be arranged alphabetically.

Below each group insert a row showing the word **Sub-Total** in the first column. Use formulae to produce the sub-totals for both groups in all columns except Item Cost.

At the bottom of the spreadsheet type **Grand Total** in the first column. Use formulae to produce the grand total for all columns except Item Cost.

Save the completed spreadsheet as SS5 and print a copy entitled ASSIGNMENT 5.

ASSIGNMENT 6

Print a copy of the completed spreadsheet, showing the formulae you have used in your calculations. This printout should be entitled ASSIGNMENT 6.

PRACTICAL COMPUTING – SPREADSHEET
SECOND LEVEL
CANDIDATE COPY

LONDON CHAMBER OF COMMERCE AND INDUSTRY EXAMINATIONS BOARD

PRACTICAL COMPUTING – SECOND LEVEL

SPREADSHEET – CANDIDATE'S COPY

PRACTICAL COMPUTING – SPREADSHEET
SECOND LEVEL
CANDIDATE COPY

239

TIME ALLOWANCE: **2 hours**

PRACTICAL COMPUTING – SECOND LEVEL

SPREADSHEET – CANDIDATE'S COPY

BACKGROUND

You work for Athena College which offers a range of courses to students of all ages. The Principal has asked you to prepare a set of figures showing the current course provision. Please follow the instructions below and prepare the necessary spreadsheets.

ASSIGNMENT 1

1   Prepare a spreadsheet with the main heading **ATHENA COLLEGE**. Include a sub-heading – **COURSE PROVISION**.

2   On the next row enter a cell to show a Lecturer Charge (per hour) of £25.

3   Enter the data given below on this page and embolden the two main headings.

4   Embolden the column headings and right justify those containing figures. Fees and charges should be shown as currency. Wrap the text so that longer headings appear on two lines (as below).

5   Insert a header to show your name and a footer with today's date.

6   Save a copy of the spreadsheet as AC1.

7   Print a copy of the spreadsheet on A4 landscape.

Course Title	Course Reference	Length (hours)	No in Group	Room Fee	Catering Charge
Time Management	BU4357	8	12	100	120
Assertiveness Training	BU3876	6	12	100	120
Health and Safety	BU8721	12	15	200	180
Communication Skills	BU9876	12	15	200	180
Internet Skills	TE3298	15	18	150	50
Presentation Skills	TE4597	12	20	200	50
Practical Computing	TE3390	20	18	180	50
Desktop Publishing	TE2190	25	18	250	50
Creative Writing	LE5572	30	20	150	0
Spanish for Beginners	LE9703	48	20	200	0
Holiday Italian	LE4497	48	20	200	0
Basic Japanese	LE2265	48	20	200	0
Practical Bookkeeping	VO2408	45	15	150	0
Business Administration	VO9765	45	15	150	0
Accounting	VO1437	45	15	150	0

ASSIGNMENT 2

1   Insert a column after the **No in Group** column and give it the heading **Lecturer Costs**.

2   Enter a formula to calculate the lecturer costs on each course by multiplying the length in hours by the lecturer charge per hour. Show these figures as currency.

3   Add a column to the right of the **Catering Charge** column and give it the heading **Total Overheads**.

4   Enter a formula to calculate the total overheads for each course. Show these figures as whole numbers.

5   The College fees are calculated on a 50% markup on the total overhead figures. Add a further column and give it the heading **Total Charge**. Calculate the figures for each course and show the figures as whole numbers.

6   Insert a column after the **Course Reference** column and give it the heading **Course Fee**.

7   For each course calculate the course fee by dividing the total charge by the number in the group. Show each course fee as currency but without decimal places.

8   Ensure all column widths are adjusted to fit headings.

9   Adjust the spreadsheet to fit on one sheet of A4 landscape.

10   Save the spreadsheet as AC2.

11   Print a copy of the calculated spreadsheet on A4 landscape. Include the header and footer as in Assignment 1, point 5.

ASSIGNMENT 3

1   Sort the spreadsheet into alphabetical order of course reference.

2   Create four sections by inserting a row under each of the following courses:

Communication Skills
Spanish for Beginners
Presentation Skills

3   Sort each section into alphabetical order of course title.

4   Entitle each of the new rows **Total** and add a final row entitled **Total**. Embolden these titles.

5   Calculate the totals for lecturer costs and total overheads only. Embolden these two sets of figures.

6   Insert a further row underneath the four **Total** rows and entitle each of these rows **Average Course Fee**.

7   Use the Average function to calculate the average course fee.

8   Display the average figures in bold.

9   Save the spreadsheet as AC3.

10   Print a copy of the calculated spreadsheet on A4 landscape. Include the header and footer as in Assignment 1, point 5.

ASSIGNMENT 4

1   The Principal wants to know how many students would be needed to cover the total overheads. Add a further column and give it the title **Break-Even Student No**.

2   Calculate the number of students needed to cover costs by dividing the total overheads by the course fee. Display the figures as whole numbers.

3   Leave a clear row at the bottom of the spreadsheet and then add the heading **TOTALS** in the first column. Embolden and italicise this heading.

4   Calculate totals for the columns headed **No in Group, Lecturer Costs, Room Fee, Catering Charge, Total Overheads** and **Total Charge**.

5   Display these figures in bold and italic.

6   Adjust the spreadsheet to fit on one sheet of A4 landscape.

7   Save the spreadsheet as AC4.

8   Print a copy of the calculated spreadsheet on A4 landscape. Include the header and footer as in Assignment 1, point 5.

9   Print a copy of the spreadsheet showing the formulae you have used. Display the column and row headings. Include the header and footer as in Assignment 1, point 5.

PRACTICAL COMPUTING – SPREADSHEET
THIRD LEVEL
CANDIDATE COPY

243

LONDON CHAMBER OF COMMERCE AND INDUSTRY EXAMINATIONS BOARD

PRACTICAL COMPUTING – THIRD LEVEL

SPREADSHEET – CANDIDATE'S COPY

PRACTICAL COMPUTING – SPREADSHEET
THIRD LEVEL
CANDIDATE COPY

PRACTICAL COMPUTING – SPREADSHEET
THIRD LEVEL
CANDIDATE COPY

244

TIME ALLOWANCE: **2 hours and 30 minutes**

PRACTICAL COMPUTING – THIRD LEVEL

SPREADSHEET – CANDIDATE'S COPY

BACKGROUND

You work for Athenaware Computer Supplies who provide computer equipment and accessories to educational establishments. You have been asked to prepare the August sales figures and analyse the sales of printers using the following two data tables:

SALES TO CUSTOMERS IN AUGUST

Date	Customer	Quantity	Item
6 August	Regency College	3	inkjet printers
6 August	Regency College	4	laserjet printers
6 August	Regency College	100	box 3.5" diskettes
9 August	Excelsior College	15	box 3.5" diskettes
9 August	Excelsior College	20	CD recordable disks
9 August	Excelsior College	10	box zip disks
10 August	Regency College	20	box zip disks
10 August	Regency College	6	box laser labels
10 August	Regency College	5	box inkjet labels
10 August	Central College	50	box 3.5" diskettes
10 August	Central College	10	box zip disks
12 August	Regency College	6	inkjet colour printers
12 August	Regency College	2	colour flatbed scanners
13 August	Central College	12	box laser labels
13 August	Central College	15	box inkjet labels
13 August	Central College	5	inkjet printers
15 August	Excelsior College	4	laserjet printers
15 August	Excelsior College	5	inkjet colour printers
15 August	Excelsior College	6	inkjet printers
21 August	Central College	8	laserjet printers
21 August	Central College	8	inkjet colour printers
21 August	Central College	2	flatbed scanners
23 August	Excelsior College	2	flatbed scanners
23 August	Excelsior College	10	box laser labels

ATHENAWARE COMPUTER SUPPLIES – PRICE LIST (EXCLUSIVE OF VAT)

Item	Unit of Supply	Price (£)
3.5" diskettes	box	11.45
CD-recordable disks	box	15.70
zip disks	box	81.25
inkjet labels	box	16.45
laser labels	box	18.25
flatbed scanner	each	85.50
colour flatbed scanner	each	159.00
inkjet printer	each	139.00
inkjet colour printer	each	209.50
laserjet printer	each	232.50

PRACTICAL COMPUTING – SPREADSHEET
THIRD LEVEL
CANDIDATE COPY

Follow the instructions given and create the spreadsheets.

Each spreadsheet must be in A4 landscape orientation adjusted to fit on one sheet. Insert a header showing the assignment number at the left of the page and your name at the right. Insert today's date at the bottom of the page in the centre. Headings and columns must be formatted and aligned consistently. Currency columns should be formatted to 2 decimal places. Headings and data may be in capitals or initial capitals and lower case.

1   Colleges are eligible for a 5% discount on each item if the total price for the item exceeds £150.

2   VAT (Value Added Tax) of 17.5% is not included in the price per item.

3   Orders equal to or in excess of a grand total of £5000 will not be liable to pay a delivery charge. Orders under £5000 will be charged a flat rate of £50. This is added to the final **Net Total + VAT** to make the **Grand Total**.

ASSIGNMENT 1

Refer to the data in the two tables given above.

1   Set up the August spreadsheet template to be used to show Athenaware Computer Supplies' sales to each of the three named colleges.

2   Insert a suitable heading and include a space for the name of the college.

3   Use the following column headings suitably formatted: **Date, Quantity, Item Description, Price Each, Total Price, -5% Discount, VAT, Net Total + VAT, Delivery** and **Grand Total**. The figures for **Delivery** and **Grand Total** should be shown only at the base of the last two columns (on the **Totals** row referred to in Point 4 below).

4   In Assignment 2 there will be 8 rows of data to input. After these 8 rows, in the **Date** column, add a heading **Totals**. Sum the totals for all columns except **Date, Quantity, Item Description** and **Price Each**. On this row insert the figures for **Delivery** and **Grand Total**.

5   Save this template as SALES1. No printout is required.

ASSIGNMENT 2

1   Use the template created in Assignment 1 to enter the relevant data from the tables above in order to compile 3 individual college order sheets for Regency College, Excelsior College and Central College.

2   Save your work as SALES2 (1), SALES2 (2) and SALES2 (3).

3   Print out the 3 individual order sheets.

4   Print a further copy of SALES2 (1) showing the formulae used.

ASSIGNMENT 3

You are asked to analyse the sales of inkjet, inkjet colour and laserjet printers to the 3 colleges in August.

1   Create a spreadsheet to show the sub-totals for these 3 items for each customer. This spreadsheet will be linked to the 3 previous individual order spreadsheets.

2   Set up the spreadsheet using the headings **Item Description, Net Total + VAT – Regency, Net Total + VAT – Excelsior** and **Net Total + VAT – Central**. Add a column for the **Final Total**.

3   After the last entry in the **Item Description** column, add a label **Total Spent on Printers**.

4   Leave a blank row and then label the next row **Grand Total for Each College**.

5   Create links between the individual order spreadsheets so that the **Grand Total** on each college's August order sheet is automatically inserted into the relevant cells on this new spreadsheet. Calculate all totals.

6   Once the totals have been inserted leave a blank row and then label the next row **Percentage Spent on Printers**. Calculate to the nearest whole number what percentage of each college's entire order was spent on the purchase of printers.

7   Leave a row and then label the next row **Average Spent on Printers**. Calculate this and insert the answer under the **Final Total** column.

8   Save your work as SALES3.

9   Print a copy of this spreadsheet.

10   Print a copy of this spreadsheet showing the links and formulae you have used.

ASSIGNMENT 4

1   Prepare 2 graphs (or charts) as follows:

a   a graph or chart to show only the total figure from Assignment 3 spent on printers by each college (use whole numbers)

b   a graph or chart to show a comparison of the Net Total + VAT for each type of printer in Assignment 3 bought by each of the colleges in August. Once again, use whole numbers.

The graphs/charts can be in any format – pie chart, bar chart etc. Give each graph a suitable heading and label the data with the figures. Label both axes. Adjust and format where necessary.

2   Print one copy of each of these 2 graphs/charts.

PRACTICAL COMPUTING – DATABASE
FIRST LEVEL
CANDIDATE'S COPY

LONDON CHAMBER OF COMMERCE AND INDUSTRY EXAMINATIONS BOARD

PRACTICAL COMPUTING – DATABASE

FIRST LEVEL

CANDIDATE'S COPY

249

TOTAL TIME ALLOWANCE: 1 hour 30 minutes

The Candidate's name must appear on every printout.

Printouts may be in portrait or landscape orientation as appropriate.

PRACTICAL COMPUTING – DATABASE
FIRST LEVEL
CANDIDATE'S COPY

ASSIGNMENT 1

It is sale time again and Athena House Handicrafts has asked you to set up a database in order to prepare the Sale Price list to be sent to customers.

1 Create the database using the specified field headings and enter the records which are given below.

Kit Ref	Item	Manufacturer	Usual Price	Sale Price
BA2	African Bead Kit	Ringold Bead Co plc	£26.99	£19.99
BN1	Naranja Indian Bead Kit	Ringold Bead Co plc	£28.99	£22.99
BS3	Sioux Indian Bead Kit	Ringold Bead Co plc	£27.99	£21.99
DB1	Sailor Teddy Bear Kit	Diana's Miniature Bears	£24.50	£19.50
DB2	Cricketer Teddy Bear Kit	Diana's Miniature Bears	£19.50	£24.50
MB1	Model Boat Kit	Mariposa Model Co	£35.00	£30.50
MH2	Model House Kit	Mariposa Model Co	£37.50	£32.50
PC1	Alice Porcelain Doll Kit	Annette's Unique Dolls	£50.00	£40.00
PC2	Emma Porcelain Doll Kit	Annette's Unique Dolls	£55.00	£47.99
TA3	Apron Cross Stitch Kit	Cassandra Crafts	£23.50	£19.00
TC1	Cushion Tapestry Kit	Cassandra Crafts	£37.25	£27.00
TS2	Stool Tapestry Kit	Cassandra Crafts	£29.99	£21.00

2 Prices should be formatted for currency and 2 decimal places.

3 Some database applications automatically sort the records after entry. Check this and sort your records in ascending order on **Kit Ref** if your data entry has not been automatically sorted for you.

4 Save your work using the filename **Hand1**.

5 Print this table.

ASSIGNMENT 2

There are some errors in the database and these need to be amended. There are also additional records to be added.

1   In record BN1 the name "Naranja" is wrong and should be amended to Navajo.

2   In record DB2 the **Usual Price** and the **Sale Price** have been reversed. Amend these 2 prices.

3   The Alice Porcelain Doll Kit (PC1) proved so popular that all the stock has now been sold. Delete this record.

4   Add the following 5 new records to the list as the items have been reduced in price:

Kit Ref	Item	Manufacturer	Usual Price	Sale Price
XDB3	Footballer Teddy Bear Kit	Diana's Miniature Bears	£28.00	£23.00
XDB4	Lawyer Teddy Bear Kit	Diana's Miniature Bears	£29.50	£25.00
XMC3	Model Car Kit	Mariposa Model Co	£33.50	£28.50
XPC3	Carmen Porcelain Doll Kit	Annette's Unique Dolls	£60.00	£52.00
XPC4	Tosca Porcelain Doll Kit	Annette's Unique Dolls	£60.00	£50.00

5   Sort the table on the **Manufacturer** field in ascending order.

6   Save your work using the filename **Hand2**.

7   Print this table.

ASSIGNMENT 3

Recall the table saved as **Hand2** (or a copy) to the screen.

1   Sort the **Usual Price** field so that the highest price is at the top and the lowest at the bottom of the list (descending sort). Make sure all the data is sorted.

2   Save your work under the filename **Hand3**.

3   Print this table.

ASSIGNMENT 4

The manager wishes to know how many kits manufactured by Diana's Miniature Bears are in the sale.

1 Select these records.

2 Sort them in descending order on the **Item** field.

3 Save your work using the filename **Hand4.**

4 Print these selected records.

ASSIGNMENT 5

The manager needs a record of the dates the usual prices were reduced for each item and added to the sale list. Using the file **Hand3** (or a copy):

1 To the right of the **Sale Price** field add a new field called **Date** and enter the dates from the table below.

Kit Ref	Item	Usual Price	Sale Price	Date
BA2	African Bead Kit	£26.99	£19.99	12/6/98
BN1	Navajo Indian Bead Kit	£28.99	£22.99	12/6/98
BS3	Sioux Indian Bead Kit	£27.99	£21.99	12/6/98
DB1	Sailor Teddy Bear Kit	£24.50	£19.50	19/4/98
DB2	Cricketer Teddy Bear Kit	£24.50	£19.50	19/4/98
MB1	Model Boat Kit	£35.00	£30.50	3/4/98
MH2	Model House Kit	£37.50	£32.50	15/9/98
PC2	Emma Porcelain Doll Kit	£55.00	£47.99	4/7/98
TA3	Apron Cross Stitch Kit	£23.50	£19.00	19/4/98
TC1	Cushion Tapestry Kit	£37.25	£27.00	19/4/98
TS2	Stool Tapestry Kit	£29.99	£21.00	27/4/98
XDB3	Footballer Teddy Bear Kit	£28.00	£23.00	31/8/98
XDB4	Lawyer Teddy Bear Kit	£29.50	£25.00	31/8/98
XMC3	Model Car Kit	£33.50	£28.50	15/9/98
XPC3	Carmen Porcelain Doll Kit	£60.00	£52.00	15/9/98
XPC4	Tosca Porcelain Doll Kit	£60.00	£50.00	15/9/98

2 Sort the **Date** field in ascending order.

3 Save your work as **Hand5**.

4 Print your work showing only the **Item, Manufacturer** and **Date** fields.

ASSIGNMENT 6

A customer has asked for a list of Teddy Bear kits in the sale. Using the information saved under filename **Hand4,** prepare this list in report format:

1 Head the report **ATHENA HOUSE TEDDY BEAR KITS**.

2 Insert today's date on the report.

3 There should be 3 fields only, **Kit Ref, Item** and **Sale Price.**   Rename these fields as **Reference, Name of Item** and **Discount Sale Price.** These field headings should be in block capitals.

4 Sort the **Name of Item** field in ascending order (A – Z).

5 Add the words **GRAND TOTAL** at the base of the columns and insert the total for the **Discount Sale Price** under that column.

6 Print this report.

PRACTICAL COMPUTING – DATABASE
SECOND LEVEL
CANDIDATE'S COPY

LONDON CHAMBER OF COMMERCE AND INDUSTRY EXAMINATIONS BOARD

PRACTICAL COMPUTING – DATABASE

SECOND LEVEL

CANDIDATE'S COPY

PRACTICAL COMPUTING – DATABASE
SECOND LEVEL
CANDIDATE'S COPY

255

TOTAL TIME ALLOWANCE: 2 hours

The Candidate's name must appear on every printout.

Printouts may be in portrait or landscape orientation as appropriate.

PRACTICAL COMPUTING – DATABASE
SECOND LEVEL
CANDIDATE'S COPY

BACKGROUND

You work for Comlon's Cattery. Today you have been asked to set up a database to record information about the cats which are listed on Comlon's register. Please carry out the following instructions.

ASSIGNMENT 1

Turn to the next page where you will find a table giving details of seventeen records to be entered in this new Feline Register table.

1   Create a database table to include the following 10 fields: a numeric **Cat Ref, Cat Type, Cat Name, Birth Date, Breed, Colour Details, Gender, Breeder, Address** and **Price.** The **Price** field should be formatted for currency but with no decimal places.

2   Set up a lookup table linked to the **Address** field. You will need to create a 2 columns x 5 rows lookup table. You should enter the following information in this table: town and county, followed by the breeder's name.

   Stockport, Cheshire; Cuddly Cats plc
   Framley, Barset; Barset Cat Breeders
   Ashton, Somerset; Jaswinder's Topcats
   Brixton, London; Tamara's Exotic Felines
   Leeds, Yorkshire; Joe Bloggs Moggies

By accessing the lookup table on the **Address** field, you can automatically enter the correct address for the breeder.

3   Create an entry screen based on the table you have designed, to enable you to enter data into the table. Give the screen a title COMLON'S CATTERY DATA ENTRY SCREEN. In the **Gender** field specify that only Male or Female should to be entered. Enlarge and embolden the text, to make it clearer.

4   Enter the first record. Save your work as **Cat1Scrn**.

5   Print a copy of the entry screen to show this first record.

6   Now enter the remaining 16 records.

7   Save your work as **Cat1Tab**.

8   Print a copy of this complete database table in landscape orientation.

Cat Ref	Cat Type	Cat Name	Birth Date	Breed	Colour Details	Gender	Breeder	Address	Price
601	Tortoiseshell	Felicity	15/10/98	Tortoiseshell	Red/Black	Female	Tamara's Exotic Felines	Brixton, London	£255
602	Siamese	Beauty	16/2/99	Siamese	Seal Point	Female	Jaswinder's Topcats	Ashton, Somerset	£350
603	Angora	Zara	22/1/99	Angora	Lilac/White	Female	Barset Cat Breeders	Framley, Barset	£395
604	Ocicat	Nanamay	14/4/99	Ocicat	White	Female	Barset Cat Breeders	Framley, Barset	£340
605	Tortie Tabby	Dumpling	17/3/99	Tortie Tabby	Blue/Silver	Female	Cuddly Cats plc	Stockport, Cheshire	£345
608	Manx	Pushkin	31/3/99	Manx	White	Male	Jaswinder's Topcats	Ashton, Somerset	£320
612	Tabby	Shamus	6/2/99	Tabby	Red	Male	Barset Cat Breeders	Framley, Barset	£345
614	Burmese	King John	14/2/99	Burmese	Brown	Male	Tamara's Exotic Felines	Brixton, London	£385
615	Tortoiseshell	Gingerbread	3/2/99	Tortoiseshell	Red/Black/White	Female	Tamara's Exotic Felines	Brixton, London	£295
616	Persian	Vanilla	27/1/99	Persian	White	Female	Pat Cloggs Moggies	Leeds, Yorkshire	£315
617	Persian	Bella	21/2/99	Persian	Black Smoke	Female	Cuddly Cats plc	Stockport, Cheshire	£325
618	Siamese	Milor	23/2/99	Siamese	Cream Point	Female	Jaswinder's Topcats	Ashton, Somerset	£298
619	Maine Coon	Whiskey	17/1/99	Maine Coon	Brown/White	Male	Pat Cloggs Moggies	Leeds, Yorkshire	£220
625	Tortie Tabby	Candyrue	1/3/99	Tortie Tabby	Blue/Silver	Female	Cuddly Cats plc	Stockport, Cheshire	£355
627	Siamese	Torquil	16/4/99	Siamese	Cream Point	Male	Jaswinder's Topcats	Ashton, Somerset	£325
644	Persian	Xanadu	13/4/99	Persian	Black	Male	Pat Cloggs Moggies	Leeds, Yorkshire	£350
666	Somali	Little Caesar	19/3/99	Somali	Lilac	Male	Cuddly Cats plc	Stockport, Cheshire	£305

257

ASSIGNMENT 2

On inspecting the database, certain amendments are required. Carry out the following:

1 A new system of coding is coming into operation so change the **Cat Ref** to an alphanumberic field instead of a numeric one to cope with future references.

2 As the data entered into the **Cat Type** column is identical to the **Breed** data, delete the **Cat Type** field from the database.

3 A new field called **Long Hair?** should be inserted between the **Colour Details** and the **Gender** columns. This indicates if the cat is a long-haired cat or a short-haired one. Make this a Yes/No field (**not** a check box field). All the cats bred by Cuddly Cats plc and by Joe Bloggs Moggies are long-haired cats. The other three breeders only supply short-haired cats.

4 As Shamus the tabby (Cat Ref 612) has now been sold, delete the record from the database.

5 Milor, the cream point Siamese (Cat Ref 618), is a male cat so amend this record.

6 Amend the colour details for the Ocicat, Cat Ref 604. This cat is chocolate coloured and not white.

7 In the past few months, 8 new kittens have been acquired by Comlon Cattery. Details are given over the page. Add these records to the database.

8 The database should be in **Birth Date** order so once all 24 records are entered, sort the records starting with the oldest date first.

9 Save your work as **Cat2Tab**.

10 Print the amended table.

Cat Ref	Cat Name	Birth Date	Breed	Colour Details	Gender	Breeder	Address	Price
671	Sultana	5/3/99	Turkish Van	Auburn	Female	Tamara's Exotic Felines	Brixton, London	£340
672	Cookienet	3/4/99	Angora	Chocolate	Female	Barset Cat Breeders	Framley, Barset	£325
673	Rolypoly	31/3/99	Persian	Cream/White	Male	Pat Cloggs Moggies	Leeds, Yorkshire	£300
676	Sterlingworth	3/4/99	Tabby	Silver	Male	Cuddly Cats plc	Stockport, Cheshire	£350
677	Caramba	24/3/99	Tortoiseshell	Red/Black	Female	Jaswinder's Topcats	Ashton, Somerset	£310
678	Saroola	4/4/99	Singapura	Sable Brown	Male	Barset Cat Breeders	Framley, Barset	£325
679	Frisky	13/4/99	Siamese	Red Point	Male	Jaswinder's Topcats	Ashton, Somerset	£330
680	Martina Babbage	14/4/99	Persian	Blue	Female	Tamara's Exotic Felines	Brixton, London	£340

ASSIGNMENT 3

1) A customer is interested in purchasing a blue and silver Tortie Tabby cat born after 10 March 1999. Search the database and when you have made your selection:

> (i) save your work as **Cat3Q1**

> (ii) print your work in table format showing only the **Cat Ref, Cat Name, Birth Date** and **Gender** fields.

2) The manager would like a list of all long-haired cats on the Register who were born before 1 April 1999. Search the database and when you have made your selection:

> (i) sort your records in ascending price order

> (ii) save your work as **Cat3Q2**

> (iii) print a list in table format showing only the **Cat Ref, Cat Name, Birth Date, Gender, Breeder** and **Price** fields.

ASSIGNMENT 4

1 Create a report showing all the cats on the Feline Register. Head this report COMLON CATTERY – BREEDERS.

2 Group the cats by Breeder. Use the full name and address of the breeder for each group heading.

3 Sort the groups alphabetically from A – Z and under each group sort the cats in **Birth Date** order.

4 Restrict the fields to **Cat Ref, Birth Date, Cat Name, Breed, Gender** and **Price**.

5 Give sub-totals under each group showing the total price of the cats supplied by that breeder.

6 Add a Grand Total at the end to show the total amount of all Prices.

7 Add today's date and your name in a footer. Do not insert a page number.

Save your work as **Cat4Rpt.** Print this report.

PRACTICAL COMPUTING – DATABASE
THIRD LEVEL
CANDIDATE'S COPY

LONDON CHAMBER OF COMMERCE AND INDUSTRY EXAMINATIONS BOARD

PRACTICAL COMPUTING – DATABASE

THIRD LEVEL

CANDIDATE'S COPY

PRACTICAL COMPUTING – DATABASE
THIRD LEVEL
CANDIDATE'S COPY

TOTAL TIME ALLOWANCE: 2 hours 30 minutes

The Candidate's name must appear on every printout.

Printouts may be in portrait or landscape orientation as appropriate.

BACKGROUND

You work for Athena House – Builders. This company has now produced plans for 5 new housing estates which are about to be developed in England. Today you are asked to use your database package to help the company's staff to manage these new developments by setting up a database in accordance with the following specifications.

Two tables will be required, the **Estate** table and the **House Details** table.

1   Set up the **Estate** table for each of the new estates to be developed, with the following 10 fields: **Estate Ref** (set the primary key on this field), **Estate Name, Town, Year Started, Site Manager, Telephone No, Building Type,** whether **Incentives?** to buy are offered (this can be a Yes/No type of field or a check box) and the actual **Offer** (make this a Memo field). The tenth field is called **Clerk** and is for your initials. When you have set up this table save your work as **EstTab1.**

2   Set up the **House Details** table with 9 fields which will have details of the types of houses to be built on the estate. These fields are the **House Ref** as the primary key, **Start Date, House Name, Detached, Bedrooms, Receptions, Garage** and **Price.** (The **Detached** and **Garage** fields are a Yes/No or check box type of field). The ninth field to be added is the **Estate Ref** (ie the primary key from the **Estate** table). This shows on which estate the house is being built.

3   In the **House Details** table **Estate Ref** field add a 3 column x 5 lines lookup box. Enter the **Estate Ref, Town** and **Estate Name** from the **Estate** table for each of the 5 new estates. This should enable you to link the **House Details** table to the **Estate** table. When you have set up this table save your work as **HseTab1.**

4   Set up a relationship of one-to-many from the **Estate** table to the **House Details** table using referential integrity.

5   You do not need to print anything at this stage.

PRACTICAL COMPUTING – DATABASE
THIRD LEVEL
CANDIDATE'S COPY

ASSIGNMENT 1

To enable staff to enter data more easily in the 2 tables, prepare 2 data entry forms, one for each table. You should first set up the field headings for the table and then create the appropriate data entry screen form ready for entering the data which appears on the following pages.

1   For the **Estate** data entry screen attach a property to the **Estate Name** field and the **Town** field so that these all appear in capital letters on the form and are saved to the table in the same format. Attach properties to most of the fields so that data is always entered in the correct manner and only valid data is accepted.

2   In the entry screen for the **House Details** table, providing you have set up the lookup box properly, when the **Estate Ref** box is selected it will automatically show a list of the 5 estate references, names, and towns. By checking which town and estate name is on the house record card staff can use this to enter the appropriate reference for the estate.

3   Add suitable headings to the data entry screens and your name and today's date in a footer for each of the two entry screens. Enter the first record for each entry screen to test the entry form. The first record for the **Estate** entry screen should be entered from the Supplied Data list shown below. Enter the first record for the **House Details** entry screen from the 16 records which appear after the Supplied Data overleaf.

4   Once you have entered the first record on each screen, save the **Estate** entry screen as **EstScrn1** and the **House Details** screen as **HseScrn1.**

5   Now print a copy of each screen in Form view.

265

SUPPLIED DATA

<u>**Estate**</u> Table.

All estates are offering incentives.

RUN65, Runway Farm, Gatwick, Year started – 1998, John Piloter, Telephone number 01293 005 622, BuildingType – houses, Offer – mortgages, £1,000 discount.

FLO23, Floodgate Meadows, Northampton, Year started – 1997, Helen Diverson, Telephone 01604 505 802. Building Type – houses, Offer – mortgages, £200 holiday voucher.

CAN41, Canal View Valley, Manchester, Year started – 1998, Billy Shipper, Telephone 0161 429 0193, Building Type – houses and flats, Offer – 1% cashback and free carpets.

JUN16, Junction Square, Clapham, Year started – 1999, Bob Signalman, Telephone 0181 0022 163, Building Type – houses and flats, Offer – mortgages, 1% cashback.

DOC78, Dockland Ponds, London, Year started – 1999, Carol Fisher, Telephone 0181 004 3761, Building Type – flats and houses, Offer – mortgages, free carpets.

House Types

There are 16 record cards giving house details to be entered on the database.
These appear on the next four pages.

PRACTICAL COMPUTING – DATABASE
THIRD LEVEL
CANDIDATE'S COPY

ATHENA HOUSE – BUILDERS

House Ref GC1

House Name Claridges

Bedrooms 4
Garage ✓

Town GATWICK

Start Date 1 June 1998

Detached ✓

Receptions 3
Price
£200,000

ATHENA HOUSE – BUILDERS

House Ref NS1

House Name Savoy

Bedrooms 3
Garage No

Town NORTHAMPTON

Start Date 7/3/97

Detached No

Receptions 2
Price
£125 000

ATHENA HOUSE – BUILDERS

House Ref MW1

House Name Waldorf

Bedrooms 3
Garage ✓

Town MANCHESTER

Start Date 9 April 98

Detached Yes

Receptions 2
Price
£130,000

ATHENA HOUSE – BUILDERS

House Ref MG1

House Name Grosvenor

Bedrooms 4
Garage ✓

Town MANCHESTER

Start Date 21 May 98

Detached ✓

Receptions 2
Price
150 000

ATHENA HOUSE – BUILDERS

House Ref   GW2   Start Date   19 July 1998

House Name   Waldorf   Detached ✓

Bedrooms   3   Receptions   2
Garage   Yes   Price

Town   GATWICK   £170 000

ATHENA HOUSE – BUILDERS

House Ref   CR1   Start Date   22 May 99

House Name   Ritz   Detached ✓

Bedrooms   5   Receptions   3
Garage ✓   Price

Town   CLAPHAM   £330,000

ATHENA HOUSE – BUILDERS

House Ref   CC1   Start Date   2nd May 99

House Name   Claridges   Detached ✓

Bedrooms   4   Receptions   3
Garage ✓   Price

Town   CLAPHAM   295 000

ATHENA HOUSE – BUILDERS

House Ref   NS2   Start Date   4 March 97

House Name   Savoy   Detached No

Bedrooms   3   Receptions   2
Garage   No   Price

Town   NORTHAMPTON   £125,000

267

PRACTICAL COMPUTING – DATABASE
THIRD LEVEL
CANDIDATE'S COPY

ATHENA HOUSE – BUILDERS

House Ref   GG1   Start Date   25 May 1998

House Name   Grosvenor   Detached   ✓

Bedrooms   4   Receptions   2
Garage   Yes   Price

Town   GATWICK   £190,000

ATHENA HOUSE – BUILDERS

House Ref   NW1   Start Date   12 June 97

House Name   Waldorf   Detached   ✓

Bedrooms   3   Receptions   2
Garage   ✓   Price

Town   NORTHAMPTON   £130000

ATHENA HOUSE – BUILDERS

House Ref   LC1   Start Date   18 April 99

House Name   Claridges   Detached   ✓

Bedrooms   4   Receptions   3
Garage   ✓   Price

Town   LONDON   £300,000

ATHENA HOUSE – BUILDERS

House Ref   SG2   Start Date   14 April 98

House Name   Savoy   Detached   No

Bedrooms   3   Receptions   2
Garage   No   Price

Town   MANCHESTER   £145,000

ATHENA HOUSE – BUILDERS

House Ref GW1   Start Date 10 July 1998

House Name Waldorf   Detached ✓

Bedrooms 3   Receptions 2
Garage ✓   Price

Town GATWICK   £165 000

ATHENA HOUSE – BUILDERS

House Ref SM1   Start Date 22/4/98

House Name Savoy   Detached No

Bedrooms 3   Receptions 2
Garage No   Price

Town MANCHESTER   145000

ATHENA HOUSE – BUILDERS

House Ref CR2   Start Date 27 March '99

House Name Ritz   Detached ✓

Bedrooms 5   Receptions 3
Garage ✓   Price

Town CLAPHAM   £350,000

ATHENA HOUSE – BUILDERS

House Ref LG1   Start Date 30 April 99

House Name Grosvenor   Detached ✓

Bedrooms 4   Receptions 2
Garage ✓   Price

Town LONDON   285000

PRACTICAL COMPUTING – DATABASE
THIRD LEVEL
CANDIDATE'S COPY

ASSIGNMENT 2

1 Using the data screens you have just set up, input the rest of the records in the appropriate tables. Enter the remaining 4 records for the **Estate** screen. (Use the Supplied Data for the **Estate** screen.) Then enter the remaining 15 records for the **House Details** screen. (Use the record cards for the **House Details** screen.) As different clerks have entered the details on the record cards, ensure you enter your data consistently on the data entry forms.

2 Once all the data has been entered into the **Estate** table, sort this table on the **Estate Ref** field.

3 Save this table as **EstTab2.**

4 Print a copy in table format.

5 Once all the data has been entered into the **House Details** table, sort this table in **House Ref** order.

6 Save this table as **HseTab2.**

7 Print a copy in table format.

ASSIGNMENT 3

1 Create a simple tabular report headed **ATHENA HOUSE – BUILDERS, PRICE SUMMARY.** This report should start with the **Estate Ref** based on the **House Details** table, followed by the **House Ref** field, and show a summary of all new houses for each of the estates forming part of Athena House – Builders. Do not list each individual estate's name. The **Estate Ref** from the **House Details** table together with all the other fields from that table will identify on which estate the house is being built.

2 Sort the summary alphabetically on the **Estate Ref**.

3 Next sort the summary in **House Name** order within each estate.

4 At the end of the report, summarise the **Price** field to show the **Grand Total** of all house prices on the 5 estates.

5 Insert today's date in a footer together with your name. A page number will not be needed so do not insert one.

6 Save your work as **Report1.**

7 Print this report.

ASSIGNMENT 4

1   Making use of the one-to-many relationship between the two tables from Assignments 1 and 2, create a further report entitled **ATHENA HOUSE – BUILDERS, ESTATE ANALYSIS.** In this report group the houses under their respective estates. For this purpose, use the **Estate Ref, Estate Name** and **Town** from the **Estate Table**. For each group show only the field heading and data for the **House Name, Start Date, Bedrooms, Receptions** and **Price** fields taken from the **House Details** table. The field headings may appear every time for each group, or they may be set out at the head of the report once only, and only the actual data will appear in each group under the field headings at the head of the report. Either type of report is acceptable.

2   Sort the groups alphabetically on **Estate Ref.**

3   Within each group sort in **Start Date** order starting with the oldest date.

4   Add a **Sub-total** under each group based on the **Price** for each house in that group, and at the bottom of the report give the **Grand Total** showing the total value of the housing stock.

5   Insert today's date and your name as footers but do not insert a page number.

6   Save your work as **Report2.**

7   Print this report.

PRACTICAL COMPUTING – WORD PROCESSING
FIRST LEVEL
CANDIDATE COPY

LONDON CHAMBER OF COMMERCE AND INDUSTRY EXAMINATIONS BOARD

PRACTICAL COMPUTING – FIRST LEVEL

WORD PROCESSING – CANDIDATE'S COPY

PRACTICAL COMPUTING – WORD PROCESSING
FIRST LEVEL
CANDIDATE COPY

TIME ALLOWANCE: **1 hour and 30 minutes**

PRACTICAL COMPUTING – WORD PROCESSING
FIRST LEVEL
CANDIDATE COPY

ASSIGNMENT 1

1   Key in the text below in single line spacing, using the default margins.

2   Key in your name at the bottom of the document.

3   Proofread your work carefully.

4   Save the document as [WP1ASS1].

5   Print a copy.

It is generally believed that the purchase of a good bed is one of the best investments a person can make. We spend, on average, a third of our life in bed and so it is important that these hours are spent in an environment which is comfortable and healthy.

We need a good night's sleep to recharge our batteries, both mentally and physically. If we sleep badly, our daily life can be adversely affected. We make more mistakes, lose our temper more easily and generally enjoy life less.

A suitable bed, which gives the comfort and support we need for a good night's sleep, can be a vital factor in our happiness. It should be comfortable and large enough to allow us to move freely. It should be purchased from a reputable retailer and changed every eight or ten years.

Choose your bed wisely, or your body will suffer!

PRACTICAL COMPUTING – WORD PROCESSING
FIRST LEVEL
CANDIDATE COPY

ASSIGNMENT 2

1   Key in the text below in single line spacing, using fully-justified margins.

2   Insert today's date.

3   Add your initials at the end of the reference.

4   Key in your name at the bottom of the document.

5   Proofread your work carefully.

6   Save the document as [WP1ASS2].

7   Print a copy.

MEMORANDUM

To   Sheila Conway
          Sales Supervisor

From   Robert Malloy
          Marketing Manager

Ref   Rm/

HOME INTERIORS EXHIBITION, OLYMPIA

Please note that our attendance at this exhibition has now been confirmed. We have been allocated Stand Number 240 which is on the first floor of the exhibition hall. This is a prime location and should enable us to show our products to a large number of visitors.

We shall need a sales team of ten people to cover the four-day event in shifts. Please prepare a list of staff from your department who would be willing to attend. The exhibition is open from 1000 to 2000 each day. It will be necessary, therefore, for some members of staff to increase their working hours for the exhibition period. Please tell them that they will be paid for the extra hours worked.

The space available to us will accommodate three double beds and one single, in addition to glass shelves on which we can display our range of bedlinen and matching accessories.

I look forward to receiving your list by Friday.

PRACTICAL COMPUTING – WORD PROCESSING
FIRST LEVEL
CANDIDATE COPY

ASSIGNMENT 3

1   Key in the text below, in single line spacing, using left and right margins of 5 cm (2 inches).

2   Leave two clear line spaces between paragraphs.

3   Use fully justified margins.

4   Make the necessary changes as shown.

5   Key in your name at the bottom of the document.

6   Proofread your work carefully.

7   Save the document as [WP1ASS3].

8   Print a copy.

CHOOSING A NEW BED?   — centre and bold

When choosing a new bed, always buy the largest you can afford. Buy the mattress and base together and select a protective cover for the mattress.

It's unhygienic to buy a second-hand bed — so don't be tempted!

PRACTICAL COMPUTING – WORD PROCESSING
FIRST LEVEL
CANDIDATE COPY

ASSIGNMENT 4

1   Recall your document saved as [WP1ASS2].

2   Make the changes to the text as shown below.

3   Proofread your work carefully.

4   Save the document as [WP1ASS4].

5   Print a copy.

MEMORANDUM

To   Sheila Conway
            Sales Supervisor

From   Robert Malloy
            Marketing Manager

Date

Ref

double line spacing for this paragraph

HOME INTERIORS EXHIBITION, OLYMPIA   — *bold*

demonstrate

Please note that our attendance at this exhibition has now been confirmed. We have been allocated Stand Number 240 which is on the first floor of the exhibition hall. This is a prime location and should enable us to ~~show~~ our products to a large number of visitors.

experienced

We shall need a sales team of ten people to cover the four-day event in shifts. Please prepare a list of staff from your department who would be willing to attend. The exhibition is open from 1000 until 2000 each day. It will be necessary, therefore, for some members of staff to increase their working hours for the exhibition period. Please tell them that they will be paid for the extra hours worked. **Travel expenses can also be claimed.**

The space available to us will accommodate three double beds and one single, in addition to glass shelves on which we can display our range of bedlinen and matching accessories.

draft

I look forward to receiving your list by ~~Friday~~ **next Monday.**

PRACTICAL COMPUTING – WORD PROCESSING
FIRST LEVEL
CANDIDATE COPY

ASSIGNMENT 5

1   Recall your document saved as [WP1ASS3].

2   Make the necessary additions to the document as shown.

3   Proofread your work carefully.

4   Save the document as [WP1ASS5].

5   Print a copy.

CHOOSING A NEW BED?

When choosing a new bed, always buy the largest you can afford. Buy the mattress and base together and select a protective cover for the mattress.

It's unhygienic to buy a second-hand bed – so don't be tempted! Always throw away your old bed.

There are many types of bed to choose from. These are our most popular lines:

Range	Mattress Type	Covering
Prestige	Continuous springs	Diamond quilting
Emperor	Open springs	Micro quilting
Ambassador	Pocket springs	Tufting

PRACTICAL COMPUTING – WORD PROCESSING
FIRST LEVEL
CANDIDATE COPY

ASSIGNMENT 6

1   Key in the text below following line spacing exactly.

2   Centre each line horizontally.

3   Make the necessary formatting changes.

4   Key in your name at the bottom of the document.

5   Proofread your work carefully.

6   Save the document as [WP1ASS6].

7   Print a copy.

DECORATING YOUR BEDROOM?

BUYING A NEW BED?

} *bold*

If you're thinking about making changes to your bedroom,
come along and see our exciting new range of beds and bedlinen.

You can find us on

<u>Stand Number 240</u>   – *bold and underline*

at the

HOME INTERIORS EXHIBITION   – *bold*

at Olympia

next month!

<u>We look forward to seeing you!</u>   – *bold and underline*

Athena Bedrooms, 4 Grove Gardens, Bexley
0181 302 0261

} *italics*

PRACTICAL COMPUTING – WORD PROCESSING
SECOND LEVEL
CANDIDATE COPY

LONDON CHAMBER OF COMMERCE AND INDUSTRY EXAMINATIONS BOARD

PRACTICAL COMPUTING – SECOND LEVEL

WORD PROCESSING – CANDIDATE'S COPY

PRACTICAL COMPUTING – WORD PROCESSING
SECOND LEVEL
CANDIDATE COPY

TIME ALLOWANCE: **2 hours**

PRACTICAL COMPUTING – WORD PROCESSING
SECOND LEVEL
CANDIDATE COPY

ASSIGNMENT 1

1   Key in the text below and edit as shown.

2   Insert today's date.

3   Expand abbreviations.

4   Insert a hard page break at an appropriate point in the text.

5   Key in your name at the bottom of the document.

6   Proofread your work carefully.

7   Save the document as [WP2ASS1].

8   Print out a copy.

ATHENA TOURS   — increase font size

Voyager House
24-28 Rodney Place   } bold and centre
LONDON EC4A 3PG

Mr James Kildare
152 Hurstwood Rd
CROYDON
CR2 9KM

Dr Mr Kildare

Chief Executive
Your letter, addressed to our ~~Managing Director~~, has been passed to me. I am sorry to hear that you were dissatisfied with your recent Athena Tours coach trip to Austria.

CHANNEL CROSSING

complain
You ~~say~~ that the timing of the Channel crossing was delayed by approx 90 minutes. I am reliably informed that on that particular day all trains were running late.~~due to an earlier emergency.~~ I ~~can only~~ apologise for this inconvenience **but wd point out that our brochure does state that 'we reserve the right to substitute alternative crossings if necessary without liability.'**

COACH SEATS

I am sorry that you were not able to be seated in row 3 as you requested. Unfortunately, seat allocations are made on a first come, first served basis and row 3 had already been reserved when yr booking was made.

run on

All seats offer panoramic views and we trust that yr seat in row 5 was comfortable.

HOTEL ACCOMMODATION IN VIENNA

You state that the Hotel Imperial in Vienna was, in yr opinion, not a 4-star hotel as described in the brochure. You mention low standards of hygiene and poor quality food. The Hotel Imperial has an official 4-star rating and is a popular choice amongst our regular clients.

I am sorry that yr holiday was spoilt by these misunderstandings. Although this co bears no responsibility for the changes, please accept the enclosed voucher which entitles you to free holiday insurance when you next book with Athena Tours.

double line spacing here

Yrs sncly

Rose Weston
Public Relations Officer

Enc

283

PRACTICAL COMPUTING – WORD PROCESSING
SECOND LEVEL
CANDIDATE COPY

ASSIGNMENT 2

1   Key in the text below and edit as shown.

2   Key in your name at the bottom of the document.

3   Proofread your work carefully.

4   Save the document as [WP2ASS2].

5   Print out a copy with justified right and left margins.

ATHENA TOURS

HELPFUL HINTS FOR COACH TRAVELLERS } bold

Thank you for booking your coach travel with Athena Tours. You can be confident of receiving professional service from our experienced staff.

Before you depart, please spend a few ~~minutes~~ moments studying the following information:

- please arrive at your pick-up point at least 30 minutes prior to the scheduled departure time
- check that you have all necessary documentation to hand
- please do not exceed the stated limit of one medium-sized suitcase per person (weight limit – 20 kilos)   [trs]
- ensure that all baggage is clearly labelled
- please do not ask your driver to make unscheduled stops

indent 2.5 cm (1 inch) from both margins

All hotels listed on the itinerary will be located centrally. All rooms will have private facilities. Colour television and air conditioning are standard. Most hotels have restaurant facilities; in exceptional cases, a local restaurant will have been designated for the exclusive use of our clients.

PRACTICAL COMPUTING – WORD PROCESSING
SECOND LEVEL
CANDIDATE COPY

ASSIGNMENT 3

1   Key in the text below and edit as shown.

2   Insert hard page breaks where shown and number each page at the bottom centre.

3   Insert a header AT/125 at the top right of each page.

4   Use double line spacing except where indicated.

5   Leave a space of at least 2.5 cm (1 inch) consistently between sections.

6   Use justified right and left margins.

7   Key in your name at the bottom of the document.

8   Proofread your work carefully.

9   Save the document as [WP2ASS3] and print out a copy.

ATHENA TOURS

HOLIDAYS WITH A DIFFERENCE!   } *centre and bold*

Thank you for enquiring about Athena Tours. We hope that you will enjoy reading our latest brochure. Here are a few of the features ~~which~~ we ~~are pleased to~~ offer to all our clients …

ACCOMMODATION ONLY

perhaps
If you prefer to make your own travel plans, ~~maybe~~ taking advantage of points gained through a Frequent Flyer programme, we can arrange your accommodation in any of the hotels listed *in the brochure at preferential rates.*

CREATE YOUR OWN HOLIDAY

leave a space at least 7.5 cm (3 inches) wide by 5 cm (2 inches) deep for a photograph

Although our brochure offers a wide range of holidays, we can arrange a customised holiday for you and your family. You can extend the length of your stay at the hotel of your choice, or you can combine two destinations for a two-centre holiday. Let us know your preference and we will quote an all-inclusive price.

single line spacing here

Assignments

PAGE 2 STARTS HERE

Ⓐ

COACH
ESCORTED/TOURS

We offer a wide range of escorted coach tours to most European countries. Numbers on board our/luxury air-conditioned coaches are restricted to 36, allowing for greater convenience and comfort.

trs   convenience and comfort.
           3   2   1

SPECIALLY SELECTED REPRESENTATIVES

trs All ~~our~~ holidays include the services of ~~one of our~~ a specially selected representatives who ~~have~~ has an excellent ~~working~~ knowledge of the language and local area. A representative will escort you on coach tours or, in the case of holidays by air, collect you from the airport and visit you at your hotel.

MOTORING HOLIDAYS   INSERT AT Ⓐ

If you ~~choose~~ wish to take your own car with you, we can arrange your Channel crossings by ferry or train. Our special ~~care~~ car insurance is also available with this service.

PAGE 3 STARTS HERE

ALL-INCLUSIVE PRICES

Check the table below to see what is included in the price of your holiday:

Type of Holiday	Transportation	Accommodation	Insurance
Accommodation only	No	Yes	Yes
Coach tour	Yes	Yes	No
Motoring holiday	Yes	No	Yes
Two-centre holiday	Yes	Yes	No

PRACTICAL COMPUTING – WORD PROCESSING
SECOND LEVEL
CANDIDATE COPY

ASSIGNMENT 4

1   Recall your document saved as [WP2ASS2].

2   Change coach to air wherever it occurs.

3   Make the necessary changes to the text as shown below.

4   Proofread your work carefully.

5   Save the document as [WP2ASS4].

6   Print out a copy.

<u>**ATHENA TOURS**</u>

HELPFUL HINTS FOR COACH TRAVELLERS

Thank you for booking your coach travel with Athena Tours. You can be confident of receiving professional service from our experienced staff.

Before you depart, please spend a few moments studying the following information:

• identify yourself to the Athena Tours Representative as soon as possible

• please arrive at ~~your pick-up point~~ the airport at least ~~30 minutes~~ 2 hours prior to the scheduled departure time
• check that you have all necessary documentation to hand
• ensure that all baggage is clearly labelled using Athena Tours labels
• please do not exceed the stated limit of one medium-sized suitcase per person (weight limit – 20 kilos)
• ~~please do not ask your driver to make unscheduled stops~~
• only take one piece of hand luggage on to the plane
• let us know if you have any special dietary requirements

All hotels listed on the itinerary will be located centrally. All rooms will have private facilities. Colour television and air conditioning are standard. ~~Most hotels have restaurant facilities; in exceptional cases, a local restaurant will have been designated for the exclusive use of our clients.~~ All hotels have restaurant facilities; most offer 24-hour room service.

Clients who have booked a two-centre holiday should check that the Athena Tours Representative knows of your second destination at least two days prior to your onward travel. Appropriate arrangements can then be made locally.

LONDON CHAMBER OF COMMERCE AND INDUSTRY EXAMINATIONS BOARD

PRACTICAL COMPUTING – THIRD LEVEL

WORD PROCESSING – CANDIDATE'S COPY

PRACTICAL COMPUTING – WORD PROCESSING
THIRD LEVEL
CANDIDATE COPY

TIME ALLOWANCE: **2 hours and 30 minutes**

PRACTICAL COMPUTING – WORD PROCESSING
THIRD LEVEL
CANDIDATE COPY

ASSIGNMENT 1

1   Key in this standard letter with a ragged right margin.

2   Insert merge points at the places shown with an X to take the information shown on page 2.

3   Print one copy of the standard letter.

4   Key in the information given on page 2 as a datafile and print one copy of the file.

5   Merge the datafile with the standard letter and print copies of the letters for those people who have registered as Full Members.

6   Ensure that your name appears on all documents.

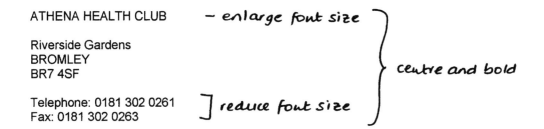

ATHENA HEALTH CLUB   – enlarge font size

Riverside Gardens
BROMLEY
BR7 4SF

                                                                    centre and bold

Telephone: 0181 302 0261   ] reduce font size
Fax: 0181 302 0263

Today's date

X
X
X
X

Dr X

With ref to yr recent letter, I have pleasure in confirming yr registration as a X member of our Club.

I enclose yr membership card, which you shd sign immed and use each time you visit the Club. I also enclose a voucher entitling you to a complimentary X in our

Treatment Suite.

I look forward to welcoming you to the Athena Health Club very soon.

Yrs sncly

Joanna Turner
Membership Manager

Encs

_____

Mrs G Stone
5 City Rd
Petts Wood
BR9 6FS
Full
manicure

Mrs W Harris
4 Bartley Pk
Sevenoaks
BR 11 1AL
Senior
pedicure

Mr J Wilson
38 London Rd
Sevenoaks
BR11 4LB
Student
pedicure

Mr F Hollis
10 Park Ave
Bromley
BR1 2AL
Senior
massage

Mr K Leavis
67 Arndale Rd
Dartford
DA2 3HM
Full
massage

Mrs D Caswell
126 The Cedars
Dartford
DA1 9Pm
Senior
facial

Miss R Timms
103 Manor Rd
Crayford
DA4 6CM
Student
facial

Ms S Boyd
14 Lark Rise
Bromley
BR4 8JW
Full
manicure

ASSIGNMENT 2

1   Key in the text below and edit as shown.

2   Use double line spacing unless otherwise instructed.

3   Insert hard page breaks at appropriate points to produce a 3-page document.

4   Insert a header with FACILITIES at the right margin and a page number at the bottom right of the page.

5   Use justified right and left margins.

6   Reorganise the text into alphabetical order of headings.

7   Leave at least 2.5 cm (1 inch) consistently between sections.

8   Key in your name at the bottom of the document.

9   Save the document under a meaningful filename.

10   Print a copy of your work.

Single spacing here

ATHENA HOUSE HEALTH CLUB   — *bold and centre*

We believe that a healthy lifestyle is of paramount importance to our members. We work hard to provide them with all the facilities they need to keep fit and healthy. Here is a brief outline of some of the ways in which we can make exercise more enjoyable ....

GYMNASIUM   — *bold*

Our superbly-equipped gymnasium offers *all* the equipment you need to keep in shape including a range of treadmills, *low impact* climbers and computerised weight machines.

, located close to the treatment rooms,

Therapy Pool   — *capitals and bold*

Our therapy pool is *only* open to members with a specific appointment. The clear blue water is maintained at a therapeutic 90° F to allow the full benefit of the pool to take effect. *Around the pool, lush vegetation grows in the tropical heat. Book now for a treatment in the therapy pool – it's an unforgettable experience!*

PRACTICAL COMPUTING – WORD PROCESSING
THIRD LEVEL
CANDIDATE COPY

PATIO AND

SUN TERRACE — bold

Come outside and enjoy a light snack on the ~~terrace~~ *patio*. This secluded area offers members an opportunity to spend a quiet moment over a cup of coffee or a soft drink. ~~The food served is healthy and fresh~~. Light lunches are served from 1130 until 1430 daily.

AEROBIC STUDIO — bold

trs

This spacious studio has fully-mirrored walls and a maple wood sprung floor. Used for low and high impact sessions, circuit training and dance classes, the studio is ~~very~~ popular with all our members.

EXERCISE POOL — bold

Ideal for the serious swimmer as well as for those who wish to take some gentle exercise, our experienced staff offer free swimming lessons at 0930 and 1230 every ~~Tuesday~~ Thursday.

Our full-sized swimming pool is open from 0700 until 2300 every day of the week.

RESTAURANT — bold

indent 5 cm (2 inches) from left margin only

but low-calorie

Our spacious restaurant serves food all day and specialises in appetizing meals for those

wide

who are watching their weight. A selection of freshly-made sandwiches and salads is always

available.

TREATMENT ~~SUITE~~ Rooms — bold

Our treatment rooms are staffed by ~~a team of~~ experienced beauty therapists who offer a caring and

trs professional service to non-members and members. Due to the popularity of the treatments,

it is advisable to make a telephone booking prior to your visit.

IF YOU WOULD LIKE TO BECOME A MEMBER OF THE ATHENA HEALTH CLUB, THIS IS WHAT YOU ~~MUST~~ SHOULD DO: *Single Spacing and bold*

trs
→ telephone 0181 302 0261 for an application form
→ enclose yr cheque made payable to Athena Health Club
→ complete the form clearly in capital letters
→ return the above in the pre-paid envelope supplied

We will contact you by return. Your membership card will be enclosed and you should *single spacing*

uc use this whenever you visit the club.

ATHENA HEALTH CLUB
Riverside Gardens
BROMLEY BR7 4SF *centre these lines*

INSERT AT ⊗ ABOVE

The full range of treatments includes aromatherapy, full and part-body massage, facial and body treatments and manicures and pedicures.

PRACTICAL COMPUTING – WORD PROCESSING
THIRD LEVEL
CANDIDATE COPY

ASSIGNMENT 3

1   Create a form from the information given below.

2   Ensure that sufficient space is left for completion by hand.

3   Key in your name at the bottom of the document.

4   Save the document under a meaningful filename.

5   Print a copy of your work.

ATHENA HEALTH CLUB   — *bold and centre*

} *insert address and telephone/fax numbers from Assignment 1*

TREATMENT BOOKING FORM   — *bold, underline and centre*

Please complete this form and return it to Julia Stevens, Treatment Room Manager.

CLIENT DETAILS — *bold*

insert space for Full Name, Address, Telephone and Date of Birth

uc   Any health problems *(please give details)*

~~SELECTED~~ TREATMENTS — *bold*

Aromatherapy	Manicure	
Body Scrub and Shower	Massage – Full Body	
Facial Treatments	Massage – Part Body	
Make Up Lesson	Pedicure	

Additional Treatments   *(please give details)*

trs   CLIENT APPOINTMENT MADE FOR

CLIENT SIGNATURE

296

PRACTICAL COMPUTING – WORD PROCESSING
THIRD LEVEL
CANDIDATE COPY

ASSIGNMENT 4

1   Key in the text below, using justified left and right margins.

2   Use a landscape page orientation (wide edge at the top).

3   Display the text in 3 columns of equal width with 1.2 cm (0.5 inches) between each column.

4   Leave a top margin of at least 5 cm (2 inches) for a photograph.

5   Key in your name at the bottom of the document.

6   Print a copy of your work.

ATHENA HEALTH CLUB PACKAGE DEALS

create a border and increase font size. Centre this heading.

Athena Health Club is ~~delighted~~ pleased to offer the following Treatment Packages to both members and non-members. To avoid disappointment, please telephone to check availability before sending us a cheque for the full amount.

centre these lines

SHEER INDULGENCE
£120

bold

Come and be pampered by our team of ~~professional~~ experienced therapists. [Start your day with an invigorating swim and sauna. Follow this with a relaxing full-body massage to relieve muscular tension. ~~and stress~~ After a light lunch, enjoy a luxurious facial. To complete the package, you will be given a manicure and pedicure.

NP

TOP-TO-TOE SPECIAL
£90
] bold

Take a day off to treat yourself to a complete body overhaul.

Begin your visit with a body scrub and shower. ~~Then~~ Follow this with a one-hour reflexology|foot massage to eliminate the toxins in the body. Then enjoy a facial to cleanse and moisturise your skin.

run on

A hairwash and style completes your day.

HEALTH AND FITNESS
£75
] bold

NP Combine fitness training with some treatments for maximum benefit. [Spend an hour with one of our fitness consultants to plan your exercise routine. Then visit the steam room to cleanse your body.

run on

A part-body massage follows, after which you may choose a manicure, pedicure or facial.

PRACTICAL COMPUTING – PRESENTATION GRAPHICS
FIRST LEVEL
CANDIDATE'S COPY

299

LONDON CHAMBER OF COMMERCE AND INDUSTRY EXAMINATIONS BOARD

PRACTICAL COMPUTING – PRESENTATION GRAPHICS

FIRST LEVEL

CANDIDATE'S COPY

PRACTICAL COMPUTING – PRESENTATION GRAPHICS
FIRST LEVEL
CANDIDATE'S COPY

TOTAL TIME ALLOWANCE: 1 hour 30 minutes

The Candidate's name must appear on every printout.

PRACTICAL COMPUTING – PRESENTATION GRAPHICS
FIRST LEVEL
CANDIDATE'S COPY

BACKGROUND

You work for Athena House Handicrafts where you help with the preparation of printed materials. Today you have been asked to use your graphics package to produce some graphic images for the firm's publications. Please carry out the following instructions.

ASSIGNMENT 1

Using your computer, create a graphical representation of the following figures.

Section	Profit (£)
Sewing	40,930
Tapestries	44,650
Beadwork	48,160
Soft Toys	37,540

It can be in the form of:

(a) a pie chart

or (b) a bar chart

Save your work as **Craft1.**

Print a copy of your work.

ASSIGNMENT 2

Retrieve the file you created, called **Craft1**. Add centrally over the chart the title **Athena House Handicrafts** in bold capitals and, on the next line, **Profit in 1999 for Each Section (£).** Use bold capitals for both titles. If the package has not added them automatically, add labels to show the sections and the figures associated with them.

Save your work as **Craft2.**

Print a copy of your work.

ASSIGNMENT 3

Import into a blank document a graphical image depicting a soft toy, a doll or another item associated with handicrafts. Centre the image on the page. Add the title **ATHENA HOUSE HANDICRAFTS** above the image and another caption **Enjoy Your Leisure Hours With Our Crafts** beneath the image. Use suitable fonts and point sizes for these captions and embolden them. Save your work as **Craft3** and print a copy. You may set out your work on A4 portrait or A4 landscape orientation.

ASSIGNMENT 4

Retrieve the file **Craft3** (any image of handicrafts) and carry out the following changes:

1   Reduce the image to approximately 2.54 cm (1 inch) square and position it at the top left hand corner of a document. Remove the captions.

2   At the top right hand corner of the document, key in the address of the firm. Use a new line for each part of the address; centre and embolden each line:

> Honeypot Lane
> LULWORTH COVE
> Dorset
> DT5 4JR

3   Position the firm's name, Athena House Handicrafts, at the head of the letter in the centre between your reduced size image and the firm's address centred at the right hand side of the document. Use a large point size and fancy font for this heading and embolden it.

4   Save your work as **Craft4** and print a copy.

ASSIGNMENT 5

Use your package to create 4 shapes. Three of the shapes are given below. Add another shape of your choice. Arrange them on the page. Label them **Figure 1, Figure 2, Figure 3,** and **Figure 4.** Save your work as **Craft5** and print a copy.

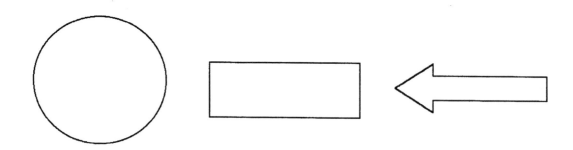

ASSIGNMENT 6

Retrieve the file **Craft5** and re-arrange the circle, square and the arrow into a compass in the following manner:

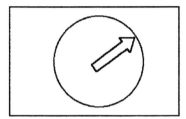

As appropriate, change the sizes and orientation of the shapes and centre the group. Increase the oblong shape to at least 10 cm (4") wide.

Add a heading under the picture, Which Way Up Is North? Embolden it, use a different font and a larger point size.

Save this new work as **Craft6** and print a copy.

PRACTICAL COMPUTING – PRESENTATION GRAPHICS
SECOND LEVEL
CANDIDATE'S COPY

LONDON CHAMBER OF COMMERCE AND INDUSTRY EXAMINATIONS BOARD

PRACTICAL COMPUTING – PRESENTATION GRAPHICS

SECOND LEVEL

CANDIDATE'S COPY

PRACTICAL COMPUTING – PRESENTATION GRAPHICS
SECOND LEVEL
CANDIDATE'S COPY

305

TOTAL TIME ALLOWANCE: 2 hours

The Candidate's name must appear on every printout.

Printouts may be in portrait or landscape orientation as appropriate.

PRACTICAL COMPUTING – PRESENTATION GRAPHICS
SECOND LEVEL
CANDIDATE'S COPY

BACKGROUND

You work for the Athena House Hotels Group where you have been assigned to the Advertising Department to help with the preparation of printed materials. Today you have been asked to use your graphics package to produce some charts and graphic images relating to the group's business. Please carry out the following instructions:

ASSIGNMENT 1

The provisional balance sheet for 1999 shows the following turnover for the 6 main hotels belonging to the Group:

Hotel Name	(£ thousands)
Athena North	169.8
Athena Park	430.6
Athena South	254.7
Athena Ferry	301.2
Athena Winston	223.1
Athena Forest	369.4

EITHER

(a) Create a pie chart to represent the highest 4 of the above figures. Explode the slice which represents the hotel with the highest turnover (to emphasise it). Add a title **Athena House Hotels Group** and a sub-title **Best Turnover in 1999 (£ thousands).** Label each slice showing the turnover figure for the hotel it represents and each hotel's name. You may also add a legend if you wish. Save your work under the filename **Hotel1** and print a copy.

OR

(b) Create a bar chart based on the figures in (a) above, to display the turnover figures for the best 4 hotels (show the hotels in the Legend). Add the title **Athena House Hotels Group** and a sub-title **Best Turnover in 1999 (£ thousands).** Save your work under the filename **Hotel1** and print a copy.

ASSIGNMENT 2

The group needs a new logo. Import a picture into A4 landscape of a large building
to use as the centre of the logo. Then key in **ATHENA HOUSE HOTELS GROUP**
around it as in the design below. Save your work under the filename **Hotel2** and
print a copy of it.

ASSIGNMENT 3

The group requires new stationery. Prepare a design for the letterhead which is to
be on A4 portrait paper.

1   Position the group's name as a centred heading in bold at the top of the letter.
    Use a large fancy font and word or text art to embellish it.

2   Retrieve the logo with text which you created in ASSIGNMENT 2. Reduce its
    size to approximately 2.54 cm (1 inch) square and position it in the top left hand
    corner.

3   Leave approximately 2-3 clear line spaces under the logo then add the group's
    address in bold and on separate lines and left justified. The address is:

    4 – 8 Portland Row   READING   Berkshire   RG1 3SL

4   Save your work under the filename **Hotel3** and print a copy.

ASSIGNMENT 4

Open the building logo which you have already created and saved as **Hotel2**.

1   Import a banner shape or word or text art shape and position this under the logo. In the banner or shape add text to read **ATHENA MILLENNIUM.**

2   Group the logo and the banner (or word art) together. Print a copy of this new image.

3   Reduce this new image to approximately 2.54 cm (1 inch) in size and insert it into the following piece of text so that the text flows round it. Position the image approximately centrally for best effect.

4   This text should be keyed in with fully justified margins of approximately 5 cm (2 inches) on either side and centre the heading.

ATHENA HOUSE HOTELS LATEST HOTEL

Athena House Hotels Group is delighted to announce the opening of the Group's newest hotel. The hotel is the ATHENA MILLENNIUM. It is set in extensive grounds on a magnificent site by Southampton Water, not far from the chemical and other industrial plants in that area. It is ideally placed for visitors being near to the M27 and the Airport. There are 200 tastefully furnished bedrooms, all with en suite bathrooms, several restaurants and other public rooms. There are conference rooms which are fully equipped with all the facilities designed to make life easier for the many business visitors who are expected to book. However, the Group anticipates that this hotel will greatly appeal to both business visitors and holidaymakers alike. It fulfils an urgent need for a large conference hotel with all modern facilities set in this particularly attractive area of the UK.

5   Save your work under filename **Hotel4** and print a copy on A4 paper.

PRACTICAL COMPUTING – PRESENTATION GRAPHICS
THIRD LEVEL
CANDIDATE'S COPY

LONDON CHAMBER OF COMMERCE AND INDUSTRY EXAMINATIONS BOARD

PRACTICAL COMPUTING – PRESENTATION GRAPHICS

THIRD LEVEL

CANDIDATE'S COPY

PRACTICAL COMPUTING – PRESENTATION GRAPHICS
THIRD LEVEL
CANDIDATE'S COPY

310

TOTAL TIME ALLOWANCE: 2 hours 30 minutes

The candidate's name must appear on every printout.

Printouts may be in portrait or landscape orientation as appropriate.

BACKGROUND

You work for Comlon's Cattery which sells cats to cat lovers. You have been asked to prepare promotional material and advertising matter to inform the general public and cat lovers in particular of the many cats which are available from Comlon's Cattery. Today you have been asked to use your software packages to produce a logo and a set of slides about various aspects of the business. Please carry out the following instructions.

ASSIGNMENT 1

Using your computer create a logo to represent the company. It should feature a picture of a cat or cats and have the words COMLON'S CATTERY as part of the logo. You may draw the picture of the cat or cats, or import it from any clip art available on your computer. The completed logo could be similar to this:

Entitle this logo **LOGO FOR INSERTION IN SLIDE MASTER.** Add the date and your name as a footer and save the image as **Comcat1**. Print a copy.

ASSIGNMENT 2

For the slide presentation described further on in Assignment 3, create the master slide. This will feature the logo you have just created in the bottom left hand corner, and the heading all on one line **COMLON'S CATS WITH CHARACTER**. This logo and heading will appear on every slide. In point size 10, 12 or 14 add the following footers to the Master, the date (in full) and your name. At this stage no printout is required. Save this logo as **Comcat2.**

PRACTICAL COMPUTING – PRESENTATION GRAPHICS
THIRD LEVEL
CANDIDATE'S COPY

ASSIGNMENT 3

Based on the Master Slide which you have just prepared, create 4 slides to form the presentation. Use your own judgement regarding fonts and formatting for all the slides. **Slide 1** must show the main heading and logo as described in Assignment 2. Add a title WHY YOU SHOULD CHOOSE YOUR CAT FROM US followed by a bulleted list to include the following phrases: **we only supply cats from healthy stock; our cats are individuals; pedigree or non-pedigree kittens; it's your choice.**

Slide 2 must show the main heading and logo as in the Master Slide. Use an organisation chart to show **CAT FUR TYPES**. There are two main fur types, Long-haired cats and Short-haired cats. The Long-haired cats are subdivided into Persian, Angora and Main Coon. The Short-haired cats have 4 main sub divisions: American Wirehair, British Smooth, Devon Rex and the "Hairless" Sphynx. Below is a sketch of how the slide will appear.

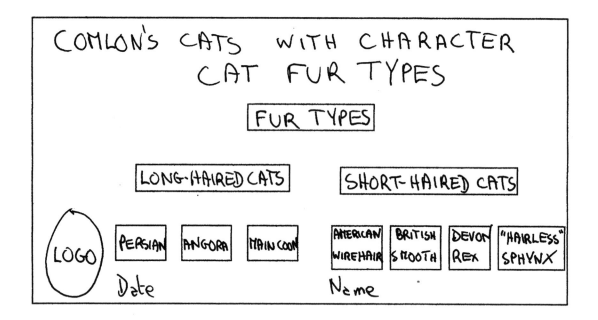

Slide 3 should show the **Cat Fur Colours**. Use an organisation chart for these. There are 5 types of colours: Ticked, Self, Tipped, Shaded and Smoke. The Smoke colour is often divided into two main colours, Blue Smoke and Black Smoke.

Slide 4 should show **Main Cat Face Shapes**. These are sub-divided into two categories: Long-haired and Short-haired cats, and each of these categories is further sub-divided into Round-faced, Intermediate-faced and Wedge-faced.

Slide 5 will be entitled **Popular Cats on our Register 1996 – 1998**. Incorporate a 3D bar chart in the slide, representing the following figures:

	1996	1997	1998
Persian	245	270	306
Tabby	310	329	350
Siamese	270	288	322

The bars should be clearly labelled with the figures.

Slide 6 should be based as usual on the master slide. Use the title CHAMPIONS EVERY ONE! Show this title as the heading for a bulleted list, giving the name and breed of Comlon's Cattery champion cats who have won top awards in regional and national cat shows throughout the country. These are Farida – a smoke blue Persian; Sherry Belinda – a tortie and white tortoiseshell; Bobby Bingo – a black and silver tabby.

Save your work as **Comcat3.**

Print the 6 slides on one printout as a handout with the date and your name as footers.

Print three full size printouts, namely **Slide 1** on "why you should choose your cat from us", **Slide 2** showing the Fur Types and **Slide 5** showing the chart.

PRACTICAL COMPUTING – PRESENTATION GRAPHICS
THIRD LEVEL
CANDIDATE'S COPY

ASSIGNMENT 4

Slide 7 must be a Notes Pages View slide. The top part must show the company's logo and a main heading as on the Master Slide, together with a heading **Rehearsing and Timing your Presentation.** Reduce the slide section in size as appropriate. Leave the footers in the slide section but remove them from the foot of the notes section.

The bottom part of the slide must show the following text. Use your word processing program to key in this text. Select suitable fonts, point size and formatting. Fully justify the margins then import this into the notes part of the Notes Pages View slide.

> *Prior to making an important presentation it is advisable to practise beforehand and time your Slide Show. At this stage you can correct any mistakes and set the timings for your slides. Most packages give you this option, thus allowing you to check all aspects of your presentation including any transitional, audio or animation effects, which you may have incorporated in your slides.*
>
> *Timings can be set beforehand. All slides can be shown for exactly the same time, or you can vary the time for each and every slide. For instance, you may want your first slide to be on screen for 20 seconds and the others for 10 seconds only.*
>
> *It is also wise to try out your presentation on the actual computer on which you are proposing to show it, as the computer may not be as fast as your own machine and may lack essential memory.*
>
> *Rehearse in good time for a striking presentation.*

Save your work as **Comcat4.**

Print this Notes Pages Slide 7.

Appendix: Advice for students taking LCCIEB practical examinations

Before starting your studies

1 Choose a school, college or private teacher who is familiar with the LCCI Practical Computing assessment scheme and who has a reputation for good results.

2 Attend your lessons regularly and practise as often as you can.

3 Look carefully at the syllabus. Check that the hardware and/or software that you are using is capable of performing all the functions to be tested. As you progress, tick off the functions you have learned.

4 If you intend to take the assignments for **Second** or **Third Level** remember that you will also be tested on the functions required for the lower levels.

5 Try to work through some past assignments. This will help you to become familiar with the layout, content and difficulty of the assignments at each level. There are examples in this book, along with the suggested answer for each assignment. Check your work carefully learn from your mistakes.

6 When you are confident that you can successfully undertake all functions at a particular level, speak to your tutor about entering for the Practical Computing assignments. He or she will advise you whether you are ready for assessment.

7 Remember that the assignments must be completed within the stated time allowance. You must practise under time-constrained conditions.

8 Make sure that you have been entered for the assessment. It is **your** responsibility, although it may be organised by your tutor or the college.

Before the assessment

1 Make sure that you know when and where the assessment will take place. Arrive in good time and check that the equipment you are using is working effectively. In particular, check that the printer is working and that the printouts are clear and legible.

2 Check that you have everything that you will need. You will need a pen, a pencil and a ruler and you may use a dictionary if you wish. Do not forget your glasses if you use them!

The assignments

1 Each assignment is given a time allowance. **First Level** assignments must be completed within 1 hour and 30 minutes; 2 hours is the time allowance for **Second Level** assignments, and assignments at **Third Level** must be completed within 2 hours and 30 minutes. Use your time sensibly. Always spend time reading through the assignment before you begin and allow time at the end to check your work carefully before handing it to your tutor for marking. Even if you finish the assignments before the end of the time allowance, spend the remainder of the time checking your work. Uncorrected errors will incur penalties.

2 Save your work regularly. At **First** and **Second Levels** you will be given filenames for your work. You may need to reprint some of your work so you must be able to find the files easily.

3 Check your work carefully, since each inaccuracy counts as an error. You may use the on-line spellchecker if you wish, but always check your work manually as well.

4 Make sure that your name appears on every printout.

5 Follow all instructions carefully. It is a good idea to tick each instruction as it is completed. Each instruction overlooked will result in a penalty.

6 Try to display your work as attractively as possible. The easiest way to display word processed work is by using the fully blocked style with open punctuation. Follow copy exactly regarding capital and lower case letters.

7 You must produce a printout of every assignment for marking. At **First Level**, all assignments will fit comfortably on one sheet of A4 paper. At **Second** and **Third Levels**, some word processing documents will be multi-page documents. You may need to reduce the font size of some spreadsheet printouts so that your work will fit neatly on the page. However, make sure that your work is legible; also, if you use non-standard fonts, make sure that the text is clear.

Finally, we hope that you will be a successful candidate. If you work through this book systematically and practise the assignments, you will soon learn what is needed for success in Practical Computing.

Good luck!

Index

Note: Figure numbers are given in bold print.